Exploring Islamic Philosophy

Global Philosophy

Series Editor—Mohammed Rustom,
Carleton University / Tokat Institute for Advanced Islamic Studies

Given the tremendous amount of interest in non-Western philosophy today, teachers, students, and the general public are beginning to come away with a clearer picture of what "philosophy" means in various civilizations and to large sectors of humanity beyond the Anglo-American and European worlds. This series in global philosophy seeks to further this interest by highlighting the epistemic diversity and profound insights of Africana, Buddhist, Confucian, Hindu, Islamic, Jain, Jewish, Latin American, Mesoamerican, Native American, Russian, and Taoist philosophy. To accomplish its goals, the series focuses on publishing accessible and lively books on these philosophical traditions and scholarly translations of their key works.

PUBLISHED

A Sourcebook in Global Philosophy
Edited by Mohammed Rustom

Exploring Hindu Philosophy
Ankur Barua

What Is Metaphysics? Ruminations on Principial Knowledge and Some of Its Applications
Seyyed Hossein Nasr

FORTHCOMING

Sacred Psychology: A Global Perspective
Samuel Bendeck Sotillos

Exploring Islamic Philosophy

SAYEH MEISAMI

equinox

SHEFFIELD UK BRISTOL CT

Published by Equinox Publishing Ltd.

UK: Office 415, The Workstation, 15 Paternoster Row, Sheffield, South Yorkshire S1 2BX

USA: ISD, 70 Enterprise Drive, Bristol, CT 06010

www.equinoxpub.com

First published 2025

British Library Cataloguing-in-Publication Data

A catalogue record for this book is available from the British Library.

ISBN-13 978 1 80050 681 7 (hardback)
978 1 80050 682 4 (paperback)
978 1 80050 683 1 (ePDF)
978 1 80050 714 2 (ePub)

Library of Congress Cataloging-in-Publication Data

Names: Meisami, Sayeh author
Title: Exploring Islamic philosophy / Sayeh Meisami.
Description: Sheffield, South Yorkshire ; Bristol, CT : Equinox Publishing Ltd., 2025. | Series: Global philosophy | Includes bibliographical references and index. | Summary: "Exploring Islamic Philosophy presents a lively introduction to the Islamic philosophical tradition by focusing on over a thousand years of Islamic philosophical theory and praxis, from Spain to Iran"-- Provided by publisher.
Identifiers: LCCN 2025026870 (print) | LCCN 2025026871 (ebook) | ISBN 9781800506817 hardback | ISBN 9781800506824 paperback | ISBN 9781800506831 pdf | ISBN 9781800507142 epub
Subjects: LCSH: Islamic philosophy--History
Classification: LCC B741 .M445 2025 (print) | LCC B741 (ebook) | DDC 181/.07--dc23/eng/20250620
LC record available at https://lccn.loc.gov/2025026870
LC ebook record available at https://lccn.loc.gov/2025026871

Typeset by Scribe Inc.

Contents

Series Foreword by Mohammed Rustom vii

Preface and Acknowledgments ix

Introduction: Entry Points 1

1. Reality and Its Parts 8

2. Knowledge and Selfhood 37

3. God and Cosmos 57

4. Virtue and Governance 85

Conclusion: Care for Others, Care for the World 109

Bibliography 117

Further Reading 127

Index 129

Series Foreword

Given the tremendous amount of interest in non-Western philosophy today, teachers, students, and the general public are beginning to come away with a clearer picture of what "philosophy" means in various civilizations and to large sectors of humanity beyond the Anglo-American and European worlds. This series in Global Philosophy seeks to further this interest by highlighting the epistemic diversity and profound insights of Africana, Buddhist, Confucian, Hindu, Islamic, Jain, Jewish, Latin American, Mesoamerican, Native American, Russian, and Taoist philosophy. To accomplish its goals, the series focuses on publishing accessible and lively books on these philosophical traditions, as well as scholarly translations of their key works.

Mohammed Rustom
Series Editor, *Global Philosophy*
Carleton University / Tokat Institute for Advanced Islamic Studies

Preface and Acknowledgments

This volume attempts to present an accessible account of what is known as "Islamic philosophy" in an inclusive and contextual manner. It includes various methods of philosophical inquiry within their historical, cultural, religious, and political contexts, which sometimes overlap. To create a seamless narrative of Islamic philosophy, I draw on metaphysical concepts as connectors among different fields of inquiry, including theories about reality, knowledge, the soul, good and evil, gender, and the environment. While highlighting major narratives and arguments in such fields of philosophical inquiry, I also include a number of those that have been overshadowed due to factors such as political and sectarian prejudices or mere historical misfortunes. This book is therefore an attempt to present a more colorful story about the intellectual discourses in the Islamic world over the centuries. Yet this is a small book, and during the course of writing it, I often faced the challenge of resisting my desire to include more ideas and more philosophers.

My focus will be on the main features of both theoretical and practical philosophy in the Islamic world. The chapters on theoretical philosophy review metaphysical problems regarding both the natural and supernatural domains. Under practical philosophy, I discuss ethics and politics with special attention paid to contemporary issues. Each chapter opens by explaining the main topic, along with its significance. This is followed by an elucidation of the key concepts that are required for comprehending the structure and meaning of the philosophical positions on the topic. Wherever necessary, I provide relevant passages from primary philosophical texts (the translations are my own unless cited otherwise). As for secondary sources, space and time would not allow me to refer to all the great works that have been written on different aspects of Islamic philosophy. Since this volume is intended for readers in English, I sadly leave out not only the invaluable secondary scholarship in Arabic and Persian (the two main languages in which Islamic philosophy took shape) but also works in other European languages, all of which I have used over the course of my academic career and to which I am indebted.

There are many great philosophers in Islamic history, but for the purposes of this book, I confine myself to a limited number of them who represent major philosophical and/or methodological contributions. In this vein, I have tried to include figures from both the eastern and western sides of the Islamic world. Moreover, selective ideas and figures in philosophical Sufism and rational theology (*kalām*) are discussed under the umbrella of Islamic philosophy because of their discursive confluence over the centuries.

The order in which I discuss philosophical figures follows the order of the themes discussed because the goal of this volume is not a survey of the history of Islamic philosophy per se but an introduction to the major ideas and arguments (with ample textual demonstration) that have animated the tradition from past to present. As for actual historical contexts, they will be brought up mostly when I speculate on their role in shaping trends and ideas.

Exploring Islamic Philosophy has benefited from my many years of experience teaching and writing about philosophy both overseas and in North America. As ever, I am indebted to everyone who taught me philosophy and encouraged me to pursue it. I am especially grateful to the book's anonymous reviewers for their incredibly insightful comments on an earlier draft of the manuscript, as well as Oussama Marei for his careful reading of its penultimate version. I am also thankful to Mohammed Rustom, Equinox Publishing Ltd.'s Global Philosophy series editor, for trusting me with this task and providing me with his generous comments along the way. Finally, as always, I have been blessed with the loving support of Amir Kalan and our wonderful son, Sam.

Introduction

Entry Points

Let us begin with a brief note about the term *Islamic* in the title of this volume. It is true that "Islamic philosophy" as a long intellectual tradition has taken shape in regions under Muslim rule, and the key players therein identified as Muslim; yet Islam is not the only influence upon this tradition. Most importantly, there is a host of philosophical doctrines in Islamic philosophy that may be accepted as "Islamic" by some Muslim interpretive communities but not so by others. Without venturing into this debate, my use of the adjective *Islamic* is primarily methodological while also acknowledging the role that Islam's sacred sources (the Quran and Hadith) and certain Islamic theological and political discourses have played in shaping the philosophical tradition in question.

Treating key Islamic philosophical concepts in a holistic fashion, the chapters in this book are dedicated to major philosophical topics, and each inquires into a problem that is broad enough to be accessible to specialists and nonspecialists alike. As such, each chapter begins with an elucidation of key philosophical concepts and proceeds to discuss important textual examples from significant authors in the history of Islamic philosophy. The chapters build off one another, proceeding from the most theoretical to the most practical. Thus, later chapters are concerned with issues in practical philosophy such as ethics and politics, but these are dependent upon key ideas developed in earlier chapters—namely, themes in theoretical philosophy such as the nature of reality and knowledge. But before moving to our theme-based presentation of Islamic philosophy, a brief sketch of its historical influences is in order.

THE ISLAMIC INFLUENCE

The nature and scope of the Islamic influence on the development of philosophy in the Islamic world have been subject to much debate. On the one hand, some major historians and scholars have grounded its very existence in Islam's sacred sources and described Islamic philosophy as "prophetic philosophy." Alongside Henry Corbin (d. 1978),[1] Seyyed Hossein Nasr (b. 1933) argues, "Islamic philosophy is essentially a philosophical

1. Corbin, *History of Islamic Philosophy*.

hermeneutics of the Sacred Text while making use of the rich philosophical heritage of antiquity."[2] Other scholars who work in both Western and non-Western academic contexts choose to focus on the influence of Greek philosophy. For them, Islamic philosophy is, for the most part, Greek philosophy in Arabic. Yet this approach is fraught with limitations, since it tends to downplay the importance and significance of the postclassical Islamic philosophical works, the vast majority of which cannot simply be reduced to Greek philosophy in Arabic garb. This approach to Islamic philosophy is, however, by no means the norm today. Indeed, the diversity of Islamic philosophy fittingly corresponds to the diversity of the kinds of contemporary scholars who study it, resulting in a much broader picture of the Islamic philosophical tradition's historical influences, philosophical concerns, and contemporary significance.

Besides content and method, both the classical and postclassical Muslim philosophers wrote their works and pursued their careers within the borders of the Islamic world, and some of them had the patronage of either Sunni caliphs or Shiʿa princes/leaders. For example, "the philosopher of the Arabs" Abū Yūsuf Yaʿqūb al-Kindī (d. ca. 870) was one of the exponents of the translation movement that was active during the Abbasid Caliphate (750–1258) and even tutored the son of Caliph al-Muʿtaṣim (r. 833–43). Al-Kindī opens his major philosophical treatise *On First Philosophy* by addressing the caliph as "the son of outstanding rulers who provide happiness, and whose guidance, when followed, leads one to bliss in this life and the next."[3] Even Abū Naṣr Fārābī (d. 950), who started as a self-made philosopher, eventually had to seek the support of the Shiʿa Prince Ṣayf al-Dawla. In addition, the life of the great Abū ʿAlī Ibn Sīnā, henceforth Avicenna (d. 1037), was divided among several patrons who competed over his service, and at one point, he even served as a minister.

Another example is Naṣīr al-Dīn Ṭūsī (d. 1274). He worked closely with the Ismaʿīlī leader Nāṣir al-Dīn Muḥtasham (d. 1257) and named two of his ethical treatises after him. Later, upon joining the Mongols and after the fall of the Abbasid Caliphate in 1258, Ṭūsī dedicated a large number of his works to the Twelver Shiʿa cause and received patronage from the Mongol court for his scientific projects.[4] The Twelver Shiʿa patronage is particularly noticeable during some periods under the Safavid (r. 1501–1736) and Qajar (r. 1794–1925) dynasties. Even in the twentieth century in Iran, the Pahlavi Queen Farah Diba (b. 1938) established an academy of Islamic philosophy under the directorship of Seyyed Hossein Nasr. What I mention here are only a few of the many examples of patronage for philosophers in Islamic history. At the same time, it was common throughout the premodern Islamic world for a philosopher to have a "day job" as a court physician. Indeed, several major Islamic philosophers were primarily known and sought after for their medical expertise.

Throughout Islamic history, the attempt to reconcile Greek ideas with major Islamic doctrines, particularly God's oneness (*tawḥīd*) and prophecy (*nubuwwa*), facilitated the acceptance and survival of philosophical works. Conversely, suspicion over the Islamic commitments of philosophers such as Irānshahrī (ca. ninth century), Abū Bakr Rāzī (d. 925), and

2. Nasr, "Qur'ān and Ḥadīth as Source," 1:37.
3. Adamson and Pormann, *Philosophical Works of Al-Kindī*, 10.
4. See Meisami, *Naṣīr al-Dīn Ṭūsī*, 10–18.

Ibn Rāwandī (d. ca. 911) led to their castigation by some of their colleagues, despite their influence on the history of Islamic philosophy in the Persianate world.[5] A good example of how Muslim philosophers engaged with Greek wisdom and integrated it into an Islamic worldview is al-Kindī. He spoke of appreciating truth "wherever it comes from" and, to that end, utilized Neoplatonism for Islamic purposes when he equated "the Neoplatonic true One with the Creator and One God of Islam."[6] As for Fārābī and Avicenna, despite their technical differences, they both forged a philosophical cosmology that transformed Aristotle's First Cause of the universe into a divine source of existence that brings things into being and is worthy of faith and worship. Both these Islamic philosophers also philosophized about prophecy, a major article of Islamic faith. Of course, not all Muslims found such engagement with theological matters "Islamic" enough. For example, in the prologue of his famous *Ḥayy Ibn Yaqẓān* (*Alive, Son of Awake*), Ibn Ṭufayl (d. 1184) of Andalusia criticized Fārābī's grounding of the prophetic mechanism in imagination, and in his *Incoherence of the Philosophers*, the famous Ghazālī (d. 1111) accused Avicenna of unorthodoxy on several grounds.

Any discourse on the religious context of Islamic philosophy would be incomplete without acknowledging the confluence and overlap among rational theology (*kalām*), Sufi theology, and Sufi metaphysics. There are several factors behind this confluence, such as the impact of Greek logic and metaphysics. But the most important factor is these disciplines' shared Islamic context, which is mostly visible in their respective employment of Quranic concepts and terminology. While in principle these three traditions are supposed to be distinguished based on their methods of acquiring the premises of their arguments and their positions on the relation between reason and revelation, a clear-cut demarcation is not always that easy to draw.

One fine example of a theologian who appears in this book in conversation with the philosophers (*falāsifa*) is Fakhr al-Dīn Rāzī (d. 1210), whose critical approach to Avicenna became a springboard for a tradition of fruitful commentaries for and against him. His approach to the philosophers was similar to that of Ghazālī, "as he takes a distanced but at the same time appreciative stance that allows for the widespread introduction of philosophical teachings into Muslim *kalām* yet also for the rejection of others."[7] As has been argued, Fakhr al-Dīn Rāzī's relation to Avicenna is similar to Avicenna's relation to Aristotle, as he is critical of Avicenna but at the same time "deeply indebted" to him.[8] Contemporary scholarship on Fakhr al-Dīn Rāzī often highlights the philosophical depth of his writings. On account of the complexity of the relationship among various intellectual traditions in premodern Islamic contexts, alongside the obvious need to define the term *philosophy* independent of truncated Anglo-European conceptions, I will speak of the various stripes of thinkers I address in this book as "Islamic philosophers."

5. For an account of Abū Bakr Rāzī's and Ibn Rāwandī's ideas and influence, see Stroumsa, *Freethinkers of Medieval Islam*. In contrast, recent scholarship by Marwan Rashed and Peter Adamson challenges the dominant narrative about Abū Bakr Rāzī's anti-Islamic worldview. See Adamson, *Al-Rāzī*, 3.
6. Gannage, "Rise of *Falsafa*," 34.
7. Griffel, "Fakhr al-Dīn al-Rāzī," 342. For more on Fakhr al-Dīn Rāzī, see Griffel, *Post-Classical Philosophy*, 264–303; and Shihadeh, *Teleological Ethics*.
8. Wisnovsky, "Towards a Genealogy of Avicennism," 326. Based on Rāzī's own notes on his methodology, Griffel discusses his approach to Avicenna as "a middle path" between "slavish emulation" and "outright rejection." See Griffel, *Post-Classical Philosophy*, 504.

Going back to the religious dimensions of Islamic philosophy, Shiʿa philosophy and Sufi philosophy are similar in their emphasis on an esoteric interpretation (*taʾwīl*) of the Quran. The Quran's references to God as the Light of heavens and the earth (Q 24:35), Muhammad's ascension (*miʿrāj*) to the Divine Presence (Q 17:1), and the important role of a divinely inspired guide such as al-Khiḍr (Q 18:65–82) compose dominant motifs in both Ismaʿīlī and Sufi discourses. The Andalusian Sufi Ibn ʿArabī (d. 1240) explains creation in terms of the divine "mercy" (*raḥma*) that *embraces all things* (Q 7:156), and the Ismaʿīlī philosopher Ḥamīd al-Dīn Kirmānī (d. 1021) builds on the throne imagery from the famous Throne Verse of the Quran (Q 2:255) to disclose his philosophical speculations about the mystery of creation.[9] Apart from these traditions, there are so many levels of engagement with the Quran in all types of philosophical texts throughout the history of Islamic philosophy. This is seen in its most fully developed form in the work of one of the most influential postclassical Islamic philosophers, Mullā Ṣadrā Shīrāzī (d. ca. 1636).[10]

THE GREEK INFLUENCE

Historians of Islamic philosophy all agree on the influence of Greek logic and philosophy upon Islamic thinkers, although they differ over the extent of this influence. It is commonly maintained that the translation movement (whose heyday was in ninth-century Baghdad) was the main conduit of this influence. What facilitated this movement was the work of mainly Christian scholars who were thoroughly competent in Greek, Syriac, and Arabic. In many cases, they translated Greek texts first into Syriac, then from Syriac into Arabic. Among these Christians, there were scholars who also helped with understanding the Greek philosophical texts, so their contribution to the movement was more than just translation. A prominent example in this regard was Ḥunayn b. Isḥāq and his circle of translator-scholars who collaborated with the circle of al-Kindī in rendering a good number of Greek texts into Arabic.[11]

It is reported that the Neoplatonic writings of Plotinus and Proclus were translated rather early in the movement, followed by Aristotle's *Metaphysics* and *De Caelo* by the circle of al-Kindī, who tended to see these texts in harmony not only with each other but also with the Quran.[12] In due course, the complexity of the task, complications in the reception of the texts, and most importantly, the interpretive tendencies of Muslim communities led to confusions regarding the authorship of some texts, most famously that which is cited in Islamic philosophical literature as the *Theology of Aristotle*. The so-called *Theology of Aristotle* is a translation of some parts of Porphyry's paraphrase of *The Enneads* by Plotinus.[13] At any rate, the *Theology*'s contents were very congenial to the concerns of the Islamic philosophers, as its cosmology and doctrine of the human soul could easily harmonize with Islamic conceptions of the cosmos and human nature.

9. Meisami, *Knowledge and Power*, 20–32.
10. See Rustom, *Triumph of Mercy*.
11. See Adamson, *Philosophy in the Islamic World*, 3:19–25.
12. See D'Ancona, "Greek into Arabic," 21.
13. For an accessible study of the so-called *Theology of Aristotle* in Arabic and its comparison with the original Greek text, see Adamson, *Arabic Plotinus*.

One possible way to explain the warm reception of Neoplatonism in the Islamic world is to regard it as a form of continuity between ancient Persian mythology and Neoplatonism, especially in view of the rebirth and flourishing of Zoroastrian discourses in tenth-century central Asia during and after the Samanid era. A major discursive link between Zoroastrianism (in all its variations) and Neoplatonism is the envisioning of the origin and reality of existence in terms of light and an emanationist hierarchy. If we add to this metaphysical hierarchy also the prevalence of social hierarchy shared by pre-Islamic Persia and its rival, ancient Greece, we may better understand the force of the reception of Neoplatonism in philosophical discourses that were developing in Persianate contexts. Moreover, one can also consider the fact that in the sixth century, the pre-Islamic Sasanian Empire (r. 244–651) hosted a group of Neoplatonic philosophers who took refuge in the Sasanian court after the extreme measures taken by the Christian Emperor Justinian against philosophical activities derived from Greece. However, this connection should not be overstated because we have no written records to support it.

Not too far from Neoplatonism, Plato's philosophy was also strongly present in Islamic philosophical contexts. On the one hand, in the classical period, the *Republic* formed the backdrop of Fārābī's political philosophy where Plato's philosopher-king becomes the model for the philosopher-prophet of Fārābī's "virtuous city." On the other hand, postclassical Islamic philosophers such as Suhrawardī, Mīr Dāmād (d. 1631), and Mullā Ṣadrā use Plato's theory of Ideas in their metaphysics despite Avicenna's refutation of it. Furthermore, Shiʿa philosophers of Ismaʿīlī affiliation relied heavily on Plato for their theories about the origin and destiny of the human soul, not to mention their adaptations of Plato's political philosophy into their theories about the Shiʿa Imams as the divinely appointed leaders of the Islamic community.

Despite the influence of Neoplatonism through the pseudo-Aristotle, the influence of the real Aristotle on Islamic philosophy cannot be overemphasized, especially with respect to his formulation of logic as well as his natural philosophy, which also includes psychology. Both Fārābī and Avicenna were indebted to Aristotle in their methods and ideas. In the Aristotelian line of influence, one must give much credit to Aristotle's ancient commentators, including both Neoplatonic and earlier commentators such as Alexander of Aphrodisias from the late second and early third centuries CE. Moreover, the development of Islamic philosophy in the western sphere of the Muslim world—namely, Andalusia—involved an intentional excising of Neoplatonism in favor of straightforward Aristotelianism. The two best examples in this regard are Ibn Bājja (d. 1138) and Ibn Rushd, henceforth Averroes (d. 1198).

One important Greek legacy in Islamic philosophy is Aristotelian logic, to which Islamic logical philosophers made valuable additions and modifications. Aristotle's corpus of logic, together referred to as the *Organon*, became available in Arabic translation by the tenth century, and many Islamic thinkers of various intellectual persuasions from then (and even to the present) made strides in developing logic as a tool to ultimately form arguments in support of matters of Islamic doctrine and practice.

THE PERSIAN INFLUENCE

The Persian influence on the rise and development of Islamic philosophy can be studied from several perspectives. First, the religious discourses of pre-Islamic Persia include some early forms of metaphysical narratives, which must have generated a continued interest in philosophy in the regions where Islamic philosophy would later take root. Second, the formative periods of Islamic philosophy coincide with a rebirth of Persian language and culture, and the early philosophical figures were, for the most part, of Persianate origin and familiar with that culture. Third, later trends in Islamic philosophy use Persian mythology in reconfiguring the Islamic philosophical tradition. Looking at the first aspect of this influence, ancient Persian traditions show an interest in inquiring into the fundamental structure of the universe, which is an early form of metaphysics. The *Avesta* of Zoroastrianism, a collection of ancient oral wisdom accompanied by later interpretations, tries to explain the origin of the universe. In spite of multiple interpretations of the original teachings—referred to as the *Gathas*, which is composed of seventeen hymns—a narrative of antagonism between light and darkness or the forces of good and evil is dominant in this tradition. The genres of the texts range over the poetic and the abstract in a manner that can be compared to their contemporary Greek works—namely, pre-Socratic philosophy. The *Avesta* narratives revolve around metaphysical concepts such as existence, time, infinity, matter, mind and free will (especially in relation to cosmology), ethics, and eschatology. The *Denkard*, a major Zoroastrian work, captures well the spirit of some of the metaphysical themes in the *Avesta* when it says, "Time was originally infinite; then it became subject to limitation; at the end it returns to the Infinite. The law of Time is [to proceed] from original infinity through limitation involving action, motion, passage and finally the return back to ultimate infinity."[14]

Since this is not the place to discuss the many possible ways to probe philosophical themes in the traditions of ancient Persia and their continuation in Islamic philosophy, suffice it to say that in the cultural context where early Islamic philosophers such as Fārābī, Abū al-Ḥasan ʿĀmirī (d. 991), Abū Bakr Rāzī, and Avicenna developed the discourse of Islamic philosophy, the stage was already set by the pre-Islamic Persianate background to welcome their urgent philosophical questions and responses.

Persian revivalism under the Samanid dynasty (875–999) is an important component of the context of early Islamic philosophy. In their best times, the Samanids ruled over Khorasan and Transoxiana and turned the cities of Samarqand and Bukhara into hotspots of learning, scholarship, and poetry. The Samanid court gave patronage to Persian poets such as Rūdakī (d. 941). This spirit was inherited and developed by Abū al-Qāsim Firdawsī (d. 1020), whose famous *Shāhnāma* is based on pre-Islamic characters and narratives.[15] In his autobiography, Avicenna says that he received his early education in Bukhara and that his father worked for the last Samanid ruler, Nūḥ b. Manṣūr (r. 976–97).[16] Also,

14. Zaehner, *Zurvan*, 386–91. For the influence of Zoroastrian metaphysics on Islamic metaphysics, see Meisami, "Light/Darkness Dualism," 371–88.
15. Axworthy, *History of Iran*, 85–86.
16. Gohlman, *Life of Ibn Sina*, 17, 36–37.

Avicenna's contemporary Abū Rayḥān Bīrūnī (d. 1048), who, alongside being an outstanding scientist and philosopher, was also a well-known doxographer and scholar of comparative religion, spent some time in Bukhara under the patronage of this ruler and was in correspondence with Avicenna. In addition to writing in Arabic for the most part, Avicenna also wrote a compendium of philosophy in Persian, not to mention his poetry (mostly in the form of quatrains). The tradition of writing philosophical texts in Persian had a precedence among the Ismaʿīlīs of Iran and continued to be a trend under the Ghaznavids, Seljuqs, Mongols, and onward. The Samanids not only used Persian rather than Arabic as the language of their court, but they were also tolerant of Zoroastrianism.[17]

17. Daryaee, "Zoroastrianism Under Islamic Rule," 112.

1

Reality and Its Parts

Although physics is expected to remain within the boundaries of nature while metaphysics is permitted to go beyond those boundaries, they are equally interested in finding realities behind appearances. Physics, for example, may attempt to explain subatomic particles and black holes, whereas metaphysics deals with essences, existences, or even divine powers. This is one reason why Aristotle's *Physics* and *Metaphysics* build on each other and why most classical compendiums of Islamic philosophy follow the same trend. It is important to mention that the distinction between what is "really real" and that which is not does not refer to a distinction between reality and illusion. Rather, it is about the distinction between the foundation of reality and what depends on it.

"What is really real" is the subject of metaphysics, or "first philosophy," in Islamic intellectual history. It amounts to what a philosopher may discover, through a variety of discursive and intuitive methods, to be the very foundation of what we observe as the world. For an Islamic philosopher, the "world" includes the inner world (i.e., the soul/mind) and its properties as well as the outer world, including one's own body. Additionally, due to the variety of influences on Islamic metaphysics—that is, Persian, Greek, and Quranic—the typical Islamic metaphysician seeks reality in both the natural and the supernatural domains. In the following chapters, I will discuss the most influential ideas about "what is really real" in the context of Islamic philosophy that revolve around several key concepts and their various applications in different philosophical schools. I will begin with the Peripatetic school and Avicenna as its major exponent, then proceed to Illuminationism represented by Suhrawardī and Transcendentalism represented by Mullā Ṣadrā. Averroes will be a prime example of Aristotelianism in the western side of the medieval Islamic world.

UNIVERSALS AND PARTICULARS

Our everyday world appears to us as a plurality of things, such as the different kinds of trees outside of my window, which I call and understand as "trees" despite their differences. Moreover, we ascribe the concept or trait of beauty to Beethoven's symphonies, the sunrise, a line of poetry, acts of charity, and even people, all of which we refer to as "beautiful." For Plato, this is because the observable trees are called so in virtue of being copies, or instances, of a singular though universal idea—that is, "tree-hood." This "tree-hood" belongs outside of space and time, existing eternally as an unchangeable idea. These are referred to by Plato as "Ideas" or "Forms." Although these Ideas or Forms for Plato are singular entities themselves, their immaterial and unchangeable character is the raison d'être of universals. Similarly, the observable, or rather audible, beauty of a piece of music is a particular example of the eternal and immaterial Beauty, hence our license for applying the universal idea of "beautiful" to many different things. In other words, the one term *tree* can meaningfully apply to many trees only if they somehow have "tree-hood" in common, and the sunrise can be called beautiful along with a symphony and many other things only if they have "beauty" in common. From a logical and linguistic point of view, "tree-hood" and "Beauty" are called "universals" because we can apply them to all trees and beautiful things, which are called "particulars." One basic way to distinguish "universals" from "particulars" is to say that universals can be predicated or said of plural things, but particulars cannot be predicated or said of anything. For example, we can predicate the idea of "humanity" to Plato and Aristotle, but we cannot predicate either "Plato" or "Aristotle" of anyone or anything, since particulars are not repeatable.

This is a metaphysical issue because Plato argues that Ideas compose a mind-independent and eternal world over and beyond the visible and concrete everyday world of ours. However, Plato's immediate philosophical successor, Aristotle, noticed a paradox, not to say contradiction, in Plato's explanation of the universal application of concepts by resorting to "Ideas" as individual entities. The problem of Plato's model comes down to identifying an individual entity, "Idea," as universal and how Ideas, as particular entities themselves, can be applicable to particular things. In his *Parmenides* (131a–133a), Plato himself struggles with this problem and speculates on a few models for relating the Ideas to the world of particulars; but he ends up unsatisfied with all of them. In this text, his critical questions seem to anticipate some of Aristotle's objections. Later, Aristotle introduced a new theory in which universals are situated in the mind, while their function is still grounded in the extra-mental world.

Simply put, for Aristotle, a universal term signifies a general concept that can be predicated of particular things based on their essential and accidental features. "Essence" is the unchanging nature of a particular, and "accidents" are its changing attributes. For example, "humanity" is predicated of Mary essentially, while "blondness" is predicated of her accidentally. These universals are necessary for knowing, defining, and categorizing the diversity of things in the world. In the study of metaphysics, Plato's position on universals falls under "metaphysical realism," in comparison to which Aristotle seems to be more of a moderate realist. Nonetheless, they both stand against nominalism, which is the belief in the nonexistence of universals altogether.[1]

The universal/particular debate has a strong and sophisticated presence in the Medieval Latin intellectual arena that is well beyond the present volume. On the Islamic side of the discussion, generally speaking, major philosophers of the classical period upheld the existence of universals, but they differed over where they reside. As a metaphysical problem in Islamic philosophy, the primary point of contention among the majority of Islamic philosophers revolves around this two-part question: (a) Do universals exist outside of the mind or not? and (b) In either case, how do they relate to particulars? In this

1. For an analytic study of the history of the universal/particular discussion, see Loux, *Metaphysics*, chapters 1 and 2.

regard, Peripatetic philosophers of the classical periods can be associated with a range of Aristotelian interpretations, while the Illuminationist, Ismaʿīlī and Sufi philosophers incline more toward Plato.

On the Aristotelian end, al-Kindī builds the universal/particular dichotomy on the division of perception into sensory and intellectual perception:

> I mean by "universal" the genera of species and the species of individuals; while I mean by "particular" the individuals of species. Particular, material individuals fall under the (perception) of senses, whereas genera and species do not fall under the senses, nor are they perceptible by sensory perception; they fall rather under the (perception of) one of the faculties of the perfect, i.e., human soul, that which is termed the human intellect.[2]

Like Aristotle, al-Kindī's point of entry into the discussion is a logical one for the purpose of definition, hence his use of the terms "genera" and "species." "Human being" as a species is a universal concept that can be a predicate of all particular human beings. "Animal" as genera is a universal concept that can be a predicate of the human species and other animals such as horses, dogs, and so on. However, al-Kindī does not always follow Aristotle in the process of grasping the universals. While for Aristotle universals are abstracted from sense experience, al-Kindī's position sometimes seems to depart from Aristotle's empirical approach, though it returns to Aristotle again later. It has been suggested that "al-Kindī's interests shifted away from Neoplatonizing metaphysical considerations and towards mathematically oriented, 'scientific' research."[3]

In the more developed and systematic philosophy of Abū Naṣr Fārābī, universals are discussed mostly in the context of the relation between language and logic. This is a major contribution to the history of philosophy by Fārābī.[4] He famously wrote commentaries on Aristotle's logical corpus, the *Organon*, as well as the widely used *Isagoge* by Porphyry, a Neoplatonic philosopher of late antiquity. Fārābī divides universals into "simple universals" (i.e., genus, differentia, species, property, and accident) and "compound universals" (i.e., definition [*ḥadd*] and description [*rasm*]). Compound universals are composed of simple universals. For example, the definition "a human being is a rational animal" consists of genus, differentia, and species; and the description "a human being is a laughing animal" consists of species, genus, and property. In adding the category of compound universals, Fārābī departs from Porphyry's *Isagoge*.[5] In his *Book of Letters* (*Kitāb al-Ḥurūf*), Fārābī has a semantical discussion of the universal in relation to knowledge formation, which suggests that the intellectual access to universals has an empirical basis:

> It is evident from the outset that here there are things perceived by the senses with similar and dissimilar things in them and that similar sense perceptions are so with respect to one intellectually perceived meaning they share in common. That is an attribute common to everything similar; so what is intellectually perceived in any one of them is intellectually perceived in the other. Let this

2. Ivy, *Al-Kindī's Metaphysics*, 62.
3. Adamson, *Al-Kindī*, 134.
4. See Hodges and Druart, "Al-Farabi's Philosophy."
5. See Fakhry *Al-Fārābī*, 56–57.

intellectually perceived thing be called "object predicated of many," "universal," and "general meaning."

The sense perception itself is any meaning that is single. It is not an attribute common to many things, nor are two things similar by virtue of it. Let these be called "individuals" and "distinct entities"; and let universals be called "genera" and "species."[6]

Avicenna's discussion of universals happens in several of his works in relation to both logic and metaphysics, which has given rise to many commentaries and debates. In his introduction (*Isagoge*) to the logic section of *The Healing* (*al-Shifāʾ*), similar to Fārābī, he follows Porphyry's classification of universals into genus, differentia, species, property, and accident. But Avicenna also addresses the late antiquity further division of the universals into logical, mental, and natural. The last type, "natural universal" (*kullī ṭabīʿī*), is the most controversial of all three and relates Avicenna's logic to his metaphysics both in the general sense and in relation to philosophical theology. Let us look at the three divisions of universals with an example. First, "humanity" as a universal (species) is individualized in every human being, and the mind can comprehend it as a concept. This is the mental form of humanity whose existence depends on our knowledge of particulars, hence Avicenna's rejection of Platonic Ideas/Forms, which ascribes a mind-independent existence to the universal of "humanity" outside of the human mind. Second, "humanity" as a logical universal refers to the logical consideration of the mental universal. In simple terms, the mind can accrue universality to humanity despite the fact that the mental form of humanity has a particular mental existence in the mind. As for the third type, natural universal, humanity as such is not conditioned by being either universal or particular.[7] Since for Avicenna, no universal can exist on its own in concrete reality, the "natural universal" cannot be identical with the individualized genus of humanity. Moreover, Avicenna seems to regard the ontological status of natural universals as prior to their individualized existence.

There have been many debates over what Avicenna exactly means by "natural universals," and one position that seems more consistent with his different texts is through the lens of his philosophical theology. When one compares different places where Avicenna discusses natural universals, it seems that he attributes to them a noetic existence within divine knowledge and, proceeding from divine knowledge, in the Intellects/angels. To explain this noetic existence, Avicenna uses the craftsman analogy and compares divine and angelic knowledge of universals to craftsman knowledge prior to crafting. His words in his *Isagoge* clarify the difference between this type of universal and a mental universal:

> In brief, sometimes a conceived form is in some manner a cause for the occurrence of the form that exists in external reality; sometimes the form in external reality is in some manner the cause of the conceived form, that is, [the latter] would have occurred in the mind after it had occurred in external reality. [69.10] Because the relation of all existing things to God and the angels is [the same as] the relation

6. Fārābī, *Book of Letters*, 210. (Slight changes have been made to the translation.)
7. For a detailed discussion of universals in Avicenna, see Marmura, "Avicenna's Chapter on Universals," 34–56.

of the artifacts we have to the productive soul, that which is in divine and angelic knowledge of the true nature of what is known and apprehended of natural things exists prior to multiplicity.[8]

This means that a natural universal may or may not have an individualized concrete existence in the external world, which is up to divine agency. As Avicenna himself reminds us, this discussion is more relevant to metaphysics.[9] Therefore, in the theological part of his *Metaphysics of the Healing*, he emphasizes the noetic existence of things in divine and angelic knowledge and introduces providence as the cause for the individualized existence of universals in concrete reality.[10]

ESSENCE AND EXISTENCE

These two concepts, both individually and in relation to each other, are not only the cornerstone of Islamic metaphysics but also the venue of its influence on the Latin West. Additionally, one's position on this subject may determine their association with a particular tradition of Islamic philosophy. Avicenna's unique position on natural universals is directly related to his metaphysical distinction between essence, or quiddity (a more technical term for essence), and existence. This distinction is significant not only for acknowledging the contribution of Islamic philosophers to metaphysics over and beyond the Greeks but also for understanding the progression of metaphysical trends within the history of Islamic philosophy. For Aristotle, who is believed to have only paved the way for the essence/existence conceptual distinction, the "essence" of a thing—that is, what the thing is—and its "existence" have the same referent in the extra-mental world, which houses all individual material and immaterial substances and the accidents of material substances. Substances are those existents that subsist in their own right, whereas accidents are the existents whose subsistence depends on the existence of a substance. For example, "redness" is an accident for an apple, which is a substance. Therefore, for Aristotle, existence "primarily" belongs to substances, and to say that something exists is the same as saying that something is a substance.[11] By this, he makes other existents—that is, accidents like qualities and quantities—only secondarily existent due to their dependence on substances. Departing from Aristotle, Islamic philosophers add more metaphysical nuances to this distinction, hence the appearance of conflicting approaches regarding the essence-existence distinction. This resulted in the establishment of two major traditions in Islamic metaphysics based on the ontological status of essence and existence.

First, for Avicenna, everything other than God is a composite of essence and existence. Although for him, essence and existence cannot be actually separated in the individual things, the Aristotelian position does not do justice to existence itself. To be more precise, "existence is neither a thing's quiddity, nor a part of its quiddity."[12] Moreover, for any essence to become a real thing, it must receive existence from God. With these principles

8. Cited in Marmura, "Avicenna's Chapter on Universals," 50. Brackets in the original.
9. Marmura, "Avicenna's Chapter on Universals," 50.
10. Avicenna, *Metaphysics of the Healing*, 339.
11. Aristotle, *Metaphysics*, Z I, 1028b, 2–4.
12. Avicenna, *al-Ishārāt wa'l-tanbīhāt*, 3:49.

combined, we can distinguish between Avicenna and Aristotle, on the one hand, and Avicenna and Islamic theologians, on the other hand. Avicenna differs from Aristotle because for the latter, existence is not additional to essence, and individual things are there in the world only by virtue of their individualized essence—that is, substance. For example, an individual human being as a substance is the universal essence of humanity individualized in a particular organic body, and there is no additional existence for this universal essence in the extra-mental world. In contrast, for Avicenna, the essences already reside in divine knowledge and come into existence by virtue of receiving external existence from God through His providence.

Furthermore, Avicenna's departure from Aristotle is often explained in the light of major theological interpretations of the Quranic doctrine of creation through the divine command "Be!" (Q 36:82). On the one hand, the theological usefulness of the distinction between essence and existence with regard to God's creative power was perhaps its main attraction for Christian philosophers like St. Thomas Aquinas (d. 1247).[13] On the other hand, the main philosophical critic of Avicenna's essence-existence distinction was Averroes, the Aristotelian philosopher from Andalusia. He dismissed Avicenna's distinction as logically problematic and blamed this departure from Aristotle on the bad influence of theologians:

> The theory that existence is something additional to the quiddity and that the existent in its substance is not constituted by it is a most erroneous theory, for this would imply that the term "existence" signified an accident outside the soul common to the ten categories—[14] and this is the theory of Avicenna. And then one may ask about this accident, when it is said to exist, if "exist" is taken here in the meaning of the "true" or whether it is meant that an accident exists in this accident and accidents would be found in it *ad infinitum*, which is impossible, as we have shown elsewhere.[15]

There is a disagreement among scholars as to whether Averroes has a correct understanding of Avicenna's distinction between essence and existence as a metaphysical distinction, meaning their distinction outside of the mind. Averroes is not wrong about the external reality of the distinction, but he is wrong in his interpretation of Avicenna's "existence" as an accident in the sense of an Aristotelian category such as whiteness. This is definitely not what "existence" means to Avicenna. For him, the divine act of existentiation through providence provides an existential bond, or the "ontological glue"[16] between God and the world that amounts to the realization of things whose essences remain dependent on this bond in order to subsist. As Avicenna puts it in *The Healing*, "Whatever is a possible existent is *always*, considered in itself, a possible existent. But, it may happen that its existence becomes necessary through another. This may either occur to it *always*, or else its necessity of existence through another may not be permanent—occurring rather at one time and not at another."[17]

13. For an accessible summary of Aquinas's complicated relationship to Avicenna, see Elders, *Thomas Aquinas and His Predecessors*, chapter 14.
14. He is referring to Aristotle's categorization of all beings into substance and nine accidents.
15. Averroes, *Tahāfut al-Tahāfut*, cited in Belo, "Essence and Existence," 421.
16. Leaman, *Averroes and His Philosophy*, 114.
17. Avicenna, *Metaphysics of the Healing*, 38. Italics mine.

As for Averroes's attribution of theological confusion to Avicenna, while Avicenna identifies God as the cause of the existence of things, he refutes the Muʿtazilite account of creation, according to which essence is a nonexistent "thing" in divine knowledge. Before explaining Avicenna's position, I need to explain the Muʿtazilite position. The Muʿtazilite were the early rationalists of Islamic history whose theological hegemony lasted only for a while, though their influence on philosophy was long lasting. They offered several controversial doctrines, and one of their famous views was their argument for nonexistent "objects" of God's intention. For the Muʿtazilites, before God brings *x* into existence, *x* must be some "thing," since God's intention cannot be of nothing. But this "thing" is still nonexistent before God's act of creation. They argue that "the objects of intentions have to be real, because intending something means to build a connection or relation to it."[18]

Avicenna addresses this doctrine. In some of his texts, he sounds like he differentiates between the referents of "thing" (*shay'*) and existent. In other texts, especially later ones, he emphatically argues for their co-extensionality and replaces "thingness" with "quiddity," a progression that is described as a sign of his departure from theologians during the course of his "intellectual development."[19] Therefore, it seems that for Avicenna, essence, or quiddity, is a thing only if it *exists*, whether it is in the external world, the mind, or the divine/angelic knowledge. For every external existent, its essence has a prior noetic existence in the divine realm and a posterior existence in the human mind that takes form upon experiencing concrete objects.

Regardless of the different interpretations of the essence-existence distinction, Avicenna's thesis becomes a cornerstone in the development of metaphysics in the east side of the Islamic world. There were different approaches to this distinction even among Avicenna's immediate followers, and the issue gave rise to hot debates among major post-Avicennian philosophers. These philosophers are primarily divided into two groups: those who consider the essence-existence distinction only as conceptual and those fewer who consider it as both conceptual and real.[20] A prominent example of the first group is Suhrawardī, and the second group may be represented by Fakhr al-Dīn Rāzī. Two later philosophers who engaged in this debate are Muḥammad Bāqir Mīr Dāmād and Mullā Ṣadrā, who, despite their differences from Avicenna and from each other, acknowledge their indebtedness to him for their overall metaphysical frameworks. With this in mind, in the rest of this section, I will discuss two related questions. First, how the essence-existence distinction leads to two radically different traditions, essentialism and existentialism, in postclassical Islamic metaphysics. Second, how essentialism becomes a venue for the return of Platonic Ideas.

Suhrawardī marks post-Avicennian Islamic philosophy with an imaginative mixture of Platonic and Persian colors. The centrality of light in his metaphysics credited him with the establishment of the philosophy of illumination (*ḥikmat al-ishrāq*), or Illuminationism, as a rival of Peripatetic philosophy, as well as a transition to the later Transcendentalist school of Mullā Ṣadrā. With respect to the essence-existence distinction, Suhrawardī only holds it true in the mind. For him, existence is only an intellectual consideration

18. Benevich, "Reality of the Non-Existent Object," 35.
19. Wisnovsky, "Avicenna's Concept of Thingness," 221.
20. See Benevich, "Essence-Existence Distinction," 206–7.

(*iʿtibār ʿaqlī*). But as Walbridge notes, this intellectual consideration is not an arbitrary one because the mind cannot ascribe existence to what does not exist in reality.[21] Suhrawardī argues against the real distinction between essence and existence in the sense of existence being conferred on essence for the latter to exist. For example, he says,

> It is erroneous to try to prove that existence is superadded in concrete things by arguing that if something were not conjoined to the quiddity by a cause, the quiddity would remain in nonexistence. The one who makes this argument posits a quiddity and then joins existence to it, so his opponent can argue that this concrete quiddity is itself from the efficient cause. The argument also can return to the question of whether the added existence itself is given something else by the efficient cause or whether it is left as it was.[22]

Suhrawardī's interpretation of the essence-existence distinction is based on two assumptions. First, he interprets Avicenna's view on the status of essences, or quiddities, to be that of nonexistence before their concrete existence in the external world. However, as previously explained, for Avicenna, before being given their external existence, essences exist in God's knowledge through a divine mode of existence. Second, Suhrawardī seems to interpret Avicenna's "existence" itself as a thing that needs to be given existence to be existent, an argument that is similar to Averroes's criticism mentioned previously. But for Avicenna, with the exception of God, who is pure Being, existence is always the existence of something whether it is in the human mind, the concrete world, and/or the divine knowledge. Based on his understanding of what is meant by existence in Peripatetic philosophy, Suhrawardī dismisses its real distinction from essence by resorting to the impossibility of infinite regress: If existence is there as an existent, then it must have received existence from another existent, and this chain can regress infinitely, which is logically absurd. Therefore, unlike essence, existence is not a reality.

In contrast to Suhrawardī, Fakhr al-Dīn Rāzī, his contemporary and peer, considers the essence-existence relation to be real, though his explanation of it is different from that of Avicenna.[23] Fakhr al-Dīn Rāzī argues extensively in support of his own position, according to which existence as the "realization" of essences is an "extra-mental phenomenon." By introducing "realization" into the discussion, he tries to dismiss the idea that "existence" is an attribute that is externally added to essences.[24] On the other hand, Rāzī disagrees with Avicenna on the preexistence of essences in the divine mind before their realization in the world. Yet at the same time, he would not want to think of them as nothing, so he concludes that essences are between existence and nonexistence before their "realization." As he says in one of his writings, "The quiddity [essence] is the substrate of inherence for existence. Furthermore, the quiddity as such (*min ḥaythu hiya hiya*) is a quiddity distinct from existence and non-existence."[25] This in-between status of essences has been subject to different interpretations as well as criticisms—for example, by Naṣīr

21. Walbridge, "*Intimations of the Tablet and the Throne*," 267.
22. Suhrawardī, *Philosophy of Illumination*, 46.
23. Wisnovsky, "Avicenna's Concept of Thingness," 29–30; Benevich, "Essence-Existence Distinction," 208, 226, 237–42; Kaukua, *Suhrawardī's Illuminationism*, 58.
24. Benevich, "Essence-Existence Distinction," 226.
25. Benevich, "Essence-Existence Distinction," 240.

al-Dīn Ṭūsī. However, some contemporary scholars try to read Rāzī more charitably in this regard. For example, in a reading of Rāzī, while essence and existence are distinct in their metaphysical reality, they are never separated in the external world.[26]

Returning to Suhrawardī's dismissal of existence, what is the ontological status of essences? Suhrawardī's answer to this question is found in his endorsement of Platonic Ideas or Forms. The Forms are stand-alone and independent essences, which are behind the existence of individual objects because the latter are "bundles" of Form-instantiations. He has several arguments to prove that the identity of individual objects against changes can only be justified if there are enduring Forms behind them.[27] Obviously, in Suhrawardī's metaphysics, where light is *the* reality, Forms are certain types of lights that issue from the Light of Lights, or God.

Suhrawardī not only envisions the wisdom of ancient Persians and Greeks in agreement but also considers them as utilizing the same philosophical methodology, which brings together discursive thinking and intuitive unveiling (*kashf*) or illumination (*ishrāq*). In the spirit of Illuminationism, Suhrawardī describes Platonic Ideas as an order of light-species, which are related to individuals through a "relation of emanation."[28] These are luminary archetypes, and according to Suhrawardī, they do not have to be the same as their individual examples in all aspects, since the individuals are complex and concrete, while the Ideas are "simple essences" and incorporeal.[29] Thus, for Suhrawardī, the Platonic Idea of *horse* "is not an ideal horse" but "the cause of the species horse."[30] Suhrawardī believes that the ancient Persians and Greeks discovered this truth through divine illumination:

> Whosoever questions the truth of this . . . let him engage in mystical disciplines and service to those visionaries that perchance he will, as dazzled by the thunderbolt . . . witness the heavenly essences and lights that Hermes and Plato beheld. . . . All the sages of Persia were agreed thereon. For them even water possessed an archetype [or idol] in the heavenly kingdom which they named "Khordad." That of trees they named "Mordad," and that of fire they named "Ordibehesht."[31]

At this point, I would like to suggest that the possibility of a modified Platonic interpretation of Avicenna's natural universals could have been one of the reasons behind the development of Platonism in post-Avicennian metaphysics, despite his own outright rejection of Platonic Ideas.[32] Several centuries later than Suhrawardī, Mīr Dāmād from Safavid Persia offers a metaphysical system that is fully conscious of its own essentialism. To prove that his essentialism is based on a correct understanding of Avicenna's metaphysics, Mīr Dāmād brings some evidence from Avicenna's writings and argues

26. Benevich, "Essence-Existence Distinction," 242.
27. Kaukua, *Suhrawardī's Illuminationism*, 160–61.
28. Suhrawardī, *Philosophy of Illumination*, 109.
29. Suhrawardī, *Philosophy of Illumination*, 109. For Suhrawardī's proof of Forms and how they function, see the interpretation in Kaukua, *Suhrawardī's Illuminationism*, 167–84.
30. Walbridge, "*Intimations of the Tablet and the Throne*," 270.
31. Suhrawardī, *Philosophy of Illumination*, 108. In modern Persian, these three titles are the names of months in the solar calendar.
32. Avicenna, *Metaphysics of the Healing*, 249–56.

that Avicenna's "existence" is not anything additional to the essence of a thing. This is because "the caused thing is its very essence and its quiddity as made by the Maker's simple act of making, and existence is the signification of the substance of its actually created essence."[33] As one contemporary scholar explains, for Mīr Dāmād, "existence" simply "signifies the very actualization of a creature through a cause."[34] Mīr Dāmād's essentialism is closely associated with his Neoplatonic distinction between the world of "perpetual" (*dahrī*) intellects and that of "transient" sensible things. In support of his view, he quotes from the *Theology of Aristotle*:

> Then he [Plato] distinguished between the intelligible and the sensible, between the [unqualified] natures of beings and sensible things; he made the unseen beings perpetual, never ceasing from their state; and he made the sensible things transient and subject to generation and corruption. When he had finished with this distinction, he said: "The cause of the unseen beings which have no bodies and the sensible things which have bodies is one and the same, and it is the first real Being." He means by this the Maker, the Creator (glorified be He). Then he said: "The First Maker, who is the cause of both the perpetual intelligible beings and the perishable sensible beings, is the Pure Good, and nothing is worthy of the Good except itself."[35]

According to Mīr Dāmād's interpretation of Plato's Ideas, each temporal and changeable object has a perpetual and unchangeable relation to the intelligible world—that is, it is perpetual from the perspective of the intellects. For him, Platonic Ideas are not separable entities but the unchangeable side of temporal things.[36] Thus, with Mīr Dāmād, who also enjoyed a high position among the Safavid nobility, a full-scale essentialism, including a new interpretation of Platonic Ideas, becomes an important metaphysical discourse in the intellectual milieu of Shiʿa Persia. His school flourished in the city of Isfahan, which also happened to be the political capital of the Safavid Empire.

However, the essentialist school birthed a rival within its own walls. In due course, a promising student of Mīr Dāmād who had come to Isfahan from the city of Shiraz started to play a different tune on the essence/existence relation. Starting as a follower of Mīr Dāmād's essentialism, this student, who would become famous as Mullā Ṣadrā, subverted the order of the dual concepts in favor of existence, a finding that he appreciated as a gift from God.[37] Mullā Ṣadrā offers several arguments across his many writings to prove that the only authentic reality is existence, while essence is only a shadow or apparition of it in the mind. In the world, there are only existences, which are different grades of the one overarching and absolute Being.

Unlike essence, existence (*wujūd*) cannot be conceptualized or defined. It is "neither universal, nor particular, neither general, nor specific,"[38] yet its reality is "the most mani-

33. Mīr Dāmād, *Book of Blazing Brands*, 37–38.
34. Brown, "Second and Third *Qabas*," 11–74.
35. Mīr Dāmād, *Book of Blazing Brands*, 107. Brackets in the original.
36. A brief summary of Mīr Dāmād's position can be found in Mullā Ṣadrā, *al-Shawāhid al-rubūbiyya*, 157.
37. Mullā Ṣadrā, *al-Ḥikma al-mutaʿāliya fī asfār al-ʿaqliyya al-arbaʿa*, 1:49 (henceforth, *Asfār*).
38. Mullā Ṣadrā, *Book of Metaphysical Penetrations*, 7.

fest of all things through presence and unveiling,"[39] and it is the ground of all that is real. In other words, there is no reality in the world but existence. Taking on Suhrawardī's objection to existence, Mullā Ṣadrā responds that existence is "the reality of all that possesses reality, and it does not need, in its possessing reality, another reality. It is by itself in the external world."[40] What he means is that existence is the one and only reality, so it is absurd to posit another reality to realize it. Other than existence is just nonexistence, and "nonexistence" (*ʿadam*) signifies nothing. Nevertheless, the world consists of a multiplicity of things with different definitions and descriptions, so Mullā Ṣadrā needs to explain this paradox of unity as diversity or diversity as unity. In simple terms, how can the one and only reality of existence appear as multiple realities to which our common sense attests? Mullā Ṣadrā's answer to this question composes the core of his theocentric existentialism, which he offers in the face of essentialism. For him, the diversity that appears to hold among things is primarily due to different degrees of existence that are reflected in the mind as delimitations or determinations (*taʿayyunāt*) of existence. While Mullā Ṣadrā tries to provide arguments for his thesis of the gradation of existence (*tashkīk al-wujūd*), he admits that the idea was inspired by the famous philosophical Sufi doctrine of the "unity of being" (*waḥdat al-wujūd*), which he often communicates with reference to light: "Verily, rather than being independent things and detached essences, the existences, despite their diversity and differentiations, are only levels of the determinations of the First Real One, manifestations of His light, and modes of His reality."[41]

With this ontological turn, Mullā Ṣadrā also offers a new interpretation of Platonic Ideas and tries to save them independently of essentialism. In several of his works, Mullā Ṣadrā begins with criticizing his Islamic predecessors such as Suhrawardī and Mīr Dāmād for their versions of Platonic Ideas, then offers his own interpretation and argues in favor of what he considers Plato's true position. In this respect, Mullā Ṣadrā first offers three arguments to prove the possibility of the Platonic Ideas rather than their specific characterization by Plato. The first argument is a cosmological one based on his thesis of motion in natural substances: (1) All natural substances are subject to motion; (2) natural motion is not accidental, but a natural substance is originally caused to be in motion; and (3) the cause of the substance-in-motion cannot itself be in motion, hence not material, otherwise the absurdity of infinite regress would ensue. Therefore, the sustainer of each natural substance must be an immaterial and intellectual substance.[42]

The second argument is as follows: (1) Every natural species exists with both a sensible existence and an intelligible existence (for example, the sensible human being as a material individual and the intelligible human being that the mind grasps as a universal), (2) the intelligible human being must exist either in the mind as a psychic accident or in the extra-mental world as an intellectual substance, and (3) if it exists as a mental accident, then it cannot be identified with substances, because substance cannot be an accident. Therefore, it must exist in the extra-mental world.[43]

39. Mullā Ṣadrā, *Book of Metaphysical Penetrations*, 6.
40. Mullā Ṣadrā, *Book of Metaphysical Penetrations*, 11.
41. Mullā Ṣadrā, *Asfār*, 1:71. For an analytical study of this thesis, see Rizvi, *Mullā Ṣadrā and Metaphysics*.
42. Mullā Ṣadrā, *Asfār*, 1:159–60.
43. Mullā Ṣadrā, *Asfār*, 1:160–61.

This is my reconstruction of the third argument: (1) All physical natures have real effects inherent in a specific matter (for example, rationality is an effect of the nature of humanity in the material Socrates); (2) inherent natures cannot have any effects independently of the matter in which they inhere, because materialized natures do not even have a separate existence from their matter; and (3) if the inherent natures caused the effects in the matter, then they should have done it independently of the matter, which is impossible. Therefore, there are agents that cause the real effects that are not inherent in matter. This is also followed by a sub-argument that a universal nature applies to its instances univocally, so there should exist a real agent that specifies the effects to a specific matter or material object.[44]

After these arguments for the possibility of Ideas, Mullā Ṣadrā proceeds to defend his interpretation of Platonic Ideas based on his existential metaphysics and his doctrine of the gradation of existence. First, he clarifies that Platonic Ideas are the origins and causes of physical individuals, and they are detached from all material attachment, which is a concomitant of lower degrees of existence in material things. He makes it clear that Ideas and their instances are different in the degree of existence.[45]

For Mullā Ṣadrā, inadequate interpretations by Islamic Platonists such as Suhrawardī and Mīr Dāmād are primarily due to their essentialism—because if you identify the foundation of reality with essence, then your only explanation for the relation between a material individual and its Platonic Idea would be based on positing gradation in essence, which is not possible. For Mullā Ṣadrā, gradation is possible only in existence because just like in the example of different lights, what differentiates two degrees of existence is nothing but existence itself. From his lens, Avicenna was correct in refuting Platonic Ideas in the sense of higher essences because he could not accept gradation in essence. However, unlike Mullā Ṣadrā, he did not uphold a gradational existentialism to support Platonic Ideas. Mullā Ṣadrā claims that he has restored the theory of Platonic Ideas in its original sense among ancient philosophers. He offers several arguments for Platonic Ideas, which also show the strong influence of Plotinus through the *Theology of Aristotle*, which he often cites in this context. He places the higher degrees or Ideas of all things in "the noblest world that is alive and perfect" because "it originates from the First Perfect Originator and encompasses every soul and every intellect, and it certainly has no deficiency and no need because all things in [that world] are brimful and rich."[46]

MODES OF ESSENCE AND EXISTENCE

The metaphysical distinction between essence and existence is closely associated with the modes of essence and existence—namely, necessary, possible, and impossible. In this section, I will discuss necessity and possibility only in Islamic metaphysics, but I should note that these two notions are the building blocks of a division in logic (i.e., modal logic) that is a rather controversial area among contemporary logicians. On the other hand, contemporary Western metaphysicians are interested in modalities in relation to the notion of "possible worlds" where logical and metaphysical studies conjoin. Furthermore, modes

44. Mullā Ṣadrā, *Asfār*, 1:161–62.
45. Mullā Ṣadrā, *Asfār*, 1:163.
46. Mullā Ṣadrā, *al-Shawāhid al-rubūbiyya*, 173.

can be modes of propositions (*de dicto*) and modes of things (*de re*). In what follows, it is the latter sense of modalities that I explain due to its significance in Islamic metaphysics.

Aristotle's discussion of modalities appears in his logical writings, and later logicians, especially Avicenna, add more nuances to it. Avicenna's discussion of different types of modalities is a significant contribution to the history of logic and metaphysics. Among the various types of modalities that Avicenna expounds, one is especially important for his metaphysics, to which contemporary scholars refer as "alethic." The three modes of necessity, possibility, and impossibility that appear under "alethic" modes are further divided, but in the metaphysical interest of the present chapter, I address only two types of possibility and two types of necessity. Possibility is either general (*al-imkān al-ʿāmm*) or specific (*al-imkān al-khāṣṣ*). The former simply means "not-impossible"; we intend this meaning when we say, "Our team's victory is possible." The latter has a more technical sense that refers to "not-impossible" and "not-necessary." This type of possibility, which is called "two-sided," can be a predicate of everything that is either already in existence or could be existent in the future, such as the existent species of horses and those species that could come into being.[47] Although both types of possibility have the same referential scope, it is only the first sense of it that we intend in everyday discourses, while the second sense appears mostly in philosophical discussion.

As for necessity, again in relation to the present discussion, I only refer to two types of it—namely, "necessity through another" (*wujūb bi'l-ghayr*) and "necessity by itself" (*wujūb bi'l-dhāt*). All that exists due to its cause exists necessarily through it. While the scope of this type of necessity is the entirety of the actual world, the other type of necessity can be predicated only of the First Cause, or God, hence Avicenna's use of the term "Necessary Existent" (*al-wājib al-wujūd*) in reference to God. Relation to a cause is the key to understanding the distinction between these two types of necessity. The First Cause is, by definition, without a cause, so it does not need to be necessitated by anything else. Everything other than the First Cause that is in existence, though possible with respect to its own essence, is necessary with respect to its cause:

> If it were not necessary, then with the existence of the cause and with respect to it, it would still be [possible]. It would then be possible for it to exist or not to exist, being specified with neither of the two states. [Once again] from the beginning this would be in need of the existence of a third thing through which either existence (as distinct from non-existence) or nonexistence (as distinct from existence) would be assigned for [the possible] when the cause of its existence with [this state of affairs] would not have been specified. This would be another cause and the discussion would extend to an infinite regress. And if it regresses infinitely, the existence of the possible, with all this, would not have been specified by it. As such, its existence would not have been realized.[48]

In sum, while two-sided possibility is the mode of every essence with respect to itself, necessity is the mode of all existent essences—that is, things—with respect to what gives

47. For a detailed discussion of modalities in Avicenna, see Chatti, "Avicenna on Possibility and Necessity," 332–53.
48. Avicenna, *Metaphysics of the Healing*, 31. Brackets in the original.

them existence. This distinction, which has one foot in logic and one in metaphysics, is an indispensable conceptual tool in Islamic philosophy, both classical and postclassical. For example, Suhrawardī envisions a hierarchy of contingent lights comprising the material and immaterial worlds issued from the Light of Lights. The only light or reality that is necessary by itself is the Light of Lights. He argues thus: "Nonbeing cannot overtake the Light of Lights; for were it contingently existent, it would be a contingent existent . . . and would need something absolutely independent—which would be the Light of Lights, since this series [of causes] must end."[49]

Like Avicenna, Suhrawardī characterizes the relation between cause and effect as necessary and believes that "if all the reasons and conditions for the existence of a thing are there . . . then the existence of that thing is necessary."[50] Suhrawardī maintains only one mode—namely, necessity—where a thing is understood only by virtue of its own essence in logical analysis. For example, "Necessarily all humans are possibly literate, necessarily animals, or impossibly stones,"[51] which means that no matter which of the three modes is predicated of the essence, the predication is always necessary because the possibility of becoming literate is necessary for humans, just as becoming rocks is necessarily impossible for them. This approach to modalities is later followed by Mullā Ṣadrā. He repeats the former's argument that all modal propositions turn into necessary ones if the mode is relocated to become part of the predicate, since "possibility is necessary for the possible just like impossibility is for the impossible and necessity for the necessary."[52]

The previous statement by Mullā Ṣadrā in his logical treatise is a simple repetition of Suhrawardī's logical theory of modalities. But moving to metaphysics of modalities, unlike his predecessor, who attributes modal notions to essences, Mullā Ṣadrā attributes them to existence. This is no surprise because for him, existence is the only reality, and what is the case in the existent world is necessarily so. This entails from the metaphysical teaching that whatever exists is just a manifestation of Absolute Existence, which is Necessary. In relation to the Necessary Being, which is "eternal necessity" (*al-ḍarūra al-azaliyya*), things are existences that proceed from the Necessary Being.[53] In the domain of conceptual analysis, "possible" only means "not-necessary to exist or not to exist," and "impossible" means necessary not to exist. But in reality, "necessary" is the only meaningful mode of reality. According to Mullā Ṣadrā,

> Next to the concept of existence and thingness in general, there is no other concept that is conceived by the human mind prior to the concepts of necessary and non-necessary. So, when necessity is attributed to existence, [the mode] becomes necessity; when it is attributed to non-existence, [the mode] becomes impossibility; and when non-necessity is attributed to either side of [existence or non-existence] or to both sides, there will respectively be general possibility and narrow-possibility, [which are the same as one-sided and two-sided possibilities].[54]

49. Suhrawardī, *Philosophy of Illumination*, 87.
50. Suhrawardī, *Shape of Light*, 61.
51. Suhrawardī, *Philosophy of Illumination*, 17.
52. Mullā Ṣadrā, *al-Tanqīḥ fi'l-manṭiq*, 212.
53. Mullā Ṣadrā, *Asfār*, 1:186–87.
54. Mullā Ṣadrā, *Asfār*, 1:83–84.

To interpret the previous quote in the light of Mullā Ṣadrā's general position on reality, while we can still analyze the mode of existence in terms of the three logical notions of necessity, possibility, and impossibility, among these three, only "necessity" has a real meaning, as it has the same referent as "existence." In addition, only necessary propositions state a fact about the real world in a meaningful way.

THE COSMOS AND ITS DYNAMICS

The concepts discussed in the previous sections are useful in understanding deeper aspects of the world at large. But philosophers are also interested in explaining the mechanism of the natural world specifically and, for Islamic philosophers, the relation between the natural and the supernatural. Classical and postclassical Islamic philosophers have written on the structure and dynamics of the cosmos, and like their philosophical predecessors beyond the Islamic world, they have created discourses where experimental sciences and metaphysical speculations reciprocate. Major Islamic philosophers build intricate discursive systems, which also incorporate the scientific methodology based on observation, induction, and deduction. The goal is to understand and explain how the universe works and how the cosmos follows a rational pattern, which in turn indicates a metaphysical structure based on a divine blueprint. This means that Islamic philosophy provides a cosmology that brings together scientific, metaphysical, and theological notions to explain the world in a holistic manner.

The key metaphysical concept used in cosmology is "causality," which has different senses depending on how the relation between the cause and effect is understood. Whereas in Aristotelian cosmology, causality is understood in terms of giving motion or bringing about change broadly construed, in classical Islamic philosophy, in addition to the causation of motion, there is also causation in the sense of the bestowal of existence to what is essentially possible. Moreover, Aristotle formulates four types of causes—namely, the material, formal, efficient, and final causes, which play an important part in explaining the mechanics of the cosmos. Let us take a table as an example. The material cause of the table is wood, the formal cause is the form/function of tableness, the efficient cause is the carpenter, and the final cause is the idea or plan of the table in the carpenter's mind before crafting it, which is identical to the purpose toward which it tends. These four concepts are used in every section of Islamic cosmology, including the origination and dynamics of the heavens and earth, as well as the soul-body relations. For Aristotle and his followers, the chain of causes cannot regress infinitely; so the cosmos is bound to have been caused/moved by the First Cause/Mover, which is itself not caused/moved. This is a mechanical and eternal relation that does not involve a creative agency of the kind normally associated with God in various religious traditions.

As early as al-Kindī, the sense of causality changes with respect to the relation between God and the world—namely, creation. Al-Kindī uses the notions of change and motion in explaining natural processes in the world of "generation and corruption" and only in a particular sense for God's creation. With regard to God's causality, one can speak of efficient causality in terms of giving existence to something previously nonexistent, and the process implies voluntary agency. However, bringing something into existence is also interpreted by him as motion in the sense of change. He says in *On First Philosophy*,

> What is brought to be has not always existed, and what has not always existed is originated; that is, its being-brought-to-be is from a cause. That which is brought-to-be is originated, and since the cause of its being-brought-to-be is the true, first One, the cause of origination is the true, first One. But the cause from which motion is originated, I mean, the mover, is the agent.[55]

Al-Kindī's position on the origination of the cosmos has strong tendencies toward Neoplatonic emanation theory. Using causality in the sense of emanation gives rise to a complex and hierarchical universe that incorporates philosophical, theological, and astronomical narratives. This hierarchical universe has God on top, with the world of Intellects and the Soul to follow. Additionally, this cosmic model incorporates Greek astronomy and includes heavenly spheres with souls, of which seven also have celestial bodies that were observed as planets and the moon.

Similar to Aristotle, Fārābī's First Cause seems to have an intellectual nature, although for the most part, he uses the language of "existence" in referring to it. This ambivalence will be resolved later by Avicenna. Fārābī pictures the order of immaterial existents, each emanating the one below. After arguing that everything that exists comes into being from the First, which is perfect and exists through itself alone,[56] Fārābī divides the world into the superlunary and sublunary, respectively the supernatural and the natural world. He says that "from the First emanates the existence of the Second," and so comes the "Third," down to "the Eleventh," with which the incorporeal superlunary world ends. Along with each descending level of emanation comes more diversity. While the First only contemplates itself, the Second has both itself and the First to contemplate. In virtue of thinking of the First, the Second Intellect emanates the Third Intellect, while as a result of thinking of itself, it generates the "First Heaven." This dual intellective process goes on to the next Intellects, with each respectively being associated with the sphere of the fixed stars and the spheres of Saturn, Jupiter, Mars, the Sun, Venus, Mercury, and the Moon, except for the last Intellect, which is in charge of the natural world.[57] The rotating motion of the spheres is caused by their souls. The last Intellect, or the Active Intellect, is given the most attention by Islamic philosophers due to its direct ontological and epistemological influence on the world of nature and humans.

Avicenna prefers to call the First Cause the "Necessary Being," or that which is necessary through itself. The Necessary Being emanates one thing—namely, the First Intellect—after which the Intellects are emanated one after the other in a hierarchy down to the Active Intellect, which is the tenth. For both Fārābī and Avicenna, the emanated cosmos is eternal in the sense of having no temporal beginning. This is reminiscent of Aristotle's conception of the cosmos, which was criticized by some late antique Christian and Muslim philosophers for running contrary to the Christian and Muslim understanding of the cosmos as having been created out of nothing at a certain point in time. Al-Kindī, too, finds the eternity of the world theologically problematic. In response, Avicenna uses modality as a tool to draw a line between God and the world while avoiding the theological position of creation out of nothing. For Avicenna, there is an ontological distinction between God and the world,

55. Cited in Adamson, *Al-Kindī*, 72.
56. Fārābī, *On the Perfect State*, 89.
57. Fārābī, *On the Perfect State*, 101–5.

which would not be undermined by the belief in the eternity of the world. This distinction is due to the necessity of God and possibility of every existent other than God. Thus, the supernatural world of the Intellects is eternal but still dependent on God as the only Existence that is necessary through itself. They are ontologically dependent on God, and with respect to their essence, they are only possible. In other words, the criterion for being created is "possibility," not emerging out of nothing at a certain point in time.

In *The Incoherence of the Philosophers* (*Tahāfut al-falāsifa*), Ghazālī lays out some logical problems in Fārābī's and Avicenna's eternity thesis, a belief that he also regards as tantamount to heresy. Ghazālī has elaborate arguments in refutation of the world's eternity—namely, its pre-eternity and post-eternity. Simply put, for Avicenna, God is the essential cause of the world, and an essential cause cannot be temporally prior to its effect, which necessarily issues from it. In other words, "the world exists as long as God exists and God cannot exist alone without the world just as there is no fire in the room without light."[58] Ghazālī has serious issues with this picture of creation. For him, this model excludes choice and real agency on God's part. After citing "the philosophers" about the logical problems of a temporal gap between God and His creation—namely, creation in time—Ghazālī gathers all his force to prove that it is possible for God to be the real cause of the world and create it in time. To do so, as is the general methodology of his book, he first tries to show the inconsistencies in philosophers' arguments and then proceeds to offer his own demonstrations. The upshot of his discussion is that "time is originated and created and before it there was no time at all. We mean by our statement that God is prior to the world and time: That He was and there was no world, and that then He was and with Him was the world."[59] So it is true that the human mind cannot imagine any state outside of time, but this does not entail the impossibility of such a state.

The Andalusian Ibn Ṭufayl, who considers himself indebted to both Avicenna and Ghazālī, expresses his puzzlement at the dilemmatic character of the issue and adopts a conciliatory approach between his two most favorite thinkers. Ibn Ṭufayl argues that whether the world was eternal or created out of nothing at a point in time would not change the fact that it is caused and sustained by "an incorporeal Agent." In his famous philosophical fiction *Ḥayy Ibn Yaqẓān*, Ibn Ṭufayl reaches the following conclusion:

> Thus the whole universe—including the heavens, earth, planets, and stars, and whatever is between them, above them, and below them—is the result of Its [God's] action and creation. Moreover, [the whole universe] is essentially posterior to It, even if not temporally posterior. It is just as when you grasp a certain body and then move your hand; for that body necessarily is moved as a consequence of your hand's moving, [in which case its] motion is essentially posterior to the movement of your hand, even if it is not temporally posterior to it, but in fact they both move simultaneously. In the same way the whole universe would be an effect and creation of this Agent without a [first moment of] time. "His command, when He wills a thing, is only to say to it 'Be!' and it is" [Q 36:82].[60]

58. Griffel, "*Incoherence of the Philosophers*," 200.
59. Ghazālī, *Incoherence of the Philosophers*, 31.
60. Ibn Ṭufayl, *Ḥayy Ibn Yaqẓān*, in McGinnis and Reisman, 293. Brackets in the original.

In contrast to his predecessor, Averroes is not ready to make any compromises on this issue. He defends the eternity of the world against Ghazālī's criticisms, though in his mature philosophy, he completely rejects the emanationist cosmology of Fārābī and Avicenna. As explained before, he was also against Avicenna's essence-existence distinction that is essential to a cosmology in which existence is issued from God as the ultimate efficient cause of all that exists.[61] Against the Neoplatonic emanationism of Fārābī and Avicenna, Averroes argues that there is no place for emanation as the cause of existence. He premises his argument on the Aristotelian view of efficient causality, according to which the power of the efficient cause lies only in actualizing a potentiality, not bringing things into existence. To put an otherwise complicated argument in very simplified form,

P1. Every efficient cause is the cause of actualizing potentiality.

P2. There is no potentiality in the incorporeal domain.

P3. The First Cause and its effects are in the incorporeal domain.

Therefore, the causal relation between the First Cause and its effects is not efficient causality.

Whereas for Avicenna, God is both the efficient and final cause,[62] for Averroes, the First Cause only functions as the final cause in the incorporeal world. This means that the First Cause as the object of their intellection motivates the Intellects to the extent that their rank of perfection allows them.[63] This position is in tandem with Averroes's efforts in understanding Aristotle's own words away from commentaries of late antiquity and the Islamic world, which, according to some scholars, "also often happens to be the truth [of Aristotle's positions]."[64] However, it is also correctly suggested that Averroes still thinks of the First Cause as the creator of the Intellects rather than a mere cause of their motion.[65] This makes it difficult to clearly understand Averroes's position between being a literalist Aristotelian and a Muslim who wishes to believe in a creator rather than just a prime mover.

Despite his different position on the type and mechanism of cosmic causation, Averroes's incorporeal world has a similar content and structure to that of Fārābī, where the First Cause is followed by the rest of the Intellects, each associated with a sphere that has a soul and body. Contrary to Aristotle and similar to Fārābī and Avicenna, Averroes's Intellects are ordered by nobility such that the higher ones are superior to the lower ones.

One point of interest about the inhabitants of the incorporeal world in Islamic philosophy is the appearance of certain interpretations under the influence of theological and poetic narratives—for example, the characterization of the Intellects as angels. To be more precise, both Fārābī and Avicenna point out the angelic character of the last

61. On the meaning of efficient causality in both metaphysical and natural senses in Avicenna, see Richardson, "Avicenna's Conception of the Efficient Cause," 220–39.
62. On the relation between efficient causality and final causality in Avicenna, see Wisnovsky, "Final and Efficient Causality," 97–124. See also López-Farjeat, *Classical Islamic Philosophy*, 193–96.
63. Davidson, *Alfarabi, Avicenna, and Averroes*, 229.
64. Druart, "Averroes," 196.
65. Davidson, *Alfarabi, Avicenna, and Averroes*, 231. For the background and nuances of this subject, see Adamson, "Averroes on Divine Causation," 198–217.

intellect—that is, the Active Intellect. The role of the Active Intellect in revealing truths to prophets is the ground for its assimilation with Angel Gabriel of the Quran. As far as the relation between cosmology and theology is concerned, Ḥamīd al-Dīn Kirmānī, an Ismaʿīlī contemporary of Avicenna, is a good example. He interprets many Quranic verses in the light of the emanationist cosmology of the Islamic philosophers. One prominent example is his equation of the First Intellect with the command of God (*amr Allah*), the Second Intellect with the Pen (*qalam*), and the Third Intellect with the Tablet (*lawḥ*), all terms borrowed from the Quran.[66]

As for the poetic rendering of the emanationist cosmology, one colorful example is Suhrawardī's *The Reverberation of Gabriel's Wing* (*Āwāz-i par-i Jibrāʾīl*). In this Persian symbolic work, "ten old men of beautiful countenance" who call themselves "the abstracted ones" stand for the ten Intellects. The only one among the old men who converses with the narrator is the one at the very end of the bench where they are all seated; this particular old man is "extensive in knowledge" and represents the Active Intellect. Also, this old man says that he is the only one among the elders who can speak to the narrator because humans are not worthy of approaching the ones above him, so he serves as their speaker. He further explains that each of them has a son who is in charge of a mill.[67] The "sons" stand for the souls of the spheres, and the mills for their planets. Suhrawardī's hierarchy of Dominant Lights closely matches the hierarchy of the Intellects down to the last one—namely, the Active Intellect, whom he refers to also as the Holy Spirit (namely, Gabriel).[68]

The emanationist cosmology of classical Islamic philosophy remains in the philosophical arena through later Islamic philosophy in Persia. Following their past masters, Mīr Dāmād and Mullā Ṣadrā structure their cosmology based on the hierarchy of the Intellects and pay much attention to the last one—namely, the Active Intellect—as the ontological and epistemological link between the divine and the mundane worlds. There are differences among Islamic philosophers in the mechanical details, but the general terminology, conceptual schemes, and relevance to theological narratives are similar. For example, Mullā Ṣadrā does not give a fixed number for the intellects, and by alluding to a verse in the Quran (Q 74:34), he refers to them as "soldiers of God, who are many, but none knows their number except for Him."[69]

Moving from the incorporeal world to the world of generation and corruption, one can argue that all the previously mentioned classical and postclassical philosophers believe in the causal influence of the former on the latter, but they differ over certain details. The relation between the two worlds includes discussions about the nature of time, motion, natural forms, bodies, and souls. Most Islamic philosophers have much to say about the natural world thanks to not only Aristotle's empirical legacy but also their own engagement with scientific knowledge and/or careers. For example, both Avicenna and Ibn Ṭufayl made a living out of practicing medicine, and all the rest of the classical figures were well-versed in the sciences of the time, not to mention the influential scientific

66. Meisami, *Knowledge and Power*, 29–32.
67. For a study of this treatise and its symbology, see Rustom, "Storytelling as Philosophical Pedagogy," 1:404–16.
68. Suhrawardī, *Hayākil al-nūr*, 84.
69. Mullā Ṣadrā, *al-Shawāhid al-rubūbiyya*, 141.

discoveries and texts of Abū Bakr Rāzī. Apparently, to be a polymath was a required part of intellectual life in the medieval Islamic world, but I cannot possibly cover here the range of scientific activities of the time, nor can I recount the technical differences among Islamic philosophers regarding the mechanics of the cosmos. The next section is only a snapshot of the role of the Active Intellect in generating life in the corporeal world, which is home to both inanimate bodies and animate/organic bodies that possess souls—namely, plants, animals, and humans—a domain of existence that undergoes the passage of time.

THE NATURAL WORLD

The inhabitants of the corporeal world are primarily distinguished from the incorporeal world above by their potentiality for change. Like Aristotle, Islamic philosophers ground this potentiality in a principle that is only found in the natural world. That principle is called "matter," which is also the reason for the plurality of individuals under species such as horses and humans. The essential properties that make a person really human are due to the "form" of humanity, which one can identify with the soul of the person. More will follow on the soul in relation to the material body, but for now, I delimit my account to the origination of matter and form, two principles that make up the corporeal world below the moon. Fārābī clarifies the subservient status of the matter in comparison to forms by saying,

> It would seem that the existence of forms is the primary aim, but since they subsist only in a given subject, matter was made a subject to bear forms. For this reason, as long as forms do not exist, the existence of matter is in vain. But none of the natural beings is in vain. Therefore, prime matter cannot exist devoid of a given form. Matter, then, is a principle and cause solely by way of being the subject for bearing the form; it is not an agent, nor an end, nor something that can exist independently of some form. Matter and form are both called "nature," although form is more aptly named such.[70]

Similarly, Avicenna regards form as the essence or reality of a substance and believes that in the corporeal world, form and matter are inseparable. He and Fārābī also agree that the Active Intellect, which in this context is referred to as the "Giver of Forms" (*wāhib al-ṣuwar*), produces forms of all natural kinds. While the forms of species or kinds are eternal, they join matter in time, hence the temporal origination of things in the corporal world. As far as the matter in the corporeal world is concerned, one must not confuse it with what makes up the bodies of the spheres, which for medieval philosophers is "ether," or the fifth element over and above the four elements of the natural world: fire, earth, air, and water. The matter in the corporeal world begins with the prime matter, which for Fārābī is caused by the celestial spheres. In contrast, Avicenna argues that the generator of the prime matter is the Active Intellect for the very reason that unlike its superior Intellects, it has reached down to a point where it cannot emanate another rank of the incorporeal world. Instead, the Active Intellect generates the prime matter, which cannot

70. Fārābī, *Principles of Existing Things*, 84–85.

exist without a form, so in its temporal origination, it receives the bodily form. The bodily form, roughly speaking, is nothing but three-dimensionality or extension in "length, breadth, and depth":

> The body is not a body by virtue of having a given [set of] three posited dimensions, since a body can exist and remain as a body even if the dimensions belonging to it are actually changed. So, [for example], a piece of wax or a drop of water may be such that there exist in it the actual dimensions of length, breadth, and depth determined by its extremities; but then, if it changes in shape, each of these definite dimensions ceases, and other dimensions or extensions exist. Yet the body continues as body, without corruption or change, and the form that we predicated of it as necessary—namely, that those dimensions can be posited in it—continues unchanged.[71]

The bodily substance, in turn, becomes matter for receiving forms of natural kinds within a temporal process. While the prime matter can be understood as receptivity and potentiality for change, the matter of particular substances accepts only certain forms and direction of change. For example, a human fetus can be the matter for receiving the form of a human baby but never a lamb. The potentiality that is inherent in matter also facilitates motion, of which time is only a measured magnitude. On the relation among matter, motion, and time, Avicenna says in the *Physics of the Healing*,

> Since it has turned out that time is not something subsisting in itself (and how could it be something subsisting in itself when it has no fully determinate being, but is coming to be and passing away?), and the existence of whatever is like that depends upon matter, time is material. Now, although it is material, it exists in matter through the intermediacy of motion; and so, if there is neither a motion nor a change, there is no time. Indeed, how could there be time without *before* and *after*, and how could there be *before* and *after* when one thing does not come to be after another? Certainly, *before* and *after* do not exist simultaneously; but, rather, something that was *before* ceases inasmuch as it was *before* because something that is *after* inasmuch as it is *after* comes to be.[72]

As for Averroes on the origination of matter and form, he dedicates many passages to this topic over the course of his philosophical career. He starts with a position similar to Fārābī and Avicenna, but as is often the case in his later works, he claims to restore philosophy to its "original" Aristotelian state. In his *Long Commentary* on Aristotle's *Metaphysics*, the Active Intellect abdicates its Avicennian position as both the generator of prime matter and the Giver of Forms. In *Long Commentary* and *The Incoherence of the Incoherence*, Averroes eliminates the emanation thesis from his cosmology altogether, along with the impact of the Active Intellect on the corporeal world. Instead, he explains the dynamics of the natural world

71. Avicenna, *Physics of the Healing*, 13. Avicenna's conception of prime matter became a topic for debate among later philosophers, and Fakhr al-Dīn Rāzī offered his own version of Avicenna's theory in response to the positions of Avicenna's detractors. See Shihadeh, "Avicenna's Corporeal Form," 364–96.
72. Avicenna, *Physics of the Healing*, 235–36. Italics in the original.

mostly in natural terms. For example, he resorts to the generation of material forms from material forms and the influence of physical forces such as the animal heat and the heat of the sun and the stars to explain both generation and reproduction.[73] He says, "The seeds are generated in earth and water by solar heat mixed with the heat of the other stars. Therefore, it is the sun and the stars which are principles of life for every natural being."[74]

One of the important subjects in natural philosophy is the nature of time. In his *Book of Salvation*, following Aristotle, Avicenna defines time as "a magnitude belonging to circular motion with respect to priority and posteriority," and as Jon McGinnis shows, he further provides proofs for the reality of time based on the reality of motion and the significance of time for explaining kinetic phenomena.[75] The famous commentator of Avicenna and polymath Naṣīr al-Dīn Ṭūsī argues that priority and posteriority are only conceived in the mind through the analysis of time, whose essence is unknown to us, though we have an intuitive grasp of its fluid existence. Time begins only with the origination of the bodily substance and is a concomitant of the bodily changes—that is, renewal and expiration in the natural substances. There is no time outside of the material world, hence no priority or posteriority. One of the implications of this argument is that there is no logical problem in considering the physical world as created in time. For example, Ṭūsī's analysis of time means to reinterpret the theological position of creation in time by attributing temporal origination to the chain of temporal events.[76] Ṭūsī's position influences later Islamic philosophy in its attempts to reconcile theology and philosophy on the debate over eternity and temporal origination.

One fundamentally different view of time is that of the earlier philosopher Abū Bakr Rāzī, who follows Plato in postulating absolute time—namely, time as a reality independent of motion. To be more precise, his view is influenced by Galen's interpretation of Plato in the *Timaeus*. The independent or absolute time is a self-evident and primitive phenomenon that does not require demonstration for its eternal existence. Interestingly, for Rāzī, the existence of absolute time is a prerequisite of God's act of creation because all acts happen according to a sequence of moments.[77]

The other significant departing position from the dominant Aristotelian view of time as the measure of motion belongs to Fakhr al-Dīn Rāzī. He discusses time in several of his works, including his commentary on Avicenna's *Pointers and Reminders*. It has been shown that after discussing the problems of the Aristotelian-Avicennian view of motion, Fakhr al-Dīn Rāzī eventually adopts the position that he ascribes to Plato as "that substance subsisting in itself and independent in itself."[78] However, Rāzī also wants to distance himself from considering time as a necessary existence on par with God. So he distinguishes between God and time by arguing as follows:

> It is established that the Necessary of Existence through itself is necessary of existence in every respect. This rules out that He, exalted be He, is a locus of alterations

73. For a detailed discussion of this topic in Averroes, see Davidson, *Alfarabi, Avicenna, and Averroes*, 242–57.
74. Averroes, "Commentary on Aristotle's Metaphysics, Book Lām," 111.
75. For a summary of the arguments, see McGinnis, *Avicenna*, 71–74.
76. Ṭūsī, *Sharḥ al-Ishārāt wa'l-tanbīhāt*, 3:65–71. See Meisami, *Naṣīr al-Dīn Ṭūsī*, 45–48.
77. Adamson, *Al-Rāzī*, 103–9.
78. Adamson and Lammer, "Fakhr al-Dīn al-Rāzī's Platonist Account," 109.

> and changes. Duration or time, however, is a locus for alterations and for changes through the fact that beforenesses or afternesses succeed one another in it. So, [time] is not the necessary of existence through itself in every respect and, thus, it is not the Necessary of Existence through itself. Rather it is possible of existence through itself. As for God, He exists as sanctified above alterations, exalted beyond any connection with what is potential.[79]

Postclassical Islamic philosophers such as Mīr Dāmād and Mullā Ṣadrā seem less interested in the science of nature than Avicenna and Averroes and, for the most part, follow the former on this subject. One exception is their discussion of time, which they address primarily in relation to the problem of eternity and temporal origination. Mīr Dāmād uses Avicenna's terminology in his tripartite division of time into "transcendent time" (*sarmad*), which only belongs to God, "perpetual time" (*dahr*), which belongs to the superlunary world; and "earthly time" (*zamān*), which is an attribute of all things and events in the corporeal world—that is, the time that we are familiar with.[80] Mīr Dāmād revisits this tripartite division primarily to solve the problem of eternity and creation in time. He is not convinced by his predecessors on the eternity of the world and tries to revive the temporal origination of the world by revisiting different senses of time. He believes that Avicenna does not consider a "real nonexistence" prior to creation, which for Mīr Dāmād must be actual nonexistence before existence. His objective is to demonstrate how God, who is outside of time, creates in time and that only God is eternal. To do so, he postulates "a rupture between the divine Essence and the cosmos, the latter being absolutely posterior to the former."[81]

Mīr Dāmād starts from the three ontological realms using terms already used by Avicenna. From top to bottom, the first realm is God's; the second belongs to all incorporeal beings, including the intellects, the souls, and the archetypes; and the last realm is that of material beings. Next, he tries to explain temporality in ontological terms. For him, except for the first realm, the existence of the other two realms is preceded by their real nonexistence in the higher realm:

> The Maker of essence and existence in perpetuity is himself the cause of the dispelling of perpetual real non-existence. We have recited to you a number of times that non-existence is the non-being of something and its absence, not some "thing" which is characterized by "absence" and that the existence of a creature in perpetuity is through the negation of its non-existence, since two distinct boundaries of existence and non-existence is incomprehensible in perpetuity, in contrast to how it is for [creatures in] time.[82]

Furthermore, he argues that once we reach the material world, the earthly time can be "gradual," "instantaneous," and "temporal." According to Mīr Dāmād, the first one "is the

79. Adamson and Lammer, "Fakhr al-Dīn al-Rāzī's Platonist Account," 116. Brackets in the original.
80. See Aminrazavi, "Mīr Dāmād," 159–65.
81. Rizvi, "Mīr Dāmād's (d. 1631) *al-Qabasāt*," 454. In his article, Rizvi also discusses the relation between Mīr Dāmād's thesis and Shiʿa theology.
82. Mīr Dāmād, *Book of Blazing Brands*, 321.

occurrence of one thing, like terminal motion, in the extension of a particular time such that that thing coincides with it and is divisible by its divisibility." The second one "is the occurrence of an existent thing in its entirety not in the extension of time but rather in an indivisible now among nows that are the boundaries and dividers [of time]." As for the third, "the event happens in a particular time bordered by a beginning and an end, not by coinciding with it or being divisible by its divisibility . . . [but] it occurs in its entirety in each of its parts and each of its nows, except for the bounding time, that is to say, the instant of the beginning and the instant of the end."[83]

Similar to Mīr Dāmād, Mullā Ṣadrā's primary goal in discussing the nature of time is to resolve centuries of conflicts between theologians and philosophers over the problem of eternity and temporal creation. To do so, he considers different senses of time and settles on one that we could understand as the fourth dimension of physical objects. His understanding of time as the fourth dimension is grounded in his general metaphysics regarding the primacy of existence and its gradational character. Briefly, for every bodily substance, in addition to the three dimensions—that is, length, breadth, and depth—there is time as its fourth dimension. This interpretation of time corresponds to Mīr Dāmād's "gradual time" in the sense that a thing in motion has an existence whose extension and divisions correspond to the extension and divisions of its time. But for Mullā Ṣadrā, this correspondence is due to the nature of reality that he identifies as existence, not essence. In his *Asfār*, he states, "A formal substance in its gradual development, has one constant temporal being from one point of view and a continuous gradual being with limits, from another point of view."[84] This is Mullā Ṣadrā's original contribution to Islamic metaphysics, which is referred to as "substantial motion" or "motion in substance." For example, the tree outside of my window is both a numerically identical one-hundred-year-old being and a gradual existence whose phases match all the divisions of its past, present, and future. In sum, every natural substance is temporal because it is an extended flow of existence between its generation and corruption.

For Mullā Ṣadrā, once we prove that motion and temporality are inherent in the very existence of material substances, then there is no longer a need to explain its relation to its immaterial cause in terms of its motion and time. This is because the immaterial cause is simply the cause of the existence of nature, and all natural properties like motion and time come along with this type of existence rather than being separately caused. So thanks to its mode of existence, nature is being constantly renewed in time, hence the temporal origination of every particle in nature at every moment. Mullā Ṣadrā dismisses the question of whether the "whole" world was created in time by arguing the whole world is merely composed of parts, and talking of the creation of the whole separately from the parts is absurd. It is important to note that Mullā Ṣadrā seems to endorse the Aristotelian-Avicennian description of time as the measure of motion, yet for him, motion is not an accident, and that makes all the difference in one's perspective of time. As he says, "Verily time is additional to motion only in the conceptual realm because, as explained before, motion and time exist with one and the same existence."[85]

83. Mīr Dāmād, *Book of Blazing Brands*, 29.
84. Mullā Ṣadrā, *Asfār*, 3:97.
85. Mullā Ṣadrā, *Asfār*, 3:200.

THE SOUL AND THE BODY

Aristotle found Plato's picture of the soul and its independence from the body contrary to both reason and observation. For him, the soul-body relation is like a form-matter relation that is characterized by inseparability, and the soul is the principle of life and spontaneous motion in all organic bodies. However, even Aristotle considered a partial immortality for the human soul through the intellectual faculty, which does not depend on the bodily organs for functioning.[86] The story of the soul-body relation is a complicated one in classical Islamic philosophy due to both the heavy influence of Aristotle and Neoplatonic thinkers, on the one hand, and the theological significance of the soul's afterlife in the Quran and the Tradition, on the other hand. There is also a wide range of narratives about the soul between extreme Platonism and Aristotelianism. The diversity of the narratives and arguments is too much to cover in this volume, so I will confine the discussion to a few representative thinkers and texts on the definition of the soul, its relation to the body, and the possibility of immortality. In the interest of time and relevance to other discussions in this book, I limit this section to the human soul rather than the soul in general, which would include the celestial, plant, and animal souls.

In the Western / Middle Eastern traditions, some of the earliest written discourses on the soul-body distinction were created in ancient Persia, followed by the Greeks. Among Greek thinkers before Socrates, Pythagoras was quite serious about the soul and its superiority over the body, and then Plato embarked on this issue more systematically in several of his writings. For Plato, the soul preexists the body, and the soul-body accompaniment is a temporary one before the soul is again bodiless and free. Similar to Pythagoras and ancient Persian narratives on the soul, Plato shows a preference for poetic/mythical techniques of inquiry and expression, which is also observed in the works of Abū Bakr Rāzī. Apart from their methodology, the Persian, Pythagorean, and Platonic narratives of the soul also agree in their commitment to not only the immortality of the soul but also a moral framing of their metaphysical psychology. In his *Spiritual Medicine*, Rāzī says,

> Plato, the chief and greatest of the philosophers, held that there are three souls in every man. The first he called the rational and divine soul, the second the choleric and animal, and the third the vegetative, incremental and appetitive soul. The animal and vegetative souls were created for the sake of the rational soul. The vegetative soul was made in order to feed the body, which is as it were the instrument and implement of the rational soul; for the body is not of an eternal, indissoluble substance, but its substance is fluid and soluble, and every soluble object only survives by leaving behind it something to replace that element which is dissolved. The choleric soul's function is to be of assistance to the rational soul in suppressing the appetitive soul and in preventing it from preoccupying the rational soul with its manifold desires so that it is incapable of using its reason. If the rational soul employed its reason completely, this would mean that it would be delivered from the body in which it is enmeshed.[87]

86. Aristotle, *On the Soul*, II, 413a 3–8, 556.
87. Rāzī, *Spiritual Physick*, in Nasr and Aminrazavi, 1:419.

Unlike Rāzī, al-Kindī tends to prove a harmony between Plato and Aristotle, and he has a commitment to reconcile philosophy with Islamic doctrines. Therefore, for him, the human soul is the form of the body, in the sense of being its very reality, but it is also immortal, just like all forms and species are immortal. As for the body, sometimes he describes it as an instrument for the soul, and at times, it can drag the soul down by over-indulging in the sensible world.[88] Al-Kindī's Platonic reading of Aristotle's theory of the soul-body relation is textually traceable in the so-called *Theology of Aristotle*:

> And the soul is also not in the body like something predicated, for something predicated is one of the impressions of the bearer of predication, for example color and figure. . . . But the soul separates from the body without corrupting or dissolving through the dissolution of the body.[89]

Beginning with al-Kindī and through Fārābī and Avicenna, the Neoplatonic survival of the human soul after the death of the body only applies to the intellectual faculty of the human soul, and the afterlife is nothing more than joining the world of intellect in its eternal pure thinking state, a philosopher's paradise. Although classical philosophers, especially Avicenna, provide a more detailed picture of the soul, they all show a tendency toward reading Aristotle in a Platonic light due to the influence of Neoplatonic texts. Since Fārābī is more occupied with the intellectual power of the soul, especially in relation to epistemology—that is, the theory of knowledge and conditions of truth—I skip to Avicenna, whose writings on the soul are exhaustive of all the aspects of the soul and its relation to the body. In addition, Avicenna goes beyond Aristotle by associating the powers of the soul, except for the intellect, with different parts of the brain, bringing together metaphysics and the science of anatomy. Moreover, for him, the individual human soul could hypothetically have primitive self-awareness, hence existence, even in the absence of bodily organs altogether. In book one of his *On the Soul*, he asks us to imagine someone created as suspended in a kind of void and barred from any contact with the external world and without any possibility of finding out about internal or external organs. In the absence of any awareness of the body or the outside physical world, Avicenna argues, the suspended person would still be aware of the self. To clarify, the suspended person has just been created, so he has no past experiences or memories. With these suppositions in mind, Avicenna concludes the following:

> Thus, the self whose existence he asserted is his unique characteristic, in the sense that it is he himself, not his body and its parts, which he did not so assert. Thus, what [the reader] has been alerted to is a way to be made alert to the existence of the soul as something that is not the body—nor in fact *any* body—to recognize it and be aware of it, if it is in fact the case that he has been disregarding it and needed to be hit over the head with it.[90]

88. For a useful summary of al-Kindī's eclectic position on the soul-body relation, see Adamson, *Al-Kindī*, 107–18.
89. Cited in Adamson, *Arabic Plotinus*, 50.
90. Avicenna, *On the Soul*, 179.

In addition to a "primitive self-awareness" of its individual existence, which does not require physical organs,[91] the soul, which is individuated through its relation with an individual body, also has powers, most of which need bodily organs to function. Like all other animals, the human soul has the power of self-nutrition, growth and reproduction, perception, and motor powers. Yet the human soul is a form or species distinguished from other animals by possessing a rational power of both theoretical and practical aspects, with the latter following the former's lead. The human potential for mathematical, scientific, and philosophical knowledge is grounded in the theoretical faculty, which also guides the practical faculty in its ethical and political functions:

> The human soul, though one substance (as will become apparent), has a relation and reference to two sides, one below it and one above it, and for each side there is a faculty through which the connection between it and that side is ordered. So, this practical faculty is the one the soul possesses for the connection with the side below it, that is, the body and its maintenance. The theoretical faculty is the one that the soul possesses for the connection with the side above it, to be affected by it, learn from it, and receive from it. . . . It is from the lower side that the moral temperaments are produced, whereas it is from the higher side that the sciences are produced.[92]

The function of the theoretical faculty of the human soul is more relevant to cognitive psychology, so I will discuss it in the next chapter. As for the present discussion of the soul-body relation, Avicenna believes that despite its reliance on the body for its activities, the individual soul is incorruptible and self-subsisting.[93] From a logical point of view, the body cannot be resurrected,[94] and in the absence of the body, the individual soul can enjoy an intellectual afterlife to the extent that is not comparable with bodily pleasures "in terms of virtue, completion, abundance," and "eternal duration."[95] This idea is condemned by Ghazālī in his *Incoherence of the Philosophers* as proof of philosophers' deviation from Islamic faith.[96]

For Avicenna, the possibility of individual immortality is based on his view that even after the death of the body, the soul retains the individuality that it gains due to its relation with an individual body. To be more precise, during its existence in this life, each soul has certain rational and nonrational "properties" in virtue of its attachment to a particular body of certain material configurations and temperaments. Although there is no actual body after death, the soul retains its individual identity as a legacy of the properties gained through its relation to the body before death.[97] By this account, Avicenna's position is distanced from Aristotle and gets closer to the Neoplatonic view. Most importantly, Avicenna's

91. This self-awareness is called primitive because the suspended man does not have second-order awareness in this state—or in other words, he is not aware that he is aware. On this distinction, see Black, "Avicenna on Self-Awareness," 63–87.
92. Avicenna, *On the Soul*, 183.
93. Avicenna, *On the Soul*, 197–99.
94. Avicenna, *Metaphysics of the Healing*, 347–48.
95. Avicenna, *Metaphysics of the Healing*, 350.
96. Ghazālī, *Incoherence*, 219.
97. For a thorough discussion of this topic, see Kaukua, *Self-Awareness*, 43–51.

position accommodates the Islamic doctrine of individual immortality. Nevertheless, as I explain later, Avicenna's view of the immortality of the soul revolves around the union of the human intellect with the Active Intellect, hence his promotion of an intellectual afterlife. Regardless of this, he "prepares the way for the later systematic thinkers of the Islamic and Jewish Middle Ages and helps to do so also for the systematizers in the medieval Christian West."[98]

In opposition to Avicenna, Averroes does not find the immortality of individual souls defensible from his Aristotelian perspective, according to which the relation between the soul and the body strictly follows the form-matter paradigm. Despite his religious adherence to the Islamic doctrine of resurrection, for Averroes, in the absence of the material body, the soul cannot retain its particular individuality. He says, "If then the soul does not die when the body dies, or if it possesses an immortal element, it must, when it has left the bodies, form a numerical unity."[99] In other words, the immortal part of the human soul—that is, the intellect, which "is a separate substance and one for all human knowers"[100]—survives the death of the body as one substance rather than many. Averroes's position gave rise to many controversies in the Latin West, but it had little impact on metaphysical psychology in the Islamic East, which, for the most part, followed Avicenna's lead.

One important doctrine about the soul-body relation, which in time also facilitated a kind of solution for bodily resurrection, revolves around the substantial evolution of the human soul. This evolutionary narrative of the soul was initiated by Ḥamīd al-Dīn Kirmānī (d. 1021), an Ismaʿīlī philosopher active in the Fatimid Cairo and a contemporary of Avicenna. For Kirmānī, the individual substance of the human soul is "ennobled" through knowledge and practice to the point of transformation and transcendence beyond bodily attachments. This evolved soul "becomes eternally and fully subsistent," which Kirmānī commends as "another creation" of the soul, an implied allusion to the "new creation" mentioned in the Quran (Q 5:15).[101] Centuries later, a full-fledged evolutionary theory of the soul was structured by Mullā Ṣadrā based on his aforementioned doctrine of "substantial motion."

To begin, Mullā Ṣadrā departs from Avicenna's substance dualism regarding the soul-body relation. Mullā Ṣadrā states emphatically that "the human soul is bodily in its origination and in its management [of the body and material objects], but spiritual in subsistence and intellection."[102] In other words, the human soul, just like other animal souls, begins as a material existence, but unlike other animals, it can move beyond this to continue as an immaterial existence. In this context, material existence refers to the original state of the soul as mere potentiality of becoming a fully developed human soul later in midlife. This notion of the soul is a departure from Avicenna because the latter regards the soul as an independent substance, which uses the body as an instrument. This departure is due to Mullā Ṣadrā's unique view of reality as a fluid existence. For Mullā Ṣadrā, the human soul

98. Hall, "Intellect, Soul and Body," 64.
99. Leaman, *Averroes and His Philosophy*, 91.
100. Black, "Psychology," 322.
101. Meisami, *Knowledge and Power*, 41.
102. Mullā Ṣadrā, *Asfār*, 8:347.

is a mode of existence capable of moving from lower to more intense degrees. Of course, we can refer to every stage of the soul's evolution as a stage of its "substance in motion," in which "substance" refers not to the developing reality of the soul but its conception in the mind throughout its existential development.

The chapter on metaphysics ends here, but in the context of Islamic philosophy, we can never be done with metaphysics because its principles are invoked everywhere—hence the aptness of its other name, "first philosophy." The systematic character of Islamic philosophy, with its major system builders such as Fārābī, Avicenna, Averroes, and Mullā Ṣadrā, requires attention to the presence of metaphysical principles in all areas of philosophical inquiry. In the same vein, metaphysical concepts such as form, matter, essence, existence, and so on play significant roles in discourses on knowledge, ethics, politics, and even philosophical theology. Thus what we consider to be the reality of natural and supernatural existence is always embedded in discussions on knowledge, good and evil, the just and the unjust, and the relation between God and the world.

2

Knowledge and Selfhood

Thus far I have discussed metaphysics, or "first philosophy," broadly construed, including metaphysical psychology. Whether we define "first philosophy" as knowledge of things in their realities, knowledge of being as such, knowledge of causes, or even knowledge about the First Cause (God), as al-Kindī put it, the actual enterprise requires that our knowledge process be a safe pathway to truth. To say that something is certainly the case in the world, or even with high probability, would be out of question if our means of accessing the world outside were not trustworthy. By way of analogy, this would be like forever looking through lenses not fitted to our eyes to verify the real shape and position of things. In this respect, premodern philosophers—with the exception of ancient Greek skeptics, a number of non-Western traditions, and many mystics, including Sufis in the Islamic context—are, for the most part, confident that human cognitive process is by default well-grounded, and epistemic errors are accidental and occasional rather than inherent and systematic. This epistemic confidence is both thanks to Aristotle and thanks to the Abrahamic faith in a benevolent God who would not have created the human mind as fundamentally flawed. The Islamic perspective on the nature and scope of knowledge is particularly endowed with this confidence due to the noble status of knowledge as a virtue in the Quran and the Tradition. Furthermore, philosophical texts and the Quran similarly regard the intellect as exclusive to the human species and their gateway to universal truths about both the material and the immaterial worlds.

THE MIND AND THE WORLD

In his seminal inquiry into the meanings and status of knowledge in medieval Islam, Franz Rosenthal correctly points out the "all-pervasive attitude toward 'knowledge' as something of supreme value for Muslim being"[1] and cites numerous definitions of knowledge by a variety of Muslim philosophers, theologians, and Sufis. The idea that Rosenthal finds mostly in common among the definitions is the "mastery" of the "object of knowledge" by the "subject," with the former being "prior" to the latter.[2] So typically, the study of knowledge would revolve around subject-object relation, alternately referred to as the relation between the mind and the world, or the knower and the known. In this chapter,

1. Rosenthal, *Knowledge Triumphant*, 2.
2. Rosenthal, *Knowledge Triumphant*, 51.

I will often use the latter terms, "knower" (*ʿālim*) and "known" (*maʿlūm*), to avoid terminological confusions that may be caused by the implications of "subject" and "object" in modern Western philosophy. The overarching question that guides this chapter is about how the mind captures realities in the world and the internal and external foundations that guarantee truth and justify our correct aiming at it. As in the previous chapter, I will roam around different times and places in the Muslim world to present a narrative about intellectual contributions and encounters. While sometimes using familiar concepts from contemporary epistemology such as truth conditions and justification, I hope to highlight the fundamental difference between epistemology in the Islamic and contemporary Western contexts. Some of the distinguishing features and approaches of epistemology in the Islamic world are as follows: (1) The implacable postulation of the possibility of knowledge; (2) the belief in the independence of the world from the mind, or the existential priority of the known over the knower (i.e., realism); (3) the ontological hierarchy of knowledge based on the ontological status of what is known; (4) an unquestioned incorporeal reality of the knower/mind in intellection; (5) a supernatural intervention in the process of intellection; and (6) the possibility of existential transformation for the knower through unification with the supernatural source of knowledge.

SOURCES OF KNOWLEDGE

In Islamic philosophy, the mind as the source of cognition is identified with the rational faculty of the incorporeal soul. To acquire knowledge of the world, the mind as the incorporeal agent cannot access the external world directly due to the obvious existential gap between the immaterial soul and the material world. This implies the necessity of certain venues or apparatuses to bridge the gap. These apparatuses can be discussed as "sources of knowledge," the most comprehensive list of which is found in Avicenna's theory of knowledge.

Avicenna divides sources of human knowledge into sense perception, imagination, estimation, and intellection, which provide content for mathematical, experimental, philosophical, theological, and prophetic sciences. One can also add "instruction" or "acquisition of knowledge" from "someone else" to the Avicennian sources of knowledge and place it under what is often referred to as "testimony" in contemporary epistemology. Avicenna does not treat the latter on par with other sources because it is not a power of the soul, but it is used when a human soul is not capable of internally knowing all things.[3] From a different perspective, "instruction" becomes a very valuable source of knowledge for both Ismaʿīlī and Sufi philosophers because it explains the epistemic/spiritual reliance on the Shiʿa Imams and/or spiritual masters. The testimony of the prophet, his companions, and Shiʿa Imams also provides premises for arguments in the science of theology. Avicenna's predecessors, Aristotle and Fārābī, already provided the scaffolding for most of the sources of knowledge and their application in different types of sciences, including most of the necessary terminology. However, Avicenna provides a full-scale account of knowledge formation and the epistemic processes for each type of science. Of course, there are alternative accounts, though not as systematic, but Avicennian epistemology

3. Rahman, *Avicenna's Psychology*, 35.

became dominant in the philosophical arena for centuries after him. Even the rise of a Platonist/Illuminationist epistemology in the Persianate context through Suhrawardī and his followers did not aim or claim to subvert the Avicennian conceptual framework of epistemology but rather simply added new dimensions to it that, in turn, helped the formation of a rather novel perspective on knowledge in later Islamic philosophy.

With the previous text in mind, I begin with the soul's primary and most basic source of knowledge: sense perception. Avicenna divides the apparatuses of sense perception into the external senses (*al-ḥawāss al-ẓāhira*) and internal senses (*al-ḥawāss al-bāṭina*). All major Islamic philosophers after him retain this division, except for some differences in the subdivisions of internal senses. External senses are our channels to the material world through the five sense organs for seeing, hearing, smelling, tasting, and touching. The initial process for gaining sense data through the organs is completely physical, though the mechanism varies among different senses. What they all have in common is the actual physical impact by the external objects on the organs and the formation of sensible forms. Avicenna describes the detailed mechanism of each type of sense perception, and his analysis of sight resulted in a full-fledged scientific theory of vision.[4] With regard to sense perception, Avicenna announces, "Whoever loses a certain sense necessarily loses a certain knowledge."[5] This is an important statement from an epistemological point of view because it seems to associate Avicennian, or rather classical Islamic epistemology, with empiricism, which grounds all possible knowledge in sense perception. This association would be a misunderstanding because for Avicenna, although all knowledge must begin in sense perception, not all knowledge comes from sense perception. Sensible forms function as raw material for the apparatus of internal senses, which in turn would provide the epistemic "material" for the higher source of knowledge—that is, reason or intellect.

Internal senses, which Avicenna locates in different parts of the brain, are not only in charge of processing and storing data but also responsible for making sense out of what is received in sense perception—that is, what is signified or intended by the sensible forms (i.e., "intentions"). Avicenna divides the internal senses into common sense, formative imagination, estimation, memory, and compositive imagination. This division of internal senses is based on certain "epistemological principles," resulting in two receptive and retentive powers that work in pairs and one compositive power.[6] The common sense can be likened to a lake into which the five streams of senses pour sensible information from the material world. Once received by the common sense, the sensible forms are simultaneously retained as images by the formative imagination, and their intentions, or meanings, are grasped through estimation and retained by memory. The last internal sense, compositive imagination, actively manipulates images and intentions by dividing and/or combining them, and it is, on the one hand, responsible for making our dreams and creative productions when it is under the control of estimation. On the other hand, when governed by reason, the compositive imagination facilitates cognition.[7] Humans and animals share all these senses except for the cognitive function of the compositive imagination

4. For a summary of Avicenna's theory of vision, see McGinnis, *Avicenna*, 102–4.
5. Avicenna, *Book of Demonstration*, 152.
6. For the three principles, see Black, "Imagination and Estimation," 59.
7. Black, "Imagination and Estimation," 60.

due to the absence of reason in animals. Among internal sources, Avicenna explains his formulation of estimation as follows:

> The distinction between the perception of the form and that of the intention is that the form is what is perceived both by the inner soul and the external sense; but the external sense perceives it first and then transmits it to the soul, as for example, when the sheep perceives the form of the wolf, i.e., its shape, form, and color. This form is certainly perceived by the inner soul of the sheep, but it is first perceived by its external sense. As for the intention, it is a thing which the soul perceives from the sensed object without its previously having been perceived by the external sense, just as the sheep perceives the intention of harm in the wolf, which causes it to fear the wolf and to flee from it, without harm having been perceived at all by the external sense. Now, what is first perceived by the sense and then by the internal faculties is the form, while what only the internal faculties perceive without the external sense is the intention.[8]

Avicenna's estimation thesis is challenged from different quarters and for different reasons. For example, Averroes tries to restore sense perception to its Aristotelian version, which lacks estimation. In his *Incoherence of the Incoherence*, while responding to Ghazālī's objections to Avicenna's estimation thesis, he finally decides that Avicenna's "estimation" is "at best superfluous" and imagination alone is enough for serving the function Avicenna assigned to estimation—namely, perceiving intentions.[9] Averroes also disagrees with Avicenna on classifying imagination into two types.

In later Islamic philosophy, Mullā Ṣadrā's list of the sources of knowledge is at first sight in accordance with that of Avicenna's, but he offers his own interpretation of estimation that cancels the ontological independence of this source. In his existential hierarchy of the sources of knowledge, which corresponds to his cosmology of three worlds, Mullā Ṣadrā reduces estimation to the engagement of the intellect with particular intentions. This he considers as the lower function of the intellect because its object is particular sensibles and images compared to the higher function of the intellect—that is, receiving and managing universal intelligibles. With respect to this ranking, we need to recall that universals are always ranked higher than particulars because of their scope of application; their essential role in cognition, philosophical thinking, and argumentation; and most importantly, their complete detachment from matter. According to Mullā Ṣadrā,

> The difference between estimation and intellection is accidental rather than essential. [The difference] lies in the relation [of the intellect] to the particular [sensation and imagination] or lack of it. In fact, perception is of three kinds as there are three worlds [viz., the sensible, the imaginal, and the intellectual], and estimation is like an intellect that has fallen from its [higher] state.[10]

8. Translated in Rahman, *Avicenna's Psychology*, 30. For a study of estimation based on the totality of Avicenna's discussion of it in response to two of his critics, see Black, "Estimation (*wahm*) in Avicenna," 219–58.
9. Black, "Estimation (*wahm*) in Avicenna," 223.
10. See Mullā Ṣadrā, *Asfār*, 3:362. The second part of this translated passage is taken from Kalin, *Knowledge*, 138.

For Avicenna, the faculty of estimation also governs the nonrational function of compositive imagination in creating novel and complex images like those produced in our dreams. In contrast, the other function of the compositive imagination as a source of knowledge is rational and governed by the intellect. Once the sensible data pours into the common sense through the external senses and the sensible forms, which are imprinted therein and stored by imagination, their intentions or meanings are received through estimation and stored by memory, followed by the cognitive operation of the compositive imagination using the stored images and intentions under the supervision of the intellect.

In addition to its previously mentioned role in cognition, imagination is also the venue of prophetic knowledge broadly construed—that is, truthful dreams, divinations, and revelations. This prophetic function of imagination originates in Fārābī's thesis that the imaginative faculty receives both theoretical and practical knowledge from the Active Intellect in dream-images and symbolic configurations in sleep or waking states. Depending on the level of intimacy or connection with the Active Intellect, the imaginative faculty can facilitate mere clairvoyance or produce revelatory knowledge in the form of religious symbols and narratives. For example, a prophet's knowledge of the afterlife is symbolically represented as images of Heaven and Hell. Fārābī's discourse on imagination is particularly important for his political philosophy, so we will revisit this topic later in the book.

For Avicenna, the ultimate source of human knowledge is the intellect. The epistemic function of the intellect as the incorporeal source of theoretical knowledge is to receive universal intelligibles necessary for knowing things in their essences as stripped from all corporeal attachments. The intelligibles provide the content for conception (*taṣawwur*), which is necessary for assent (*taṣdīq*). The latter is linguistically expressed as a proposition that is subject to truth or falsity—for example, the conception of "tree" as a universal in the mind and the assent that "every tree can grow." Avicenna discusses conception and assent under his theory of logic because for him, logic is a tool that protects thinking from errors, and thinking is "to move from things present in his mind—including what is conceived or assented to . . . to things not present in it."[11]

For Fārābī and Avicenna, the intellect as a source of theoretical knowledge must primarily receive intelligibles in the form of "primary intelligibles" (*al-ma'qūlāt al-ūlā*), or universal concepts and primary truths. Primary intelligibles are in the sense of single concepts like "tree" or "triangle." An example of a primary truth is "the whole is bigger than the part," which in modern philosophical parlance is an "a priori proposition" because its verification does not depend on experience. Once primary intelligibles are at the intellect's disposal, thinking or movement from known to the unknown begins, which includes the production of secondary intelligibles (*al-ma'qūlāt al-thāniya*). For example, when the intellect receives the tree-universal as a primary intelligible, it can consider it as a "species" (*naw'*) of plants. Here, "species" is a secondary intelligible. Classical Islamic philosophers follow Avicenna in confining secondary intelligibles to logical concepts such as genus and species. Secondary intelligibles are further divided into logical and philosophical intelligibles in later Islamic philosophy. Beginning with Naṣīr al-Dīn Ṭūsī's ambiguous treatment

11. Avicenna, *Remarks and Admonitions*, 47.

of secondary intelligibles and Mullā Ṣadrā's formulation of them in relation to his existential metaphysics, secondary intelligibles end up in two divisions: logical secondary intelligibles and philosophical secondary intelligibles. Logical secondary intelligibles are produced by the intellect and have no direct ground in the world outside of the mind—for example, genus and species. Philosophical secondary intelligibles are fixed attributes of real objects but occur to primary intelligibles in the mind. For example, "existence" as a secondary intelligible occurs to "tree" in the mind, but the existence of a tree is not just a consideration of the mind; rather, it is a reality or, better, *the* reality of a tree. It is in this latter sense that the secondary intelligible turns into a topic where metaphysical and logical discourses in later Islamic philosophy overlap.[12]

Classical Islamic philosophers all agree that the human intellect only has the potential for receiving the intelligibles. In other words, it is potentially intellect and passive, hence its need for an Active Intellect as the actualizing or efficient cause of knowledge. The highest status of the human intellect is when it undergoes conjunction (*ittiṣāl*) with the Active Intellect, which is a separate immaterial and immortal substance of divine nature. Before reaching this stage, the potential human intellect must go through several stages of actualization, which will be discussed in the next section of this chapter. The ontological status of the Active Intellect, as well as its epistemic function and relation to the potential intellect, is a matter of contention among philosophers. While major exponents of Islamic philosophy regard the Active Intellect as a separate and immortal substance, they have different views on its function with respect to the material world and the human soul.

The Greek ancestor of the Active Intellect in Aristotle functioned as an actualizing force, which was interpreted as either separate from the human intellect or a faculty of the human intellect. Some commentators of Aristotle and Islamic philosophers chose the first reading and even attributed angelic characteristics to the Active Intellect. This interpretation of the Active Intellect was also inspired and reinforced by Neoplatonism. In the context of his cosmic trinity of the One, the Intellect, and the Soul, in *The Enneads*, Plotinus places Platonic Forms, or intelligibles, in the second principle or "hypostasis" of the universe—namely, the Intellect. Later commentators refer to this cosmic principle as either "the First Intellect" or "the Active Intellect." The former term is sometimes used by al-Kindī, and his treatment of the epistemic role of this intellect differs across his various texts.[13] After Fārābī, the term "Active Intellect" (*al-ʿaql al-faʿʿāl*) became a common coin among philosophers, and its role in securing human knowledge was firmly established.

In his *Treatise on the Intellect* (*Risāla fi'l-ʿaql*) and several other works, Fārābī devotes a good number of passages to describing the nature and function of the Active Intellect as the source of intellectual knowledge. While his different texts may seem to treat the function of the Active Intellect differently, they all agree that conjoining with the Active Intellect is necessary for the human intellect at the final stage of intellection. According to the dominant reading of Fārābī, this process is only epistemological rather than ontological, which means that the two intellects never become one entity. The necessity of conjoining is because for Fārābī, the Active Intellect facilitates intellectual knowledge by emanation,

12. Mullā Ṣadrā, *Asfār*, 1:332–33. For a study of the overlap between metaphysics and logic with respect to secondary intelligibles, see Meisami, "Mullā Ṣadrā Shīrāzī," 57–58.
13. Davidson, *Alfarabi, Avicenna, and Averroes*, 15–17.

whether we understand the emanation (*fayḍ*) as the direct bestowal of intelligibles or simply illuminating what is stored in the imaginative soul—that is, the imaginative forms, which the faculty of imagination abstracts from sensible forms. In both these scenarios, the mind needs the Active Intellect to transform it into an active knower of intelligibles occasionally.[14] For Fārābī, the Active Intellect is the mediator of that type of knowledge, which the human soul needs for ultimate felicity (*sa ʿāda*) and which qualifies a perfect leader who can also happen to be a prophet. He argues that a person at the highest stage of the rational soul is "through the emanation from the Active Intellect to his Passive Intellect, a [perfect] wise man and a philosopher and an accomplished thinker who employs an intellect of divine quality."[15]

The Active Intellect is a clear point of divergence between Islamic philosophy and modern Western philosophy on the sources of knowledge. The unique place of the Active Intellect in Islamic philosophy is the main reason why efforts to argue for a fully "naturalized epistemology," in the sense of an epistemology with no supernatural intervention, would be impossible. Even those scholars who emphasize the empirical character of acquiring scientific knowledge in classical Islamic philosophy acknowledge the necessity of investigating both sense perception and the Active Intellect for understanding the process of cognition in a philosopher like Avicenna.[16] The Active Intellect remained present in the history of Islamic philosophy.

An alternative position on the intellect is offered in Sufi philosophy. For example, Ghazālī questions the intellect as the highest stage of knowledge and postulates a source that is nobler. After undermining the authenticity of sense perception through the lens of the intellect, he says,

> Perhaps, therefore I can rely only on those rational data which belong to the category of primary truths, such as our asserting that "ten is more than three," and "one and the same thing cannot be simultaneously affirmed and denied." . . . Then sense data spoke up: "What assurance have you that your reliance on rational data is not like your reliance on sense data? . . . But were it not for the reason-judge you would still accept me as true. So there must be beyond the perception of reason another judge."[17]

For Ghazālī, this higher source is God. In his famous interpretation of the Light Verse (Q 24:35), Ghazālī identifies five types of "luminous human spirits" and places the rational and reflective spirits under "the holy prophetic spirit" (*al-rūḥ al-qudsī al-nabawī*), which according to him belongs to "the prophets and some of the friends of God" (*awlīyā'*). Here, he says that "there is another stage beyond the rational faculty within which there becomes manifest that which does not become manifest to the rational faculty."[18] Ghazālī's formulation of knowledge acquisition in terms of illumination and the manifestation of divine light lays the grounds for later philosophers and Sufis, such as the Sufi philosopher

14. Fārābī, *On the Intellect*, 74–75.
15. Fārābī, *On the Perfect State*, 245.
16. See McGinnis, "Avicenna's Naturalized Epistemology," 144.
17. Ghazālī, *Freedom and Fulfilment*, 65.
18. Ghazālī, *Niche of Lights*, 37.

ʿAyn al-Quḍāt (d. 1131), to explain the relationship between regular epistemic states and suprasensory ones.[19] It is true that already in classical Islamic philosophy, the Active Intellect has affinities with the divine, and it is sometimes equated with the Angel of Revelation. Nonetheless, the philosophers' perspective on its relation to the human mind in this life is primarily an epistemic one rather than an ontological one. Moreover, Fārābī and Avicenna consider the conjunction of the human intellect with the Active Intellect as a temporary connection, which does not transform the substance of the soul.

In contrast, for Sufi-oriented philosophers like Ibn Ṭufayl and Mullā Ṣadrā, what happens between the Active Intellect and the human intellect is both epistemic and ontological, hence the priority of the term *unification* over *conjunction* in this context. Toward the end of Ibn Ṭufayl's philosophical tale *Ḥayy Ibn Yaqẓān*, the protagonist, Ḥayy, who is approaching the end of his intellectual journey, makes a transformative discovery. He realizes that the ultimate happiness of the soul lies in the "attainment of the pure beatific experience, submersion, concentration on Him alone Whose existence is necessary. In this experience the self vanishes; it is extinguished, obliterated—and so are all other subjectivities."[20] A full-fledged spiritual turn in epistemology, which culminates in the "spiritualized epistemology"[21] of Mullā Ṣadrā, is discussed further in the section that follows.

ABSTRACTION, INTUITION, AND PRESENCE

Islamic philosophers explain how knowledge is acquired by using the pair concepts of potential and actual, with "potential" being associated with the material and "actual" with the immaterial. But whereas in Islamic metaphysics both material and immaterial substances can be referred to as "actual," in epistemology, actual knowledge is obtained only in the absence of matter. In other words, at all levels of knowing (sense perception, imagination, and intellection), what is immediately available to the soul should be abstracted from matter. Even at the level of actual sense perception, which is triggered by bodily sensation, what is formed in the soul as actual sensible and imaginative forms are immaterial in their mental existence. That said, when we hear the term *material* with respect to a phase of knowing, it is often a figure of speech and simply stands for "potential."

A full-scale theory of abstraction is developed by Avicenna to explain how the human soul can arrive at conceptual and universal knowledge about the world. In the second book of *On the Soul*, he explains the mechanism of abstraction in knowing the material world by ranking the levels of abstraction based on the degrees of detachment from the matter and its associations:

> So if the perception is of something material, it takes its form abstracted from matter in a certain way. The kinds of abstraction, however, are different and their degrees are dissimilar; for owing to the matter, the material form happens to have certain states and factors that do not belong to it essentially from the perspective of what that form is. So sometimes the extraction from matter is together with

19. See ʿAyn al-Quḍāt, *Essence of Reality*.
20. Ibn Ṭufayl, *Ḥayy Ibn Yaqẓān*, trans. Goodman, 143.
21. *Spiritualized epistemology* is a term I borrowed from Kalin, *Knowledge*, 198.

> either all or some of those associations, whereas at other times the extraction is perfect, that is, in that the formal aspect is abstracted from the matter and from the concomitants that it has on account of the matter. An example of it is that the human form and essence is a nature with respect to which all the individuals of the species are without doubt equally common.[22]

To explain the previous abstraction levels, let us use the example of my neighbor's cat who stands outside of my window from time to time, curiously staring at me while I am typing these words. In perceiving the cat, the first level of abstraction happens when I am in the presence of her concrete existence right in front of my eyes. What occurs to my mind during my sense perception of this curious cat is via sensing features such as color, size, and position. This is the lowest level of abstraction from matter because my sense organs need to be exposed to the particular cat for the perception to begin. My neighbor's cat is so quick to disappear, and she is gone when I look up again. But I can still "see" her in my imagination thanks to the next level of abstraction that provides my imaginative grasp of the cat. The imaginative form of the cat still possesses her material features such as color, size, and position, but my mental access to the image is independent of sensory exposure to the material cat, and I can summon the image in my mind whenever I wish. With this partially abstracted form stored in my imagination, my mind can move up to the next level—namely, intellection, which provides me with conceptual knowledge about cats in general. It is only at this level that total abstraction from all material features takes place, and the mind moves from everyday knowledge of particulars to universal knowledge, which we use in universal propositions of sciences and philosophy.

Classical Islamic philosophers explain the rational activity of the human soul through several stages that the intellect goes through. Avicenna uses the analytic tool of the potential/actual distinction to explain the whole process that results in conceptual knowledge. Like Fārābī, he characterizes the epistemic process of obtaining universal truths based on a movement from potential and passive to actual and active, with the last stages transcending the individual human mind. The rational process involves what Avicenna calls "primary intelligibles" and "secondary intelligibles," which are the building blocks of truth-bearing propositions about the world such as "all cats are mammals." For Avicenna, any process in nature requires the actualization of a certain potential, and this applies to the mental process that composes discursive thinking. The potential/actual dynamic that explains all natural phenomena is also utilized in explaining the epistemic process of intellection. Avicenna discusses the nature and function of the human soul under natural philosophy.

Based on the potential/actual model, Avicenna starts the rational mechanism of the soul with the potential or "material intellect," which is "present in every individual of the species and is called 'material' simply because of its similarity to the disposition of Prime Matter, which in itself has no particular form being a subject for any form." At this level, the rational soul only has the capacity or potential for receiving the primary knowledge, such as "the whole is greater than the part." Once this primary knowledge exists in the

22. Translated in McGinnis, "Making Abstraction Less Abstract," 177.

material intellect, we are at the stage of "dispositional intellect" (*al-ʿaql biʾl-malaka*). After the first potentiality of the "material intellect," every stage of the rational intellect has a degree of actuality in relation to the preceding stage, and the degree of actuality culminates in an epistemic agent that has no potentiality—that is, the Active Intellect. Avicenna also uses the term "perfection" (*kamāl*) in speaking of the growth in epistemic actuality. The third stage of the theoretical intellect, which he calls "the actual intellect" (*al-ʿaql al-biʾl-fiʿl*), is the mental power of reflecting on primary intelligibles, which can provide the secondary intelligibles necessary for thinking beyond evident truths. According to Avicenna, "It is called an actual intellect because it is an intellect that intellects whenever it wants, without the burden of acquiring [it], although it can be called a potential intellect in comparison to what comes after it."[23]

The next and last stage of the human intellect is more actual and perfect compared to the previous stages because "the intelligible forms are present in it, and it is actually reviewing them. So it intellects them, and intellects that it is actually intellecting them." This last stage of the human intellect is called "the acquired intellect" (*al-ʿaql al-mustafād*) for the very reason that it is "in some kind of contact" with an agent outside of the human soul whence it acquires its content.[24] The acquired intellect is the last actuality, or perfection, of the human intellect because the epistemic process cannot be completed without the intervention of the Active Intellect as the external agent of universal knowledge. Although the relation between the human mind and this ultimate activator and source of universal knowledge is interpreted differently, no Islamic philosopher has questioned the necessity of its role, especially as an explanation for the possibility of universal knowledge, which does not vary from one person to another.

The epistemic function of the external agent of knowledge, or the Active Intellect, is often discussed in relation to the function of abstraction. As explained previously, in knowing the world, the rational soul begins with particular objects of sense perception and eventually acquires their universal and intelligible essences through abstraction from all material features. Avicenna argues that what becomes actually intelligible for the soul is only potentially intelligible in itself, just as the rational soul is only potentially an intellect. Since acquiring universal knowledge is just a potential for the rational soul and every potential needs to be actualized by an agent other than itself, an intellect that is by nature actual and active must be the activator of the epistemic process, not to say the "cause" of it:

> The human soul is at one time something intellecting in potentiality, and thereafter becomes something intellecting in actuality. Now whatever emerges from potency to act does so only by means of a cause in act that causes it to emerge, and so in this case there is a cause that causes our souls to emerge from potency to act with respect to the objects of intellection. Since it is the cause with respect to providing the intellectual forms, it is nothing but an actual intellect in whom the principles of the intelligible forms are abstracted [from matter], and whose relation to our souls is the relation of the Sun to our vision. Just as the Sun is actually visible in itself

23. Avicenna, *On the Soul*, 185.
24. Avicenna, *On the Soul*, 185.

and through its light it makes actually visible what is not actually visible, so likewise is the state of this intellect vis-à-vis our souls.[25]

Avicenna's use of the "Sun" imagery, which closely recalls the Sun in Plato's cave allegory, is a lead on understanding the role of the Active Intellect as a force that actualizes knowledge by making visible the universal intelligibles. Based on this imagery and other evidence, some scholars argue that the Active Intellect has no direct role in the abstraction process itself, but it illuminates what is already abstracted by the mind, like when colors become visible in light—a function that is "irreducibly distinct" from abstraction.[26] Alternatively, if we take the Platonic resemblance more seriously, then the Active Intellect is to be understood as the source of the intelligibles because Plato's Sun, which stood for "the Good," was the cause and source of the Ideas. Furthermore, as Plotinus (whose influence on classical Islamic philosophy is unquestionable) notes, the pursuit for intelligibles should only occur in the Intellect. In the latter reading, the Active Intellect would have a more direct role in the epistemic act, which is also reinforced by Avicenna's use of the notion of "conjunction" and "emanation" to explain the soul's temporary connection with the Active Intellect to acquire the intelligibles at the level of intellection.[27]

As expected from Averroes, his theory of abstraction is clearly devoid of the "emanation" component. Moreover, unlike his Islamic predecessors, he postulates an imperishable material intellect that all humans share and could be interpreted as the species' epistemic potential. In his mature career, Averroes considers the material intellect to be "directly below the Active Intellect in the hierarchy of existence as the last of the incorporeal intelligences."[28] For him, the abstraction of the intelligibles from material objects is completed by the intervention of the Active Intellect as the one agent that makes the potentially intelligible forms actually intelligibles for the theoretical intellect. The mechanism of actualization happens when the knower willfully conjoins with the Active Intellect. Like Fārābī and Avicenna, Averroes regards the Active Intellect as a separate immaterial substance whose uniqueness explains the universality of scientific knowledge. But for him, this universality is also guaranteed by the uniqueness of the separate material intellect because it is common to all human beings. The same abstraction mechanism and common access of human minds to the same actualizing agent guarantees the truth of theoretical assertions, including scientific propositions for those who take the right epistemic path. Similar to Fārābī, he uses the "light" analogy to explain the role of the Active Intellect in causing conceptual thinking. As he says in his most detailed account on the subject in his *Long Commentary* on Aristotle's *De Anima*,

For just as light is the entelechy of the transparent, so the active intellect is the entelechy of the material [intellect]. Just as the transparent is not moved by color nor receives it unless illuminated, so the material intellect does not receive

25. Avicenna, *On the Soul*, 180 (with slight modifications).
26. See Avicenna, *On the Soul*, 173.
27. For the centrality of the Active Intellect in Avicenna's epistemology, see Azadpur, *Analytic Philosophy and Avicenna*.
28. Davidson, *Alfarabi, Avicenna, and Averroes*, 295. For Averroes's argument for the common material intellect, see his *Long Commentary*, 322–25. A comparison among Fārābī, Avicenna, and Averroes on abstraction can be found in Taylor, "Epistemology of Abstraction," 273–84.

> intelligible thoughts of objects in the physical world except when it [the material intellect] is perfected and illuminated by the active intellect. And just as light renders potential color actual and capable of moving the transparent, so the active intellect renders notions [in the imaginative faculty] which are potentially intelligible, actual and capable of being received by the material intellect.[29]

The foregoing brief account of the abstraction mechanism in classical Islamic philosophy shows that the variety of views on this process stems from different interpretations of the dynamics between the immaterial Active Intellect and the human passive intellect. In addition, the abstraction process, broadly construed, involves the dual though interrelated process that actualizes both the potentially intelligibles (i.e., the known) and the potentially intellect (i.e., the knower). Nevertheless, abstraction is not the only path to universal knowledge. Avicenna's texts on the epistemic role of the Active Intellect also point to "intuition" (*ḥads*) as a less common mechanism used by the theoretical intellect. Unlike the act of abstraction, which is a process with duration and mental effort, intuition, generally speaking, is instantaneous and effortless on the part of the knower. It often points to a direct and nondiscursive access of the known by the knower, whether it be through sensation, intellection, or inspiration. Avicenna uses this concept in several of his texts in the context of his theory of knowledge and sometimes places intuition beyond the access of average human minds and associates it with the prophets. But more often than not, he uses "intuition" when discussing syllogisms by describing it as the "quickness of apprehension" or "an act of the mind by which the mind itself immediately perceives the middle term."[30] Based on comments like these, one can consider the Avicennian "intuition" as an alternative epistemic mechanism next to abstraction, which is more common.

The formation of discourses around "intuition" is influenced by many factors, but Avicenna has been credited with the most consistent account of it.[31] In the psychology part of the *Metaphysics of the Salvation*, although Avicenna seems to introduce "intuition" as an alternative to "instruction," the latter cannot be the origin of knowledge due to its secondhand nature. So all knowledge by instruction must be grounded in knowledge by intuition. As he argues, "Even the first principles of instruction are obtained through intuition since all knowledge can be reduced ultimately to certain intuitive principles." Given this crucial role of intuition, Avicenna describes it as a capacity of various "degrees of intensity," which means that every rational soul may possess this capacity ranging from those "who are wholly without intuition" to "people who possess intuition regarding all or most problems," or "in people who have intuition in the shortest possible time." With regard to the highest degrees of intuition, Avicenna also mentions an "intense purity" of the soul, which keeps the mind focused on "rational principles" at all times. As for the source of intuitive knowledge, we must return to the Active Intellect.[32] This means that intellective abstraction and intuition rely on the same source, and their difference is primarily due to the absence of intellectual effort in the latter. Furthermore, given that intuition can be present in different degrees, one may conclude that the same rational soul utilizes

29. Cited in Davidson, *Alfarabi, Avicenna, and Averroes*, 317. Brackets in the original.
30. See Rahman, *Avicenna's Psychology*, 36.
31. Gutas, *Avicenna*, 170.
32. See Rahman, *Avicenna's Psychology*, 35–36.

both abstraction and intuition, while the degree to which the latter works, based on the strength of the soul and its purity, determines the time and intellectual effort on the part of the rational soul.

Despite their differences, abstraction and intuition in Avicennian epistemology both function through noetic forms or concepts. Additionally, Avicenna mentions "presence" (*ḥuḍūr*) as the way the soul becomes aware of its own existence, amounting to a type of knowledge that does not involve noetic forms or concepts—that is, "knowledge by presence" (*al-ʿilm al-ḥuḍūrī*). But in Avicennian philosophy, "presence" is not functional in knowledge about the world, so it cannot be considered as an epistemic mechanism. In his commentary on Avicenna, Ṭūsī uses knowledge by "presence" to explain God's knowledge of the world without the intermediary of concepts or noetic forms based on the premise that the effect is always immediately present to its cause.[33] Similar to Avicenna, Ṭūsī does not use "presence" as a kind of human act of knowing. But this is not the case in later Islamic philosophy, which links it with suprarational knowledge and higher forms of awareness.[34] Later Islamic philosophers, most importantly Mullā Ṣadrā and Hādī Sabziwārī (d. 1881), follow Suhrawardī in integrating knowledge by presence into their epistemologies.

Based on the narratives of light and unveiling that recur throughout his philosophical texts, Suhrawardī explains all types of knowledge as the presence of the known for the knower. His epistemology is premised on the rejection of Avicenna's universals as the known and of abstraction as the mechanism of grasping realities. For Suhrawardī, all knowledge is knowledge of particular realities, which are essentially different types of light. He uses vision as a model of all knowledge and characterizes it as an unmediated perception—that is, perception without the mediation of the Avicennian abstracted forms. Vision happens once a particular object is present to the eyes in light and there is no veil or obstacle. He rejects all major theories of vision before himself by arguing that "vision is not conditioned on the imprinting of an image or on the emission of something: it is sufficient for there to be no veil between the seer and object of vision."[35] This is based on one of the two major metaphysical principles in Illuminationist philosophy. According to the first, "light is that which is evident in its own reality and by essence makes another evident."[36] As for the second principle, realities, or lights, compose a hierarchical order according to which a lower light is "dominated in its effects by that light more perfect than it."[37] For Suhrawardī, this means that the known becomes present to the knower through a process of illumination by which the nobler light (i.e., the rational soul) dominates or encompasses a lower light (i.e., the essence of the external object). In the words of Mullā Ṣadrā, Illuminationist epistemology characterizes different kinds of perception as "an illuminative relation between luminous things."[38]

33. For a summary of Ṭūsī's arguments in this regard, see Meisami, *Naṣīr al-Dīn Ṭūsī*, 30–35.
34. For the relation between knowledge by presence and mysticism, see Haʾirī Yazdi, *Principles of Epistemology*.
35. Suhrawardī, *Philosophy of Illumination*, 104.
36. Suhrawardī, *Philosophy of Illumination*, 81.
37. Suhrawardī, *Philosophy of Illumination*, 114.
38. Mullā Ṣadrā, *Asfār*, 3:286.

In later Islamic philosophy, Mullā Ṣadrā finds both Avicenna's and Suhrawardī's uses of "presence" very useful. But "presence" in Mullā Ṣadrā's epistemology is more systematically explained and utilized in terms of the "unification of the knower and the known" (*ittiḥād al-ʿāqil wa'l-maʿqūl*), a mechanism that is grounded in his ontology of existential unity and gradation (*tashkīk*). As explained before, in classical Islamic philosophy, the hierarchy of the sources of knowledge is based on the level of abstraction from matter on the part of the immediately known. In his theory of knowledge, Mullā Ṣadrā does not rely on abstraction for explaining either knowledge formation or hierarchy of knowledge. For him, what is obtained through each type of knowledge—namely, sense perception, imagination, and intellection—is one of the three possible grades of the mental existence of an external object. Second, through each type, or rather phase, of knowledge, the knower is actualized by the known, like matter is actualized by form. In other words, the soul/mind does not use the phases of knowledge as mere venues of receiving the known. Rather, the process is an ontological one through which the soul actually *becomes* the sensible soul, the imaginative soul, and the intellective soul while retaining its unity as a single graded existence. The ascent of the sensible soul to the imaginative soul is due to its unification with the imaginal existence of the known after the soul has become unified with the sensible existence of the sensible known. At the final phase of knowledge, the intelligible existence of the known is unified with the intellect. For Mullā Ṣadrā, unification in the previously mentioned sense is possible because knowledge itself is existence, or more precisely, "knowledge is the mode of the existence of an immaterial thing."[39] This means that sense perception, imagination, and intellection are the realization of three forms of existence in the soul and unified with it. According to Mullā Ṣadrā,

> The existence of the sensible qua sensible is its very existence for the substance that is sensing it and this is a mode of existence, meaning being sensible; just like the existence of the intelligible qua intelligible and its intelligibility are really one with the intellecting substance.[40]

To explain the realization of knowledge through unification, Mullā Ṣadrā uses the conceptual framework of natural philosophy. He compares the actualization of the potential intellect with the actualization of matter by the "bodily form." Although neither the knower nor the immediately known is material, the ontological dynamic between them is similar to matter and form in nature. Mullā Ṣadrā argues that first, just as matter is realized and perfected as a thing only by substantial forms, the potential or material intellect is actualized as a knower by intelligible forms. Second, in both cases, the process is that of unification that results in one thing, not that of the conjunction of two different things or the addition of accident to substance.[41]

Mullā Ṣadrā's thesis of knowledge as realization and perfection is based on his view of reality as one graded existence. For him, the knower and the immediately known are two immaterial modes of existence, and their unification means that the former is perfected by the latter because the immediately known is of a higher degree of existence. In other

39. Mullā Ṣadrā, *Asfār*, 3:286.
40. Mullā Ṣadrā, *Asfār*, 3:299.
41. Mullā Ṣadrā, *Asfār*, 3:319–21.

words, the potentially sensing soul is perfected by the sensible form to become an actual sensing substance, the potentially imagining soul is perfected by the imaginal form to become an actually imagining substance, and the potentially intellecting soul is perfected by the intelligible form to become an actually intellecting substance. The three souls are all but different existential stages of one and the same soul that can evolve in its soul-ness by acquiring knowledge to the point of unification with the Active Intellect during the act of intellection.[42] Unification of the human soul with the Active Intellect was already a debatable matter among Mullā Ṣadrā's predecessors and rejected by Avicenna. However, Mullā Ṣadrā tries to demonstrate that previous objections to unification were premised on the authenticity of essence, or quiddity, and the impossibility of unification among different essences. Once existence becomes *the* reality, which is a graded unity, then we can understand the unification of the human intellect with the Active Intellect as the perfection of one grade of existence through the nobler one. On this subject, Mullā Ṣadrā cites the following from the so-called *Theology of Aristotle*: "Indeed the higher world is alive and perfect, encompassing all the things because it issued from the perfect, first, Transcendent Originator; so [the Intellect] includes all intellects and souls."[43]

Taking Plotinus's *Enneads* to be a text by Aristotle, a common error of his time, Mullā Ṣadrā attributes the intellectual and spiritual inclusiveness of *The Enneads*'s second hypostasis—that is, the Intellect that emanates from the One—to the Active Intellect of peripatetic philosophy. This means that the unification of multiple souls with the Active Intellect does not imply multiplicity in the latter, pace Avicenna. The possibility is there because the Active Intellect already contains all intellectual and spiritual realities without suffering from multiplicity in its own existence. All immaterial realities exist with one simple (*basīṭ*) existence in unity with the existence of the Active Intellect, and the rational soul in its perfect immaterial existence can be unified with the Active Intellect.[44] After all, for Mullā Ṣadrā, this is an existential unification, since in reality, there are only existences. I end this section with a reminder that in Islamic philosophy, epistemology is grounded in ontology, and this dependence is most obvious as we move away from the classical abstraction mechanism to the unification thesis in later Islamic philosophy due to its characterization of knowledge as a mode of existence.

JUSTIFICATION AND TRUTH

Contemporary epistemology takes Plato's definition of knowledge declared in his *Theaetetus* as "justified true belief" quite seriously but has a lot more to offer by analyzing the concepts of "justification" and "truth." Also, it is now common knowledge among epistemologists that although justification is necessary for a true belief to be regarded as knowledge, not every justified belief is knowledge, since one may have good reasons for believing something that is not true. Broadly speaking, for knowledge to be justified, it must be grounded in certain experiences, correct inferences, or even a trustworthy testimony. There are a variety of theories about the structure of knowledge, its grounds and

42. Mullā Ṣadrā, *Asfār*, 3:339.
43. Mullā Ṣadrā, *Asfār*, 3:340.
44. Mullā Ṣadrā, *Asfār*, 3:337–39. For more on this subject, see Kalin, *Knowledge*, 151–53.

truth conditions. A contemporary epistemologist discusses, on the one hand, the types of internal and/or external grounds that justify our beliefs and, on the other hand, those conditions that make a certain belief true. According to the "internalist" theory of justification, one must have access to the grounds, or reasons, for justification in the sense of being aware of what justifies one's own beliefs. In contrast, an "externalist" theory of justification defines justification not in terms of our awareness of the grounds of our beliefs but in terms of external conditions. Epistemology in Islamic philosophy seems to be more in line with internalism regarding justification. However, there are also places in Islamic philosophy where true knowledge is not conditioned on consciousness of its grounds. To resolve some apparent contradictions in this respect, I suggest a form of compatibility between internalism and externalism by associating the former with justification and the latter with truth.[45]

To begin, Islamic philosophers' position on knowledge is in tandem with "foundationalism," according to which "any indirect (hence non-foundational) knowledge there is depends on direct (and thus in a sense foundational) knowledge."[46] Classical Islamic philosophers seek the foundations of knowledge in both extra-mental sources and mental functions, which are governed by rules of logic. For this reason, their discourses on knowledge draw on logic, natural science, and metaphysics, including metaphysical psychology. Regardless of their differences, Islamic philosophers share some epistemological principles about the grounds of knowledge or justification. First, an epistemic process originates in the potential of the mind for knowing the world, a potential that is actualized by external causes. Second, the external causes of knowledge formation consist of both material and immaterial forces. Third, the human rational apparatus is not inherently flawed, so it is capable of facilitating true knowledge if logical methods of induction and deduction are utilized properly. Fourth, to know something for certain, one must have a second-order knowledge that one knows; in other words, one must be aware of the reasons for believing that something is true.

To reconstruct a kind of justification theory in Islamic philosophy, I limit the discussion to the relation between justification and truth because Islamic philosophers are only interested in justification when true beliefs are concerned. With respect to the relation between justification and truth, as Robert Audi says, "Normally, the internal states and processes that justify our beliefs also connect our beliefs with the external facts in virtue of which those beliefs are true."[47] This seems to be an implicit principle among Islamic philosophers, both classical and postclassical. This fact is reinforced by their understanding of "truth" as a correspondence (*muṭābaqa*) between the immediate object of knowledge in the mind and the state of affairs, or the known, in the extra-mental world. This is in line with the Islamic philosopher's commitment to realism in the sense that truth is not dependent on the mind. For example, my belief that "I am typing these words on my computer now" is true by virtue of the fact that this state of affairs is *really* the case outside of my mind.

45. My approach is inspired by R. Audi's suggestion with respect to compatibilism in epistemology. See Audi, *Epistemology*, 239.
46. Audi, *Epistemology*, 194.
47. Audi, *Epistemology*, 246.

To begin, Fārābī considers knowledge to consist of "conceptions," which are acquired by the mind, and "assents," which the mind arrives at by connecting conceptions using logical methods. He opens his *Book of Demonstration* by dividing knowledge into conception and assent and proceeds to argue that only assent is subject to truth and falsity.[48] Avicenna follows Fārābī in dividing knowledge into conception and assent. Like Fārābī, Avicenna assigns "truth" only to assent and understands it in terms of correspondence with reality:

> Every assent, then, is together with a conception, but not conversely. In the case of what this [statement] means, the conception informs you that [both] the form of this composite [statement] and that from which it is composed (like "white" and "accident") occur in the mind, whereas [in] assent, this form's relation to the things themselves occurs in the mind, that is, [the form in the mind] maps unto [the things themselves].[49]

Avicenna's epistemology is very attentive to the empirical grounds of knowledge. In his *Book of Demonstration*, he argues that not only inductive knowledge but also deductive knowledge, or demonstration, is grounded in empirical experience.[50] However, the *Book of Demonstration* is primarily concerned with the epistemology of the natural sciences from the point of view of a philosopher-scientist, hence Avicenna's overemphasis on the empirical grounds of knowledge therein. In his wider epistemic perspective, Avicenna offers a theory of knowledge that grounds knowledge in both material and immaterial conditions.

One important question with respect to epistemic justification is that of second-order knowledge—that is, knowing that one knows. Fārābī and Avicenna both discuss second-order knowledge in relation to certainty. In his *Conditions of Certainty*, Fārābī offers his theory of truth as correspondence between the belief and the external world. However, for him, "external does not mean 'external to the soul' but rather 'external to the belief.'"[51] So for Fārābī, the truth of a certain belief can be judged by another belief, and "if a person is certain that *p*, [they are] able to generate a potentially infinite series of meta-beliefs about the truth of *p*, and their own belief that *p* is true."[52] For Fārābī and his succeeding philosophers, when second-order knowledge is concerned, in addition to rules of logic, certain metaphysical principles are negotiated to justify the first-order true beliefs, most importantly the belief that the Active Intellect is the source of universal knowledge.

As explained previously in this chapter, the mind's use of the abstraction mechanism to translate sense data eventually into intelligibles is only partly down to the human powers because its full operation relies on the Active Intellect that is outside of the human mind. The nature and function of the Active Intellect is a matter of controversy among Islamic philosophers, but there is strong evidence that they involve the Active Intellect in the whole of the epistemic process.[53] From this perspective, believing the soundness of our physical and mental apparatuses and use of logical techniques is only *necessary* for justifying our true beliefs when we arrive at truth, whereas the *sufficient* condition of

48. Fārābī, *Book of Demonstration*, 63–64.
49. Cited in McGinnis, *Avicenna*, 29 (with slight modifications). Brackets in the original.
50. Avicenna, *Book of Demonstration*, 152.
51. Black, "Knowledge (*ʿilm*) and Certitude (*yaqīn*)," 19.
52. Black, "Knowledge (*ʿilm*) and Certitude (*yaqīn*)," 37.
53. One recent example of this position is presented in Azadpur, *Analytic Philosophy and Avicenna*.

justification for our epistemic success must also include the role of the Active Intellect. Reference to the function of the Active Intellect is an unbridgeable gap between Islamic epistemology and contemporary epistemology. Fārābī uses the "vision" analogy to explain the relation between the Active Intellect and the human potential intellect, which is later used by Avicenna too. According to Fārābī,

> The principle by which vision becomes actual vision after having been potential vision, and by which visible things that had been potentially visible become actually visible, is the transparency that comes about in vision from the sun. In a similar manner, there comes about in the potential intellect a certain thing whose relation to it is like that of actual transparency to vision. The Active Intellect gives that thing to [the potential intellect], whereby it becomes a principle through which the potential intelligibles become actual intelligibles for [the intellect].[54]

I discussed the epistemic role of the Active Intellect earlier in this chapter. With respect to justification, for an Islamic philosopher, when we know that *p*, our reason for knowing that *p* is true lies not only in our confidence in the soundness of our logical inferences and a healthy physical/psychological apparatus but also in our trust in the unfailing agency of the Active Intellect. In other words, among the metabeliefs that justify *p*—"the tree outside of my window is alive"—is the second-order belief that "*p* is true on the grounds that the Active Intellect actualizes my potential knowledge that trees are alive, by bestowing on my mind the universal of tree-hood that corresponds with the essence of tree-hood." In Islamic philosophy, the guarantee for this correspondence is a metaphysical principle: The Active Intellect has also bestowed the form of tree-hood on the natural matter that receives this form. So we are justified in our true knowledge about the world because the same source that bestows forms on things also facilitates our knowledge of them by giving the mind the noetic version of the same forms when the mind is ready for their reception.

With the previous discussion in mind, for Fārābī and Avicenna, certain knowledge, which is universal, is internally justified because we are certain about a belief only if we are also certain that all mental processes are sound and an infallible source of knowledge, the Active Intellect, facilitates our knowledge. On the other hand, contingent knowledge, which can also be true but short of the kind of certainty that is only found in universal/necessary knowledge, is grounded in factors of which one may not be directly aware. In the latter case, the truth of our beliefs is externally justified because we do not know how we know that *p* is true. This becomes especially relevant to the status of natural science in Islamic philosophy, especially for scientist-philosophers like Avicenna who investigate how we come to know scientific principles.

Avicenna's epistemology of scientific knowledge includes what he calls "methodic experience" (*tajriba*), through which we learn the first principles of natural sciences. Methodic experience is distinguished from induction as a logical mechanism that needs to explain the relation between concepts in a syllogism. Avicenna ascribes methodic experience to "the observer and perceiver seeing and sensing that certain things belong to a single kind, upon which follows the occurrence of a given action or affection."[55] Based on

54. Fārābī, *On the Intellect*, 75. Brackets in the original.
55. McGinnis, "Avicenna's Naturalized Epistemology," 146.

the importance of methodic experience in acquiring basic scientific principles and his use of sciences to describe "the psychological processes by which one becomes aware of causal relations in the case of first principles," McGinnis uses the term "naturalized epistemology" to describe Avicenna's epistemology of natural sciences.[56] This could mean that with respect to contingent knowledge that is short of certainty, the truth of our beliefs is justified externally. However, similar to Fārābī, when Avicenna addresses certain knowledge that necessarily corresponds to reality, he understands justification in terms of our internal access to the reasons for the true belief. As part of this justification, Avicenna also "suggests that certitude is always marked by an inner feeling of confidence or conviction that functions as the primary indicator that actual knowledge has been attained."[57] However, "confidence" is a psychological state, and its causes and degrees can be discussed from a psychological point of view, so despite "a strongly internalist streak in Avicenna's epistemology," a form of externalism can also be attributed to it.[58]

Constructing a theory of justification and truth in postclassical Islamic philosophy is best possible through the lens of the ontology of epistemology. This is because postclassical Islamic theories of knowledge depend on the immediacy of "presence" as an ontological state to explain knowledge about the world. Mullā Ṣadrā's epistemology is unquestionably in agreement with a strong form of foundationalism. I call his foundationalism "maximalist" due to the maximal involvement of the Active Intellect in all phases of knowledge, including sense perception. To begin, for Mullā Ṣadrā, "every transition from non-inferential to inferential knowledge is either through learning from a human teacher or not; In case it comes through learning, it must necessarily end in what does not come in this way but it is reached on its own, otherwise the infinite regress of teaching and learning would ensue."[59] All knowledge that corresponds with reality, beginning with sense perception, is founded on emanation from the Active Intellect. According to Mullā Ṣadrā,

> Sensation is through what is bestowed by the Giver of illuminative perceptual form and through it [i.e., the perceptual form], perception (*idrāk*) and awareness (*shuʿūr*) become possible. At this point, sensation becomes the actually sensor and the actually sensed, but before this it was only potentially sensing and potentially sensed. On the other hand, the existence of the [natural] form in a specific matter is one of the preparatory conditions for the emanation of the form that is the actually sensed and the actually sensor. This is exactly the same as what happens in the case of the intelligible form being intellect, intellector, and intellected.[60]

Thus, all inferences we make on the grounds of empirical experiences go back to non-inferential forms, which the soul receives from the Active Intellect. In sum, different forms of sense perception through different organs prepare the soul for acquiring primary conceptions and assents, which combine to infer more conceptions and assents, ad infinitum.[61]

56. McGinnis, "Avicenna's Naturalized Epistemology," 147.
57. Black, "Certitude, Justification, and Principles of Knowledge," 140.
58. Black, "Certitude, Justification, and Principles of Knowledge," 140.
59. Mullā Ṣadrā, *Asfār*, 3:384–85.
60. Mullā Ṣadrā, *Asfār*, 3:317.
61. Mullā Ṣadrā, *Asfār*, 3:381–82.

Understanding Mullā Ṣadrā's epistemology depends on his position on his view of knowledge as a form of existence. Similar to his predecessors, he begins with dividing knowledge into conception and assent:

> Knowledge is either assent that is a preponderant belief [regarding the relation between subject and predicate] which in case it is an assertion, if it corresponds to reality, is certitude; otherwise it is a total lack of knowledge. And, in case it is a conjecture, it could be true or false. Apart from assent there is conception. Sometimes "conception" is used as a general term that applies to both [conception and assent], in which case it is synonymous with "knowledge."[62]

As we can see in the previous quotation, the only assent that counts as knowledge is that which is true in the sense of correspondence with reality. What connects Mullā Ṣadrā's position on truth with epistemic justification is his understanding of the nature of assent as a simple existence. He describes conception and assent as "two ways of mental existence through which things are known in the mind," and "they are two simple things . . . because they are two ways of existing, and all existence is simple and as such is individualized by itself and not through some additional thing."[63] If we consider Mullā Ṣadrā's identification of knowledge as a form of existence, we can sum up his argument as follows: (1) Knowledge is a form of existence, (2) existence is simple, and (3) assent is knowledge. Therefore, assent is a simple existence.

If we add Mullā Ṣadrā's foundationalism to his view of the nature of assent and his previously explained thesis on the unification of the knower and the immediately known, we can infer an implicit internalism regarding justification. To adopt an internalist position regarding the knower's access to the grounds of their true beliefs, I imagine Mullā Ṣadrā arguing as follows: (1) The assent that *p* is an immaterial existence in the mind; (2) any immaterial existence is aware of itself;[64] (3) the mind of the knower as an immaterial existence is aware of itself; (4) due to the unity of the knower and the known, the mind is unified with the assent *p* as a simple existence; and (5) therefore, the mind knows that it knows *p*.

In the end, modern epistemology develops primarily in response to skepticism, which does not have a real significance for Islamic philosophers. For this reason, it is not possible to provide a neat theory of justification and truth among Islamic philosophers within the contemporary epistemological framework. However, in this section, I tried to report some of the efforts at applying theories of justification to the theory of knowledge in classical Islamic philosophy and offered my understanding of Mullā Ṣadrā's theory of justification in relation to truth based on some general principles in his ontology and theory of knowledge. The relation between epistemology and ontology is not exclusive to Mullā Ṣadrā, and this chapter must have shown that any discourse on the nature, function, scope, and grounds of knowledge in Islamic philosophy is based on metaphysical claims about the nature of reality and the place of the human soul in the universe.

62. Mullā Ṣadrā, *al-Tanqīḥ fi'l-manṭiq*, 197.
63. Mullā Ṣadrā, *Treatise on Conception and Belief*, 110–11.
64. For Mullā Ṣadrā's theory of self-awareness and its application to immaterial existence, see Kaukua, *Self-Awareness in Islamic Philosophy*, chapter 7.

3

God and Cosmos

A study of Islamic philosophy cannot happen without God. Not only has Islamic philosophy developed within the context of the Abrahamic faiths, but also both Persians and Greeks understood the beginning of the world and its structure in relation to a first originator. In the formative years of Islamic intellectual history, theologians got engaged in many controversies about the nature of God's involvement in the universe, with both theoretical and practical implications. As we shall see in this chapter, philosophers have an active part in generating philosophical discourses on the existence of God and His attributes, including those that relate Him to the world. Their approach to understanding God and His attributes may not have appealed to all mainstream Muslims and theologians, but they have had a long and profound impact on the development of intellectual Islam. Significantly enough, their attempts to rationalize God's existence and attributes, as well as the God-world relationship, have connected Islamic philosophers to wider intellectual and spiritual contexts.

THE EXISTENCE OF GOD

The history of Western and Islamic philosophies is replete with arguments for the existence of God. As discussed previously, the Islamic philosophers were heavily influenced by Greek philosophy, especially by Aristotle and Plotinus in their formulation of the God-world relationship. Whereas Aristotle fulfills the logical expectations of Islamic philosophers by proving the necessity of the First Cause, Plotinus's idea of the One best fits the Islamic intellectual milieu that is immersed in the principal doctrine of Islamic faith—namely, *tawḥīd*, which is acknowledging the oneness of God. Philosophers, theologians, and Sufis alike all reflect on the meaning of *tawḥīd* and interpret it from their own perspectives. The absence of the notion of creation in Aristotle's view of the First Cause distinguishes him from Islamic philosophers who prefer to envision God as a being who brings the world into existence rather than just motivating its motion, as Aristotle believed. On the other hand, despite their belief in the transcendence of God, Islamic philosophers do not follow Plotinus's description of the One as beyond existence. Plotinus's approach reappears, for the most part, in negative theology—namely, the study of God in terms of what He is not, as when we say that "God is not a substance," "God is not mortal," and so on. One group of Islamic philosophers who adopt negative theology are the Ismaʿīlīs. For example, in his

Book of Wellsprings, which is strongly influenced by Neoplatonism, the Persian Ismaʿīlī Abū Yaʿqūb Sijistānī (d. after 971) tries to prove that God "transcends being and non-being."[1] His successor, Kirmānī, despite his Aristotelian inclinations, regards God as beyond all the Quranic attributes and believes that what the Quran describes as God with attributes like seeing and hearing is actually the First Intellect or "Word of God."[2] On the other hand, Sufis interpret Plotinus in favor of the unity of being. In their theology, God is the only reality, and the rest are manifestations of Him. The Andalusian Sufi thinker Ibn ʿArabī likens God as both the central point and the circumference of the circle of the cosmos. Inspired by Ibn ʿArabī, the Persian Sufi poet Maḥmūd Shabistarī (d. after 1337) says, "From your fancy alone appears this visage of the other / As a circle is a point going around in fast motion." His commentator explains this statement as follows:

> The faculty of fancy perceives particular meanings such as Zayd's friendship and Amr's enmity. The poet says, "From your fancy alone appears this visage of the other" because the reality of affairs is only accessible through unveiling and witnessing (*kashf wa shuhūd*) since outer and inner senses are prone to many errors. [The line] means that the apparent otherness of things is the work of one's fancy that perceives particulars and has no grasp of the universals and realities of things. There is only one reality that appears as the diverse forms in both the invisible and the visible worlds.[3]

In contrast to Ismaʿīlīs, Fārābī and Avicenna try to reconcile divine transcendence with a God that can be positively characterized. They also depart from Sufis by acknowledging the reality of creation and do not consider it an appearance. They both revisit Aristotle's First Cause by characterizing it as the noblest existent. Fārābī opens his treatise *On the Perfect State* by discussing this topic:

> The First Existent is the First Cause of the existence of all the other existents. It is free of every kind of deficiency, whereas there must be in everything else some kind of deficiency, either one or more than one; but the First is free of all their deficiencies. Thus, its existence is the most excellent and preceded every other existence. . . . No existent at all can be like its existence; nor is there any existence of the same rank of its existence.[4]

While in this context Fārābī avoids a theological tone and Quranic terminology, his emphasis on the uniqueness of the First Cause perfectly resonates with *tawḥīd* and calls to mind such verses of the Quran as "There is nothing like Him" (Q 42:11). However, how is it possible for God to be the source of the existence of His creation without there being any resemblance between the cause and effect? Fārābī distinguishes between the First Existent and other existents based on the assumption that only the First Cause is perfect, in the sense of being pure from all kinds of deficiencies such as compositeness/divisibility,

1. See Sijistānī, *Book of Wellsprings*, 2:129–30. For the details of his negative theology, see Sijistānī, *Le dévoilment des choses chachées*, chapter 1.
2. Kirmānī, *Rāḥat al-ʿaql*, 101–7.
3. Cited from Meisami, "Point of Reality," 38 (with slight modifications).
4. Fārābī, *On the Perfect State*, 57.

potentiality, corporeality, temporality, and partnership in divinity and worship. But this does not explain the existential relation between the perfect and the imperfect. To clarify the existential relation between God and the world, Avicenna refines Fārābī's conceptual framework through the modal concepts of necessity and contingency. Using these concepts, Avicenna not only offers a novel proof to the existence of the First Cause as the Necessary Existent but also identifies it as the Quranic Allah with His major attributes as the All-Knowing and the Good.[5]

To begin, there are several principles that guide Avicenna's philosophical presentation of divine reality and attributes in general and continue to guide the study of God by philosophers after him. These principles are as follows:

1. The Necessary Existent has no quiddity other than His existence (*al-inniyya*), but everything other than Him has quiddity.
2. The Necessary Existent is necessary in all respects.
3. The Necessary Existent both causes and sustains the existence of what is possible.
4. The Necessary Existent created in eternity.

In this section, we especially need the first principle because it is pertinent to God's existence and the proof of it. Briefly, what has quiddity must be caused because quiddities do not have existence on their own, and in order for them to become existent things, existence must be given to them. For Avicenna, denying this would lead to the contradiction that a quiddity exists before it exists in order to give itself existence! This means that on the one hand, all quiddities need a cause to exist, and on the other hand, the First Cause of their existence has no quiddity and therefore exists in its own right. Here is Avicenna's proof of God's existence, which is often categorized under ontological proofs because it does not rely on matters of fact, such as motion or design. A snapshot of the argument would look like this:

P1. It is evident that there are existent things.
P2. Every existent thing is either possible in itself or necessary in itself.
P3. The line of possible existents cannot go back infinitely.

Therefore, the line of possible existents must end in a Necessary Existent (with no quiddity other than its necessary existence, which causes the possible existents).

To consolidate his argument, Avicenna imagines possible counterarguments and refutes them—for example, that the totality of possible things could exist self-sufficiently. He dismisses this option by responding that "then what exists necessarily subsists by means of things that exist possibly, which is absurd."[6] Likewise, for Avicenna, it is absurd to assume that each possible existent is cause for another because in that case, "each one of them would be a cause and an effect of its own existence, where *x* comes into existence from *y* only after *y* itself comes into existence, but anything whose existence depends on

5. On this topic, see Adamson, "From the Necessary Existent to God," 170–89.
6. Avicenna, *Metaphysics of the Salvation*, 214.

the existence of what exists only after its own later existence cannot exist."[7] One important advantage of this proof is that even eternal things are not self-sufficient, as they too are possible in their essence and need the Necessary Existence for being there. This is in harmony with Fārābī's and Avicenna's choice of Neoplatonic emanationism, according to which the world necessarily originated in the First Principle (the One) without the intervention of the time factor or any sort of existential gap.

Two major Islamic thinkers from opposite quarters confront Avicenna's approach to proving God's existence. For Ghazālī, the necessity of divine causality, with its delimited application to what is possible and the existence of an eternal world, flies in the face of belief in God's will and creative power. In his *Incoherence of the Philosophers*, Ghazālī equates being eternal with being uncaused and argues that philosophers like Fārābī and Avicenna just contradict themselves by postulating an eternal world and a Maker (*al-ṣāni'*) at the same time.[8] Despite his criticism of Avicenna's approach to God, Ghazālī is still in agreement with him on understanding God as an efficient cause in the sense of the Giver of existence. As for the other contender, Averroes, his target is efficient causality in the sense of giving existence through emanation, and unlike Ghazālī, he supports the eternity of the universe. Averroes's God is modeled on Aristotle's unmoved mover that actualizes the potential of the incorporeal world directly as its final cause, or "object of love," and actualizes the rest of the world indirectly via the incorporeal creation. As he says,

> Thus this first mover (God) imparts motion, without being moved to the first object moved by it, just as the beloved moved his lover without being moved itself, and it imparts motion to what is below its first moved by means of the first moved. By its first moved, he (Aristotle) means the celestial body, and by all the other moved, that which is below the first body, namely all the other spheres and that which is subject to generation and corruption (namely the natural world).[9]

In sharp contrast to the Aristotelian representation of God by Averroes, key Islamic thinkers followed Avicenna in understanding God as the Necessary Existent with efficient causality. However, they created new speculative frameworks, which were inspired by Persian mythology, religious texts, and Sufi visions. Four representative figures with influential theories about God's existence are Ghazālī, Suhrawardī, Ibn 'Arabī, and Mullā Ṣadrā. While indebted to Avicenna for their philosophical ideas and principles, they offer their own interpretations of God as the Necessary Existent. In his intellectual and spiritual dedication to the Persian myth of God as light, Suhrawardī ranks reality as different types of lights, with God being the "Light of Lights" and the only self-sufficient light that generates and sustains all the others. In his attempt to prove the existence of God, he describes Him as "the Light of Lights (*al-nūr al-anwār*), the All-Encompassing, the Eternal Light, the Holy Light, the Highest Almighty Light, the Dominating Light," and he argues, "It is absolutely independent because there is nothing beyond It . . . [and] everything other than It is in need of It and has existence from It."[10]

7. Avicenna, *Metaphysics of the Salvation*, 215.
8. Ghazālī, *Incoherence*, 78.
9. Averroes, "Commentary on Aristotle's Metaphysics, Book Lām," 154.
10. Suhrawardī, *Philosophy of Illumination*, 87.

Suhrawardī's use of light imagery in describing God is also rooted in the Quran and possibly indebted to Ghazālī's Sufi reading of the Light Verse (Q 24:35), which speaks of God as being the "Light of the heavens and the earth." The Sufi Ghazālī describes a hierarchy of lights that "climbs to the First Source, which is light in itself and by itself . . . [and] from this light all the other lights shine forth."[11] He also proceeds to equate light with existence and the hierarchy of lights with the hierarchy of contingent existents, which depend on God as the "Real Existent" or "Real Light."[12] Based on the "light = existence" equation, Ghazālī offers his version of proof for the existence of God:

> Since you have recognized that lights have a hierarchy, know that this hierarchy does not continue on to infinity. Rather it climbs to the First Source, which is light in itself and to which no light comes from another. . . . Thus it is verified that the name "light" is more appropriate for the Furthest, Highest Light, beyond which there is no light and from which light descends to others.[13]

In later Islamic philosophy, God as the Necessary Existent, or better say "Necessary Existence," is the center of Mullā Ṣadrā's metaphysics, which is profoundly inspired by the Sufi vision that culminates in the work of Ibn ʿArabī. Mullā Ṣadrā's understanding of God is rooted in his general metaphysics of the unity of being (*waḥdat al-wujūd*). While he follows Avicenna in regarding God as the efficient cause or Giver of existence to the universe, his view of efficient causality is different from Avicenna's and is more inclined toward Ghazālī's Sufi position. In his *Commentary on the Metaphysics of the Healing*, Mullā Ṣadrā discusses causality and causal relations. The selection of passages and the points of emphasis all point to Mullā Ṣadrā's attempt to prove that for Avicenna, "causality" as such only applies to the efficient cause in the sense of giving existence. It is true that Avicenna's own position on the priority of the efficient cause and his emphasis on the primary place of God as the First Principle "that gives reality to others"[14] lends itself to Mullā Ṣadrā's interpretation.

However, unlike Mullā Ṣadrā, Avicenna does not dismiss the material and formal causes as mere considerations of the mind. In his comments on Avicenna's classification of causes into four, Mullā Ṣadrā says, "The consideration of priority, posteriority, causality and being caused and their divisions in the quiddities are only accidental and in virtue of considering existence; otherwise, there are no causal relations among them whatsoever."[15] This interpretation is premised on one of the major principles of Mullā Ṣadrā's metaphysics, so his argument could be structured as follows:

P1. All quiddities and their relations are considerations of the mind.

P2. Material and formal causes belong to quiddities and their relations.

Therefore, material and formal causes are considerations of the mind.

11. Ghazālī, *Niche of Lights*, 14.
12. Ghazālī, *Niche of Lights*, 16.
13. Ghazālī, *Niche of Lights*, 14.
14. Avicenna, *Metaphysics of the Healing*, 215.
15. Mullā Ṣadrā, *al-Taʿlīqāt ʿalā ilāhiyyāt al-Shifāʾ*, 2:992–93.

Furthermore, Avicenna says that efficient causality "is the cause which bestows an existence that is other than itself."[16] In his commentary, Mullā Ṣadrā criticizes that part of the description that says "other than itself" and argues that this cannot be the case in either a natural interpretation of the efficient cause as the agent of motion or a metaphysical cause as bestower of Forms. He believes that in both cases, what the efficient cause bestows is "coupled with" the bestower, and there is no escape from this coupling.[17] In sum, true causation could not possibly make sense if what is given is other than the giver. In this light, Mullā Ṣadrā offers his proof for the existence of God in which the contingency of things "other than" God is understood in terms of their existential poverty:

> The existent is either the reality of *wujūd* (existence), or something else. What we mean by the reality of *wujūd* is that which is not mixed with anything other than pure *wujūd*. . . . And it is called the Necessary Being. . . . That which is other than the reality of *wujūd* is either a quiddity among quiddities [which are merely considerations of the mind] or a particular *wujūd* mixed with non-existence or deficiency. . . . All particularity other than *wujūd* is non-existence or non-existent. Furthermore, all that is compound is posterior to that which is simple. . . . Therefore it is evident that for all things the principle and source of the act of existing is the pure reality of *wujūd* which is not mixed with anything other than *wujūd*.[18]

In his unifying vision, Mullā Ṣadrā is deeply influenced by Ibn ʿArabī, whom he cites frequently. There is no actual proof that Ibn ʿArabī read Islamic philosophers, but his use of the language of necessity and contingency resonates with Avicenna's use of these terms in discussing the God-world relationship. Ibn ʿArabī uses several other terms as well, and he is especially interested in addressing God as "Light." For Ibn ʿArabī, the whole cosmos, which is "contingent" in itself, is a self-disclosure of the existence of God. In the words of William Chittick, "*Wujūd* is one in itself, but infinitely diverse in its self-delimitations. The diversity of the universe represents a true diversity of realities, but in the matrix of a single *wujūd*."[19] Thus, in His reality or essence, God has no differentiation, hence no attributes. It is only at the level of His manifestations when differences and attributes show up. For this reason, as Ibn ʿArabī argues, one cannot rationally know or define divine essence.[20]

GOD'S ATTRIBUTES

The question of God's attributes is a pressing one in the Islamic context. This is due to the fact that in the Quran, God is invested with a number of attributes such as knowledge, power, will, mercy, life, speech, and so on. Except for one chapter, all the chapters in the Quran open with "In the Name of God, the All-Merciful, the Ever-Merciful." However, the doctrine of divine oneness makes it hard to understand how any diversity makes

16. Avicenna, *Metaphysics of the Healing*, 194.
17. Mullā Ṣadrā, *al-Taʿlīqāt ʿalā ilāhiyyāt al-Shifāʾ*, 2:997.
18. Mullā Ṣadrā, *Book of Metaphysical Penetrations*, 49–50.
19. Chittick, "Ibn ʿArabī," 1:505.
20. See Ibn ʿArabī, *Meccan Revelations*, 1:32.

sense at the level of divinity, hence the issue of how to relate all the different Quranic attributes to the one God. This gave rise to controversies among different groups of theologians, which even put one group or another in jeopardy of inquisition depending on what was considered theologically correct at the time. Classical Islamic philosophy is invested in the issue of God's attributes too, especially because of its emphasis on the simplicity of God. In this section, I discuss some of the most important problems related to the attribute of divine knowledge, which is one of the most philosophically studied attributes.

Avicenna's position on divine attributes is guided by the principle that God does not have a quiddity other than His existence. This means that the Necessary Existent is pure simplicity because any form of composition is due to quiddity. The Necessary Existent has no composition, either the logical one of genus and differentia or the metaphysical one of matter and form. He argues, "The Necessary Existent cannot be of any characterization that entails composition so that there would be some quiddity such that the quiddity would have a meaning other than its reality."[21] In this respect, Avicenna obligates himself to reconcile the pure simplicity of God with the Quranic assertion that God has knowledge of all. He finds it necessary to clear God's knowledge of all those components of knowing that entail change, corruptibility, and temporality. To do so, he proposes the notion of knowing individual things in a "universal" manner.

Avicenna says, "The Necessary Existent intellects everything only universally, but nevertheless no individual thing escapes Its notice, 'not even the weight of a dust speck, whether in the heavens or on earth, escapes His notice' (Q 10:61)."[22] His famous analogy in this context is an astronomer's knowledge of celestial dynamics, which gives him the knowledge of the time and location of a particular eclipse without his need to observe any individual eclipse in its particular time and place.[23] In God's case, He does not even need to look at anything outside of His own reality. As the Necessary Existent, all perfections must be necessarily His, which means He cannot be devoid of self-knowledge. On the other hand, God is the source of all that exists; therefore, by knowing Himself, God knows all in an a priori manner and before their occurrence. This knowledge is also necessary in the sense that just like His existence, it is impossible for it not to be. Using the eclipse example again, the astronomer's knowledge of a particular eclipse is because of his knowledge of its causes. In a similar vein, God has knowledge of all causes of things and occurrences because He *is* the primary cause of all and knows them through knowing Himself:

> There is among the things that exist, nothing that is not in some manner necessitated by Him [as] cause. . . . The collision of these causes result in the existence of particular things. . . . The First knows the causes and their corresponding [relations]. He thus necessarily knows to what these lead, the time [intervals] between them, and their recurrences. For it is not possible that He knows [the former principles] and not this. He would thus apprehend particular things inasmuch as they are universal.[24]

21. Avicenna, *Metaphysics of the Healing*, 274–77.
22. Avicenna, *Metaphysics of the Salvation*, 217.
23. Avicenna, *Metaphysics of the Salvation*, 218.
24. Avicenna, *Metaphysics of the Healing*, 288. Brackets in the original.

Avicenna's position on God's knowledge has not convinced everyone. Aside from Ghazālī's critique out of his theological fear of limiting God's omniscience and omnipotence, even Avicenna's follower and commentator Naṣīr al-Dīn Ṭūsī struggles with the idea of restricting God's knowledge to a priori knowledge of universals. To solve this problem, Ṭūsī revisits the nature of God's knowledge in terms of the presence of the known for the knower. From his perspective, universal forms or intelligibles do not mediate God's knowledge of the world. For him, God's knowledge is active perception in the sense of having immediate access to what proceeds from Him. This means that God knows all that proceeds from Him directly—that is, not through any noetic forms.

To be more precise, for Ṭūsī, God's knowledge of the incorporeal existents—namely, the intellects—is identical with their existence for Him, and His knowledge of the material things is through their intellectual existence for the intellects. Therefore, God's knowledge of particulars does not entail multiplicity in His essence, as Avicenna fears, and it is not limited to knowledge before the existence of particulars.[25] This idea is originally stated by Suhrawardī based on his metaphysics of light and the model of direct vision, although unlike Ṭūsī, Suhrawardī does not differentiate between the incorporeal and material and applies his principle to all "things":

> Therefore, the truth about the Necessary Existent's knowledge is given in the Illuminationist principle—that is, Its knowledge of Its essence is Its being a light in Its essence and evident to Its essence. Its knowledge of things is their being evident to It, either in themselves or in their connections which are the locations where the higher managing lights [i.e., souls of the spheres[26]] continuously perceive them. . . . Thus the relation of the Necessary Existent to anything evident to it is Its vision and perception of that thing.[27]

Influenced by both Avicenna and Suhrawardī, Mullā Ṣadrā's position on God's knowledge shifts across different periods of his writing. In one of his later works, he talks about divine knowledge in detail. He starts the discussion with a critique of previous theories held by the Peripatetic and Illuminationist philosophers. For Mullā Ṣadrā, these theories have merits with regard to God's knowledge as posterior to His essence—namely, when they come to exist as particulars.[28] At this level, God's knowledge of things is identical with His act of creation, so He knows all particulars when they come to exist through His creative act. But Mullā Ṣadrā considers previous theories problematic in explaining God's knowledge at the level of His essence. Because of the esoteric nature of God's knowledge at the level of His essence, Mullā Ṣadrā resorts to analogy and argues that God's essence is where the intelligible forms of contingents manifest themselves as if in a mirror. So just like what is reflected in a mirror is not the object itself but a manifestation or reflection, the forms of things that are manifested in the mirror of God's essence are not the actual forms of objects but their reflections.

25. Ṭūsī, *Sharḥ al-Ishārāt wa'l-tanbīhāt*, 3:285.
26. Suhrawardī, *Philosophy of Illumination*, 182.
27. Suhrawardī, *Philosophy of Illumination*, 106.
28. Mullā Ṣadrā, *al-Shawāhid al-rubūbiyya*, 37.

Mullā Ṣadrā tries to solidify this position by reminding the readers about his metaphysical principle that quiddities are not existent in their own right, but their "reality" is simply "accidental" and derived from the reality of the one graded existence.[29] This principle entails that the universal forms, or quiddities, which are reflected in the mirror of God's essence, can by no means detract from the absolute simplicity and oneness of God's essence because quiddity is nothing but a reflection of existence. With these comments, Mullā Ṣadrā proceeds to address God's knowledge with a Quranic tone that is colored by the Sufi theology of divine names and says, "Thus the world is the face of God and His name, so the invisible world is the referent of His hidden name and the visible world is the referent of His manifest name."[30]

Mullā Ṣadrā's identification of God's attributes with divine names is rooted in the Quran and in Akbarian Sufism—namely, the Sufi tradition established by Ibn ʿArabī. Ibn ʿArabī considers himself a commentator of the Quran and, in his mystical reading of its verses, argues that whatever exists is a manifestation of a divine name. The unity of God's essence with His names or attributes entails that His knowledge of everything is the same as His knowledge of Himself, or as Ibn ʿArabī puts it, "He knows all things; [and] He mentioned that concerning Himself by way of lauding His own Essence."[31]

Philosophers and Sufis both accept the principle of the simplicity of divine essence and its unity with attributes. Since the origin of the discussion of attributes is the Quran, the discourse is informed by both the doctrine of divine oneness and the distinction between two types of divine attributes, which are subsumed under God's names of Beauty (*jamāl*) and names of Majesty (*jalāl*). Technically, these are the names that God calls Himself in the Quran. For example, "Ever-Merciful" (*al-Raḥīm*) is a name of Beauty, while "Avenger" (*al-muntaqim*) is a name of Majesty. Since God's essence is without either real or conceptual parts and therefore cannot be defined, the names are the only way to approach a kind of understanding of Him, at least in relation to His creation.

Classical Islamic philosophers such as Fārābī often refer to the First Cause as "Knowing," "Living," "Wise," "Existent," and "True." For him, "Since the First is in the most excellent state of existence, its beauty surpasses the beauty of every other beautiful existent, and the same applies to its splendor and brilliance. Furthermore, it has all these in its substance and essence by itself and by thinking (intelligizing) its essence."[32] Fārābī's approach and terminology influenced Avicenna and his followers, but in a more systematic manner, Avicenna premises the nobleness, or rather transcendence, of God's attributes on His necessary existence.

Avicenna addresses some of the key attributes of essence and beauty such as "knowledge," "power," "life," "will," "munificence," and "good" and interprets them in terms of God's necessary existence. While he uses the same terms for referring to those attributes that we apply to both God and His creation such as "life," Avicenna's treatment of the former assumes a different nature for God's attributes in comparison to those of the same names attributed to His creation. The reason for this distinction is that the attributes of

29. Mullā Ṣadrā, *al-Shawāhid al-rubūbiyya*, 40.
30. Mullā Ṣadrā, *al-Shawāhid al-rubūbiyya*, 43.
31. Ibn ʿArabī, *Meccan Revelations*, 1:48.
32. Fārābī, *On the Perfect State*, 85.

an existent that is necessary cannot be the same as those of contingent existents. To show the difference, Avicenna relies on the notion of "negation" that is related to the Necessary Existent being uncaused and the notion of "relation" with respect to the Necessary Existent being the cause of everything other than Him. According to Avicenna,

> If he says of Him "willer," he would mean only that the Necessary Existent's being with His intellectuality—that is the negation of matter of Him—is the principle of the entire order of the good, and that He intellectually apprehends this. This would hence be composed of a *relation* (*iḍāfa*) and a *negation* (*salb*). . . . If one says of Him "good," he would only mean either [the fact] that this existence is free from mixing with what is potency and deficiency—and this is negation—or His [state of] being the principle of every perfection and order, this being a relation.[33]

While Ghazālī regards Avicenna's account of God's knowledge as a deviation from the All-Knowing Allah in the Quran, for Averroes, it is a deflection from Aristotle's self-thinking God. As Richard Taylor argues, Averroes reinterprets theological terms such as "knowledge" to align his position on theological matters with Aristotelian philosophy. For example, with respect to God's knowledge, Averroes argues against describing it as either of "particulars," like Ghazālī, or of "universals," like Avicenna, because these notions rely on our understanding of human knowledge. For Averroes, "God's knowledge is purely an unchanging and eternal activity of self-knowing and radically unlike the human forms of knowing."[34] This view of God's knowledge is the best example of approaching divine attributes from the perspective of "incomparability" (*tanzīh*), which is the epitome of radical rationalism in the Islamic context. Although Avicenna is against an anthropomorphic understanding of God's attributes, his position is not based on the "incomparability" of God and the world as we find in Averroes. Recently, it has been argued that Averroes's position had a strong influence on some major thinkers during the late Safavid period.[35]

Sufi thinkers regard as deficient all philosophical positions on God's attributes, including knowledge. The attachment to the incomparability approach was widely the case among the philosophers of Andalusia, where Ibn ʿArabī started his intellectual career. Averroes; his predecessor Ibn Bājja (d. 1138), who was an Aristotelian rationalist; and Maimonides (d. 1204), who regarded the application of similar attributes to God and the world as mere homonymy, were all from this part of the Muslim world. The Sufi Ibn ʿArabī separates himself from them without lapsing into the anthropomorphism of "common people." On the other hand, he also separates himself from Muʿtazilite theologians, whose rationalism regarding divine attributes influenced philosophers in the first place. To do so, he tries to find a middle path between the incomparability and similitude when approaching God's attributes, or better referred to as "Names." Ibn ʿArabī sets up his theoretical framework based on a theological/mystical worldview wherein similarity and incomparability come together. Basing himself off the Quran, Ibn ʿArabī classifies God's attributes into those of similarity (*tashbīh*) and those of incomparability (*tanzīh*). The

33. Avicenna, *Metaphysics of the Healing*, 296. For a study of Avicenna's negation-relation strategy, see Adamson, "From the Necessary Existent to God," 172–76. Italics mine.
34. Taylor, "Averroes," 189.
35. See Pourjavady, "Introduction."

Quran (38:75) says that God created human beings with his "two" hands, which Ibn ʿArabī and many others take to refer to God's two attributes of similarity and incomparability. To know God in terms of similarity and incomparability, Ibn ʿArabī states in his *Meccan Revelations* one needs to use imagination and intellection respectively:

> The Real (God) described Himself by things with which the rational proofs declare Him incomparable. Hence, these things can only be accepted by way of faith and submission, or, for Him who adds it, by interpretation in the mode appropriate for rational consideration. The People of Unveiling, who possess the divine faculty that is beyond the stage of reason, recognize this, just as the common people understand. . . . So the common people stand in the station of declaring similarity, the People of Unveiling declare both similarity and incomparability, and the rational thinkers declare incomparability alone. Hence, God combined the two sides in His elect.[36]

As mentioned before, Ibn ʿArabī was a significant influence on later Islamic philosophy of the school of Mullā Ṣadrā. With respect to the method of reconciling incomparability with similarity, Mullā Ṣadrā's view of God's nature points to securing this method in his metaphysics of the graded unity of existence. As for God's existence, he says, "The Simple Reality (*baṣīṭ al-ḥaqīqa*) is all things of existence (*al-ashyā ʾal-wujūdiyya*) to the exclusion of imperfections and non-existences."[37] This guides his approach to divine attributes, three of which he discusses in detail—namely, knowledge, power, and will. I think he applies the method of incomparability when he ascribes these attributes to God "in a higher and nobler way" when they are purified of all limitations and imperfections.[38] On the other hand, when he ascribes those attributes at their lower and impure ways to human beings, he is acknowledging their similarity in meaning. So one can say that for Mullā Ṣadrā, from the perspective of incomparability, there is no knowledge, power, and will except for God's. Yet human knowledge, power, and will are somehow similar to their divine origins because where there is no existential breach, differences are only a matter of degrees. Mullā Ṣadrā's use of this methodology in solving the problem of free will is a good example of this dual perspective, which I will discuss later in the book.

GOD AS CREATOR

One of the names of God in the Quran is "the Creator" (*al-khāliq*), which captures the fundamental existential relation between God and the world. Philosophers normally discuss God's creative action in terms of causal relation, which is characterized by the mode of necessity. Most prominently, Avicenna's principle that "the Necessary in Himself is necessary in all His aspects"[39] shapes his position on the God-world relationship in the sense of necessary causation. The causal relation between God and His creation is a necessary relation in the sense that there could not be any time at which the cause

36. Chittick, *Sufi Path of Knowledge*, 75.
37. Mullā Ṣadrā, *Asfār*, 6:110.
38. Mullā Ṣadrā, *al-Mabda ʾwa'l-ma ʿād*, 374. See also Meisami, *Mulla Sadra*, 107.
39. Avicenna, *Metaphysics of the Healing*, 300.

(God) existed and the effect (world) did not. On the other hand, the existence of the effect can never be independent of the existence of the cause, which must sustain it as long as it exists, hence God's name of "Sustainer" (*al-qayyūm*) in the Quran. Avicenna's argument for God's necessary causation and sustenance of the world found its way into major philosophies after him, such as the light system of Suhrawardī and the existential gradation of Mullā Ṣadrā. Gradually, the influence of Sufi interpretations of divine oneness, in the sense of encompassing all existences, led to a new vision of the God-world relation.

In his commentary on Avicenna's text, Mullā Ṣadrā interprets Avicenna on the continuation of the need for the cause based on his principle of the primacy and unity of existence. Mullā Ṣadrā refers to Avicenna's example of the builder and the building as real causality for common people, which makes them wrongly believe that the continuation of the effect in the absence of the cause is possible. As Avicenna explains, contrary to what seems to be the case, the builder is only one of "the intermediary causes." The real causes are the natures/forms that are bestowed by the Giver of Forms following "God's permission and determination."[40] Mullā Ṣadrā takes Avicenna's position on causality to what he thinks to be its logical conclusion:

> Nothing is realized in either the mental or extra-mental realms except through existence as it encompasses them all together through its reality and sustains all things because without existence there would be nothing either in the mind or in the world; And it is the existence which manifests itself in its various degrees and appears in its various forms and realities in the mind and in the world, which are [respectively] called quiddities (*māhiyyāt*) and the fixed entities (*al-aʿyān al-thābita*).[41]

Given that the all-encompassing existence he mentions is God, Mullā Ṣadrā concludes that "all existences annihilate in His dominant existence that precedes all."[42] Also, in his discussion of the way the Absolute Existence encompasses all, he points out that only the "recognizers, those who are 'firmly-rooted in knowledge' (Q 3:18)," know how it is in reality, basing himself on Ibn ʿArabī's doctrine of the "Breath of the Merciful" (*nafas al-raḥmān*), which explains the God-world relationship.[43] Similarly, we read in Ghazālī's Sufi interpretation of God's oneness that "He is the First and He is the Last, the Evident and the Hidden. . . . He is the First in relation to all existing things that emanate from Him only, one after the other, and He is the Last in relation to the path the followers follow to Him . . . until they reach His presence, which is the end of [their] journey."[44]

Nevertheless, in *The Incoherence of the Philosophers*, Ghazālī criticizes the notion of necessary causation primarily motivated by theological concerns. There he argues that to be the creator of the world implies the involvement of will and choice both logically and from the point of view of religious orthodoxy:

40. Mullā Ṣadrā, *al-Taʿlīqāt ʿalā ilāhiyyāt al-Shifāʾ*, 2:1015.
41. Mullā Ṣadrā, *Asfār*, 1:260.
42. Mullā Ṣadrā, *Asfār*, 1:260.
43. Mullā Ṣadrā, *Book of Metaphysical Penetrations*, 9.
44. Ghazālī, *Revival*, 4:378.

> "Agent" is an expression [referring] to one from whom the act proceeds, together with the will to act by way of choice and the knowledge of what is willed. But, according to you [philosophers], the world [proceeds] from God [exalted be He] as the effect from the cause, as a necessary consequence, inconceivable for God to prevent, in the way the shadow is the necessary consequence of the individual and light [the necessary consequence] of the sun.[45]

What concerns Ghazālī about necessary causation seems to be the absence of alternative possibilities in the act of creation. For example, does God have the power to create a mountain without a valley? On the other hand, could God choose not to create the world in the first place? Avicenna's answer to both questions is negative. However, Avicenna attributes "life," "power," and will to God in his own way, which, like his treatment of God's "knowledge," is guided by the principle of divine simplicity. In the *Metaphysics of the Salvation*, he first argues that these attributes are unified with the essence of God, then clarifies the meaning of life, power, and will through God's knowledge. He believes that we are justified in calling God the "Living" because His knowledge of Himself is also His creative knowledge or "active perception" of His creation. Likewise, when knowing something leads to its existence, there will be no difference between knowledge and power. According to Avicenna, "If the rise of a certain intelligible form in our mind would result in external existence of an artifact . . . then our intellection would be identical to our power [to bring something into existence]." As for God's will, the same identity argument applies to it, but he also emphasizes the negation of any motive or purpose from the divine will. According to Avicenna, "This Will—as established here, that is, the Will to emanate existence—is for no other motive or purpose than the emanation of existence itself which is the same as [God's] Munificence."[46]

Avicenna's treatment of God's attributes in relation to His existential munificence and knowledge must have influenced Suhrawardī because Suhrawardī only speaks about knowledge without even calling it an "attribute." In *The Philosophy of Illumination*, at first, he sounds like he negates all essential attributes (namely, life, knowledge, power, and will) from God when he says, "The Light of Lights may have no attribute in any respect."[47] Later, however, he clarifies that he speaks against those who view the divine attributes as eternal entities additional to God's Essence.[48] Nevertheless, power and will have no place in his discussion of God as the Light of Lights.

In contrast, Mullā Ṣadrā discusses the full range of God's attributes, including power and will. Similar to his discussion of God's knowledge, his treatment of power and will is informed by the thesis of existential gradation. Mullā Ṣadrā argues that only God has real power in the sense of being free in His actions because all other "agents" are determined by motives and are "forced to choose in their actions." This is because what we call "power" in us is "only potency and contingency whereas power in the Necessary [Existent] is actuality and necessity."[49] Like all other attributes of God, which are identical with

45. Ghazālī, *Incoherence*, 56.
46. Avicenna, *Ilāhiyyāt al-Najāt*, 2:106–7; Avicenna, *Metaphysics of the Healing*, 295.
47. Suhrawardī, *Philosophy of Illumination*, 88.
48. Suhrawardī, *Philosophy of Illumination*, 115.
49. Mullā Ṣadrā, *Asfār*, 6:312.

His absolute and necessary existence, God's power is all-encompassing, infinite, and necessary. This means that it is a mistake to understand God's power in terms of the possibility to choose between different alternatives, which would mean contingency in divine action. The identity principle also implies that it is a mistake to distinguish between God's power and His will and consider His will as "actualizing one side of two alternatives." Rather, God's will, like His existence, is all-encompassing and necessary. Mullā Ṣadrā says,

> The Simple Reality is the entirety of all existent things to the effect that the most perfect order of the contingent world follows the noblest order of the Necessary Reality, and that is the same as the Knowledge and the Will. Therefore, the First's knowledge of the emanation of things from Him, which is not other than His essence, is the same as His will for it and His contentment [with it]. And this Will is pure from deficiency and contingency, and is different from an interpretation of power as adopting or quitting a course of action.[50]

All said previously regarding the God-world relation is from the perspective of God's relation to the world at large. However, inspired by their religious texts, Muslims also believe in the special relation of God to human beings. I discuss this in the next section.

THE GOD-WORLD RELATIONSHIP

The majority of Islamic philosophers try to explain and rationalize the divine-human relationship through predetermination, love, revelation/prophecy, divine appointments, and answering of prayers. In this context, there is also a confluence among philosophy, theology, and Sufism. I begin with predetermination for three reasons. First, for the majority of Muslims, this is an article of faith that they must embrace as Muslims. Second, predetermination directly relates to the topic of divine knowledge, which was discussed in the previous section. Third, the apparent conflict between predetermination and the existence of evil in the world is an important and controversial topic for philosophers, theologians, and Sufis alike, not to mention common people.

Avicenna discusses divine predetermination (*al-qaḍāʾ al-ilāhī*) in relation to the problem of evil (*sharr*). While he distinguishes between natural and moral evil, both kinds are explained as derivative and accidental due to the limitations of the material world. The Necessary Existent according to His providence (*ʿināya*)—namely, foreknowledge of the good order—predetermines all. Evil enters the material world only as an accidental concomitant of things that are in essence good. He uses the example of fire to explain how evil only accidentally exists and is not primarily intended by God:

> For example, it is necessary that every possible existent should be given the good existent [proper to it]; and [since] the existence of composites derives from the elements (it being impossible for the composites not to be formed from the elements); and [since] the elements belonging to the composites cannot be other than earth, fire, water, and air, and [since] it is impossible for fire to exist in a manner that leads to the good end for which it is intended unless it burns and

50. Mullā Ṣadrā, *Asfār*, 6:316–17.

disintegrates [things], it follows necessarily from this that fire is such that it would harm good people and corrupt many composites.[51]

However, Avicenna regards natural evil as "rare" and believes that to ignore the good in creation because of the rare occurrence of evil would "become a greater evil than that evil." In response to those who wonder if God could possibly create a world "free from evil," he envisions such a world as only limited to the supernatural because the natural world cannot be without matter, and evil is a concomitant of the latter. For him, "All that is in the sublunar sphere [the corporeal world] is insignificant in comparison with the rest of existence. . . . And evil, moreover, afflicts individuals at certain moments of time, whereas the species are preserved."[52] As for moral evil that is manifested in "blameworthy acts," although not regarded as rare, it is likewise derivative from the nature of the animal parts of the human soul. For example, "injustice" comes from the "irascible soul" because it is in its nature to seek "subjugation," and "it is only an evil to the sufferer of the injustice, or to the rational soul whose perfection [includes] subduing this power and controlling it."[53] It seems that the way to curtail evil action in the human world is to fortify the power and function of the rational faculty. Like in the case of natural evil, human immoral actions are an accidental derivation from the animal soul that is predetermined as "good" in God's providence.

Avicenna's characterization of evil as derivative and relative had a long impact on thinkers who followed him. For example, in his metaphysical system based on the hierarchy of lights, Suhrawardī blames all kinds of evil on the "darkness and motion" that are associated with lights below the Light of Lights (God), who has no "dark states or aspects." Also, similar to Avicenna, he considers evil in the world to be "much less than good," which would make this world the best of all possible worlds. But unlike Avicenna, Suhrawardī is not limiting evil to the natural world, as he believes that the source of evil is "need" (*faqr*), which is in the very nature of all quiddities. Thus, only God is totally pure from evil.[54]

Averroes struggles with the problem of evil as an Aristotelian philosopher and an expert of the Islamic law. One instance of evil that preoccupies him is the evil of injustice. One of the solutions he offers is that injustices are committed by individuals, while divine providence applies only to species, not individuals. Therefore, the capacity of doing injustices is in the nature of humankind, and God does not cause the minority of unjust individuals to commit evil. This is in agreement with Avicenna's example of "fire," which Averroes too uses in his treatment of natural evils. But as George Hourani observes, Averroes himself is not completely satisfied with this solution and wonders, "What need was there to create a class of creatures who by their nature would be predisposed to go astray—the extreme of injustice?" He then responds to his own question that if humankind were not created at all, this would lead to a world with less good.[55]

Mullā Ṣadrā discusses the God-world relation in terms of the occurrences of evil in the natural and human domains in several of his works. His overall position on evil is premised

51. Avicenna, *Metaphysics of the Healing*, 225–26. Brackets in the original.
52. Avicenna, *Metaphysics of the Healing*, 341.
53. Avicenna, *Metaphysics of the Healing*, 344.
54. Suhrawardī, *Philosophy of Illumination*, 150.
55. Hourani, "Averroes on Good and Evil," 27.

on his principle metaphysical doctrine that only existence is truly real, and existence is pure good. This means that what is not good is not existent, and what is not existent cannot be caused.[56] Nevertheless, evil is not an illusion either, so there must be a way to explain both natural and moral evils. To explain this, Mullā Ṣadrā refers to the potentiality that is in quiddities because they are delimitations of existence, and he argues, "All existence qua existence or inasmuch as it is an effect of an existence is good with no evil or ugliness (*qubḥ*) in it; but evilness and ugliness is due to its lack of perfection or due to its conflict with another good."[57]

Among things in the world, the prime matter (*hayūlā*) is the furthest from perfection in the hierarchy of existence, so it is "the origin of the world below (*dunyā*) and the source of its evils." But even the prime matter is a grade of the light of existence, and it is not evil per se.[58] Mullā Ṣadrā agrees with an earlier philosopher from his hometown, Quṭb al-Dīn Shīrāzī (d. 1311), on dividing the notion of evil into essential and accidental. Essential evil is impossible because for something to be essentially evil, it means that it should be the source of its own nonexistence, or it should nullify its own essential perfections. For example, the essential evil of fire would be for it not to have the nature of fire, which is impossible. God is the source of existence and has predetermined in His providence that everything must reach its essential perfection, so He would never cause essential evil. As for accidental evil, it "causes harm" to another thing,[59] or it makes some good nonexistent in another—for example, when fire burns a farm. Therefore, this type of evil belongs to the category of nonexistence, and as nonexistence, it is not caused by God, who is the source of existence.

One cannot be content just to grant that God is not the source of evil because the Quranic God is also said to care for creation and guide it toward its perfection. So the main question is whether in Islamic philosophy God is pictured in such a relationship with His creation. This relationship is of special significance when it regards humankind and their journey to God as their ultimate happiness. For this reason, major Islamic philosophers have discussed the meaning and mechanism of divine revelation (*waḥy*) and prophethood (*nubuwwa*), with the Shiʿa philosophers also discussing divine appointment in the case of the imamate (*imāma*). There is also an influential narrative about love between God and humankind that is predominantly present in Sufi philosophy, while in classical Islamic philosophy, the object of God's love is just Himself, as when Avicenna says, "His self is the greatest lover and object of love."[60] Even for Muḥammad Ghazālī, "He Almighty loves none but himself, and all narrations about His love for His servants should be construed as allegorical and not literal."[61] Philosophers' views on divine love and guidance also lead to the question of humans reaching out to God through supplication (*duʿāʾ*), which has a strong presence in the Islamic religion and culture.

To begin with prophetic revelation, most philosophers believe that the truths revealed to prophets have the same content as philosophical truths, though they are received in a

56. Mullā Ṣadrā, *Asfār*, 6:375.
57. Mullā Ṣadrā, *Asfār*, 6:375.
58. Mullā Ṣadrā, *al-Shawāhid al-rubūbiyya*, 148.
59. Mullā Ṣadrā, *al-Taʿlīqāt ʿalā Sharḥ Ḥikmat al-ishrāq*, 232–33.
60. Avicenna, *Metaphysics of the Healing*, 297.
61. Ghazālī, *Revival*, 4:486.

different manner and address a different audience. Philosophers believe that for the average person, philosophy may not be the most accessible pathway to happiness, hence the necessity of an alternative medium of truth through prophets. Despite their differences over the mechanism of revelation, the vast majority of Islamic philosophers consider prophetic revelation as an effective way for God to guide people to truth and happiness, and they believe that prophets have a major role in the governance of human affairs.

For Fārābī, everything that happens in the world is "according to order, perfection, providence, justice and wisdom," and the human capacity to make free choices requires proper guidance and governance so they can reach true happiness, which for Fārābī consists in the immortality of their souls. It is in this context that Fārābī mentions "revelation" and associates the power to the "first ruler"—namely, a prophet.[62] Fārābī's concern about religion and revelation results from his political philosophy, in which true happiness—namely, immortality—can only happen if we live in a rational society governed by rational principles. Fārābī's major texts suggest that prophets are philosophers in the first place, as they receive truths from the Active Intellect. However, prophets enjoy a very strong power of "representation" or imagination to represent rational concepts in symbolic forms,[63] which the prophets use in order to communicate philosophical truths to average people. This means that different prophets may communicate with their people using diverse symbols and images for the same truths, hence the existence of diverse societies of different religions. According to Fārābī, these different communities and cities "all have as their goal one and the same felicity and the very same aims."[64] Thus, for Fārābī, human beings receive guidance through divine revelation, whether from philosophers or philosopher-prophets, whom he often mentions under the title of "the first ruler."

Avicenna follows Fārābī in his attempt to rationalize the existence of revealed religions as a necessary aspect of God's creation. Avicenna holds that the existence of prophets is necessitated by divine providence. His proof is based on the premise that human beings live in societies, and social life needs to be governed by rules of justice, which a prophet establishes "by the permission of God, by His command, revelation and *the descent of the Holy Spirit* on him (Q 16:102)."[65] In order for this role to be fulfilled, God equips a prophet with miracles so "the people would recognize him." Moreover, prophets are not to reveal their knowledge of the true nature of God and the afterlife to common people, so they "should let them know of God's majesty and greatness through symbols and similitudes." This is all determined by God's knowledge of what is good, and as Avicenna says,

> It follows, then, that that which God knows to be the good must exist in the way that [He knows it], as you have known from [our preceding discussion]. But there is no harm if the legislator's words contain symbols and signs that might call forth those naturally disposed toward theoretical reflection to pursue philosophical investigations.[66]

62. Fārābī, *On the Perfect State*, 279.
63. Fārābī, *On the Perfect State*, 225.
64. Fārābī, *On the Perfect State*, 281.
65. Avicenna, *Metaphysics of the Healing*, 365 (with slight modifications).
66. Avicenna, *Metaphysics of the Healing*, 366.

Similar to Fārābī, Avicenna considers prophets as philosophers too. However, unlike Fārābī, his position is not susceptible to vagueness about whether non-prophet philosophers can lead a society to its happiness in the absence of a revealed religion. As suggested by the previous text, for Avicenna, human societies cannot survive without a prophet, although it is possible for a minority of human intellects to go beyond the symbolic language used by prophets and grasp intellectual truths. As for the mechanism of receiving truths, in several places, Avicenna mentions "the sacred faculty" as a rare and most powerful faculty of the rational soul, which receives universal truths directly and effortlessly. As long as this power alone is used by the prophets, they are philosophers with pure intellectual knowledge about the divine. But in their position as prophets with a sociopolitical and religious task, they also use their power of imagination to communicate the truths to people. The imaginative power is also used during prophetic visions—for example, the appearance of the Angel of Revelation or events from the past and future.[67]

Averroes's account of divine guidance through prophets is interesting, and it has given rise to many interpretations and disputes. This is partly in virtue of the fact that he regards religion and philosophy as having their own truths, although their truths do not contradict each other. This doctrine is famously known as Averroes's "principle of double truth." Moreover, in his different works, he gives apparently different accounts of prophecy. But one thing that we should take into consideration is that in his personal life and choice of career as a jurist, Averroes was a professed Muslim, and as such, he believed that Prophet Muhammad received divine revelation. So in his writings that investigate religious themes, he attests to the necessity of prophecy in the same sense that the Quran suggests. However, his purely philosophical writings, which only follow a rational method of analysis, diverge from the previously mentioned texts in their treatment of prophecy.[68] As Richard Taylor argues, in his philosophical works, Averroes struggles with the idea of God's or even the Active Intellect's engagement with the imagination of individual prophets in the process of revelation.[69] He is aware of his predecessors' involvement of the faculty of imagination in explaining prophecy. A thorough analysis of his ideas in this respect is beyond this study. Yet one thing that can be said for certain is that as a philosopher, Averroes acknowledges the practical value of religion; and as a practicing Muslim, he is committed to prophecy as a cardinal doctrine of Islam.[70]

The necessity of prophecy is also confirmed by Suhrawardī, but for him, the scope of divine guidance goes beyond just prophets and includes all "perfect humans," such as the "Friends of God" (*awliyā ʾAllāh*). What he contributes to the discussion is a new interpretation of the function of imagination because unlike the previous philosophers, he postulates an imaginal world that subsists in itself and is the source of true dreams and prophetic visions, such as the vision of the Angel of Revelation. It is from this world that secrets are revealed to the elect as they "descend upon their souls in a thought, or they may see suspended forms."[71] According to Suhrawardī, images are not inherent in our imaginative

67. On the functions of imagination in prophecy, see Lizzini, "Representation and Reality," chapter 8.
68. Davidson, *Alfarabi, Avicenna, and Averroes*, 351–52.
69. Taylor, "Averroes and the Philosophical Account," 295.
70. See also Taylor, "Averroes and the Philosophical Account," 193.
71. Suhrawardī, *Philosophy of Illumination*, 153.

faculty, but our imagination is only like a mirror that makes the suspended images (*al-ṣuwar al-mu ʿallaqa*) from the imaginal world apparent to us. Regardless of the philosophical technicalities of his discussion, Suhrawardī believes that the prophets are "sent by Allah" to guide people to the right path. In general, with respect to God's relationship to human beings, Suhrawardī insists, "The guidance of God has reached a people standing in ranks with hands outstretched in expectation of heavenly sustenance."[72] Suhrawardī's position on prophecy had a strong influence on later thinkers such as Mullā Ṣadrā.

Similar to Suhrawardī, Mullā Ṣadrā includes all perfect humans in the plan of divine guidance, although his view of the role of imagination in prophecy is different. Mullā Ṣadrā does not agree with Suhrawardī on the independent existence of the suspended images in the imaginal world between the intelligible and the physical worlds. According to Mullā Ṣadrā, the imaginal forms are like acts of the soul that "subsist in the soul—not like something inhering in something else, but rather like an act subsisting through its agent."[73] On the other hand, while he follows Avicenna in considering the Active Intellect as the source of both philosophical and prophetic truths, he departs from him by postulating the unification of the human intellect with the Active Intellect:

> Just as the embryo is in actuality an embryo, and an animal only potentially, so (at first) the soul is in actuality a mere mortal man but potentially (realized) intellect. It is to this that His saying—May He be exalted—alludes: Say "*I am a mere mortal like you. It is inspired in me that your God is One God*" (Q 18:110). The resemblance mentioned here between the soul of the Prophet—God's blessing and peace be with him!—and the souls of other mortal men refers to this (initial) state of being in the soul. But, when through divine inspiration, his soul moved from potentiality to actuality, he became the noblest of all creatures and nearer to God than any other prophet or angel as indicated in his words: "I have a time with God which I do not share with a proximate angel, nor with any prophet and messenger."[74]

In addition to his disagreement with Suhrawardī on the role of imagination in prophecy, Mullā Ṣadrā also departs from Suhrawardī in excluding the medium of the Angel of Revelation to prophets alone. For Mullā Ṣadrā, while prophets receive revelation (*waḥy*), other perfect humans—namely, the Friends of God and the Shiʿa Imams—receive inspiration (*ilhām*). While the bestower of truths in both inspiration and revelation is the same, to which Mullā Ṣadrā refers as "the Angel that inspires truths on behalf of Allah" and "the Active Intellect that inspires forms of knowledge to the passive intellect," they differ in one important characteristic: Only the receivers of revelation are aware of the identity of the angel that bestows truths on them and are able to have a vision of it. As Mullā Ṣadrā explains, "Revelation and inspiration do not differ in any of the things mentioned above [i.e., receiving intelligible forms from the Active Intellect/Angel] though they are different in the degree of clarity and luminosity and the vision of the angel who bestows the intelligible forms."[75] So we can say that although Mullā Ṣadrā follows Suhrawardī in pos-

72. Suhrawardī, *Philosophy of Illumination*, 156.
73. Mullā Ṣadrā, *Wisdom of the Throne*, 138.
74. Mullā Ṣadrā, *Wisdom of the Throne*, 149 (with modifications).
75. Mullā Ṣadrā, *al-Shawāhid al-rubūbiyya*, 349.

iting an imaginal world, he modifies the theory by regarding human imagination as active rather than a passive receiver.

The attribution of the divine charge of guiding humanity beyond the scriptural prophets to the "perfect human" (*al-insān al-kāmil*) has its grounds in Sufi discourses. This is a significant concept because it is one of the places where Sufism and Shiʿism connect. Here, I say a few words about the notion of the "perfect human" in Ibn ʿArabī, since it was through him that this idea found its way into later Islamic philosophy. In his usual esoteric rhetoric, Ibn ʿArabī combines theological and mystical narratives to explain the status of the perfect human in relation to the world at large. For him, the ultimate examples of perfect humans are the prophets. In one of his key texts, *The Bezels of Wisdom*, he titles his chapters under the names of twenty-seven prophets from the Quran, beginning with Adam and ending with Prophet Muhammad, with different aspects of the divine wisdom manifesting through each prophet. There, he says,

> [God] has described Himself as being possessed of beauty (*jamāl*) and majesty (*jalāl*), having created us as combining awe [of His majesty] and intimacy, and so on with His attributes and Names. He has expressed this polarity of qualities [in the Quran] as being His Hands devoted to the creation of the Perfect Human (*al-insān al-kāmil*) who integrates in himself all cosmic realities and their individual [manifestations].[76]

In many places, Ibn ʿArabī refers to saints, or Friends of God, as perfect humans. For example, he says that as a perfect human, "God makes the Friend travel through His most beautiful Names to the other Names."[77] So all perfect humans receive truths from God; however, the charge of revealing the truths to others is designated only to prophets and messengers of Allah, as the Angel of Revelation with a divine command and law (*sharīʿa*) only comes to prophets, with Muhammad being the last one of them.[78] So perfect humans all receive true knowledge from God, but only prophets teach them to people in the form of the law. One could consider prophecy as one of the signs of God's love for humanity, and as far as His love is concerned, Ibn ʿArabī believes that it is "more intense than their [people's] love for Him."[79]

The idea of the perfect human finds its ultimate home in the philosophical Shiʿism of both the Ismaʿīlī and Twelver branches. The Shiʿa Imams are not only receptors of divine knowledge but also divinely appointed to guide their community as the rightful heirs of Prophet Muhammad. Major Shiʿa philosophers even devoted treatises to the meaning and function of the imamate, what we can refer to as their "philosophical imamology." For example, the Ismaʿīlī philosopher of the Fatimid period, Ḥamīd al-Dīn Kirmānī, considers the Imam as chief of humanity "because of God singling him out with superior excellence just as is the case with every other species."[80] For Kirmānī, God's wisdom and care necessitate the appointment of Imams after the death of Prophet Muhammad.

76. Ibn ʿArabī, *Bezels of Wisdom*, 55 (with a slight modification).
77. Ibn ʿArabī, *Meccan Revelations*, 1:214 (with slight modifications).
78. Chittick, *Sufi Path of Knowledge*, 261.
79. Ibn ʿArabī, *Meccan Revelations*, 1:186.
80. Kirmānī, *al-Maṣābīḥ fī ithbāt al-imāma*, 70.

Although ahead of Ibn ʿArabī in time, Kirmānī's position on the status of the Imam in relation to God and the world is in harmony with the perfection narrative of Sufis. The Sufi tone becomes more evident as we reach later Ismaʿīlī texts on the imamate such as those by Naṣīr al-Dīn Ṭūsī, who was at a point in correspondence with Sufis, most importantly Ibn ʿArabī's student Ṣadr al-Dīn Qūnawī (d. ca. 1274), who spread Ibn ʿArabī's ideas beyond Andalusia. According to Ṭūsī, the Imam is "the manifestation of the Sublime Word [of Allah]," and "God has made him the center of the heavens and the pole (*quṭb*) of the earth."[81] Here, the cosmic status of the Imam and the use of the famous Sufi term *quṭb* reinforce my interpretation of Ṭūsī's narrative of the imamate. In his synthesis of Sufism and Shiʿism, Ṭūsī anticipates the more systematic confluence of the two in the works of Sayyid Ḥaydar Āmulī (d. 1385) in the Twelver context.[82]

The Shiʿa climate of the Safavid period led to extensive attempts toward rationalizing the imamate, and Mullā Ṣadrā is an exponential contributor to this agenda. He has a systematic way of proving the necessity of the imamate after the death of Prophet Muhammad. First, he argues that the existence of Shiʿa Imams is necessary because only they can reach the deep meanings of verses in the Quran, owing to their perfect knowledge. The Imams' knowledge is perfect because of the perfection of their intellectual faculty and reception of divine inspiration. He says, "Just like God made a hidden gate or a hidden proof for every knowledge, He made a manifest gate or manifest proof, meaning, the Messenger of God and the infallible Imams."[83] Second, as "the perfect human," the Imam is the pole of the universe, without whom the world would not sustain in existence. He argues that in the hierarchical order of existence, lower existence always relies on the higher rank and seeks it as its ultimate goal. While this is premised on his key metaphysical principle of the gradation of existence, Mullā Ṣadrā is also indebted to Ibn ʿArabī's previously mentioned conception of the perfect human as the pole of existence.

Thus, for the previously discussed Islamic thinkers, God has provided guidance for human beings so they would find their right path to salvation. However, Islamic texts also encourage people to seek divine guidance and assistance through prayers. In addition to the daily ritual of praying, there is a long tradition of occasional reaching out to God not only for forgiveness and spiritual intimacy but for the betterment of one's situation, cure of illness, protection from evil, success, and so much more. Among classical philosophers, Avicenna has a more systematic approach to prayer in the sense of supplication. As reported in his autobiography, he even went to the mosque to pray for solutions to difficult philosophical problems.

According to Dimitri Gutas, for Avicenna, "prayer and other acts of worship . . . purify the rational soul and render it receptive to divine effluence" of the middle terms of a syllogism.[84] This is true about the function of prayer for a philosopher qua philosopher, but Avicenna also discusses prayer in the context of his discussion of God's providence in relation to the efficacy of people's supplication for things like rainfall. In such cases, prayer can invoke the celestial power of conceiving something in the celestial souls, which can

81. Ṭūsī, *Paradise of Submission*, 120.
82. On this subject, see Meisami, *Knowledge and Power*, 84–102.
83. Cited from Meisami, *Knowledge and Power*, 151 (with slight modifications).
84. Gutas, *Avicenna*, 182.

actually influence nature. Avicenna compares this power to the power of the human soul to cause bodily warmth just by the conception of it. However, Avicenna clarifies that what results from the connection between the supplicant and the celestial power is ultimately caused and predetermined by God. This means that for Avicenna, human supplications do not cause any change in the divine plan. According to Avicenna,

> The relation of supplication to invoking this power is [similar to] the summoning of expression [all of which] emanate from above. This does not follow the celestial conceptions, but the First Truth [i.e., God] knows all this in the manner we have said is appropriate to Him, and from Him begins the existence of all that comes to be although through mediation [of secondary causes].[85]

Prayers have a special place in Suhrawardī's works. He has not only several texts about prayers, with instructions for them, but also many prayers of his own. Suhrawardī's prayers, which can be categorized as "inrushes" (*wāridāt*) and "holy magnifications" (*taqdīsāt*), synthesize notions and images from the ancient wisdom of Persians and Greeks, the Quran, astrology, occult sciences, and most importantly, his own cosmology of lights. While angels, intellects, and celestial spirits have a strong presence in his prayers, they are only intermediaries between the human soul and God, who gives the ultimate answer to the supplicant, and this is predetermined in God's providence. As he says, "God has inscribed in the Book and decreed to the Trusted Spirit [i.e., Gabriel] that He will answer the prayers of those who are weighed down with gloom." Then he explains the role of the angels by saying, "The angels have heard the cries of the virtuous in their fear of God and beseech their Lord on their behalf."[86] In general, for Suhrawardī, praying is a component of his philosophy as a way of life that is conducive to intellectual and spiritual perfection.

Mullā Ṣadrā, too, confirms supplication/prayer as a path to spiritual perfection. Like his predecessors, he discusses prayer in the context of divine providence, and his presentation of it is in agreement with his general philosophy. Mullā Ṣadrā's understanding of prayer is profoundly influenced by Ibn ʿArabī, and he uses the latter's theory of creative imagination especially to explain the power of prayer on the natural world:

> And at times the soul may reach such a degree of sagacity and purification from bodily concerns and sensual pleasures that there shall be bestowed on her from the Supreme Origin such a power and dignity by which the soul becomes influential on the world of natural elements. As a result, the soul would heal the sick, sicken the evil, transform one element into another, and move those objects that she is not typically capable of moving like in [ʿAlī b. Abī Ṭālib] unhinging the door of Khaybar. This is due to the fact that bodies are subject to influences by the souls.[87]

85. Avicenna, *Metaphysics of the Healing*, 361 (with slight modifications). Brackets in the original. Elsewhere, Avicenna states that God makes prayer a cause for the existentiation of a particular thing, much like medicine effectuates a cure for the ill. See Meisami, "Mullā Ṣadrā on the Efficacy of Prayer," 74.
86. Suhrawardī, *Philosophy of Illumination*, 158 (with a slight modification).
87. Mullā Ṣadrā, *Risala fī'l-qaḍā ʾwa'l-qadar*, 208 (with slight modifications).

While emphasizing the creative power of the evolved souls, Mullā Ṣadrā clarifies in several places that the whole process of praying, including the soul of the supplicant with her creative power and the changes that happen in the universe because of the prayer, are all "from the command of God."[88] Mullā Ṣadrā attempts to answer his teacher, Mīr Dāmād, about the paradoxical nature of praying in relation to God's providence. He says, "If the fulfillment of prayers is not predetermined by God, what is the point in praying to Him, and, if it is, why should we take the trouble of praying in the first place?"[89] Similar to his position on power and will, Mullā Ṣadrā regards the influence of a prayer as one of the intermediary causes, with God being the real cause. Despite the similarity of his position to Avicenna, whom he also quotes in this context, the relation between God and the intermediary causes, including the heavenly and earthly ones, is that of a gradational unity. On this basis, one could interpret the power of prayers as the lower degree of God's power, which is identical to His providence. In any case, all the philosophers mentioned previously picture a universe where humankind also has a role in the state of affairs and is encouraged to reach out to the divine world above. Given their place in the world, human beings are also given certain responsibilities, which I will discuss in the next chapter.

GOD'S REWARD AND PUNISHMENT

As in the case of divine oneness and prophecy, believing in the Return to God (*ma ʿād*) is a cardinal principle of Islamic faith, and philosophers in the Muslim world often address it. Belief in the afterlife becomes especially important in the light of divine justice, which entails reward and punishment for all in the afterlife. Since the immortality of the soul is a predominant idea among Islamic philosophers, they have to explain the quality of the afterlife. But philosophers' interpretations of the afterlife have, for the most part, appalled religious scholars, such as the famous example of Ghazālī's harsh critique of Fārābī and Avicenna on this issue. The main reason for the controversy is in virtue of the fact that classical Islamic philosophers agree on the spiritual nature of the afterlife but cannot rationalize bodily resurrection. For al-Kindī, Fārābī, Avicenna, and Averroes, the soul is disengaged from all her bodily attachments in her life after the death of the body, and the ultimate reward for a pure soul is nothing similar to the joys of the body; rather, it is the eternal life of the intellect. For al-Kindī, the soul is essentially an intellect, and the lower faculties of the soul "belong accidentally to the living body" to facilitate living in the corporeal world.[90] He says, "O ignorant man, know you not that your stay in this world is but a brief instant, and that you shall then come to the true world, there to stay in it forever and ever?"[91] The true world is the incorporeal world of the intellects, souls, and celestial bodies, which have no need for the lower faculties.[92]

Avicenna openly argues against the resurrection of the body from a logical point of view. He argues that the only way of believing in bodily resurrection is through the

88. Mullā Ṣadrā, *Risala fʾl-qaḍā ʾwaʾl-qadar*, 207.
89. Meisami, "Mullā Ṣadrā on the Efficacy of Prayer," 72. My summary is based on Mullā Ṣadrā, *Asfār*, 6:403.
90. Adamson and Pormann, *Philosophical Works of Al-Kindī*, 182.
91. Adamson and Pormann, *Philosophical Works of Al-Kindī*, 118.
92. Adamson and Pormann, *Philosophical Works of Al-Kindī*, 182.

teachings of the Islamic revelation as confirmed and expanded upon by Prophet Muhammad.[93] He believes that the real nature of resurrection is not accessible to the masses, hence the scriptural representations of life after death in "parables." Avicenna acknowledges the truth of eternal bliss and damnation in the afterlife, but not in the same corporeal sense as most people understand. As he puts it, "Of the true nature of [afterlife], he [the Prophet] should indicate only something in general, and that is something that no eye has seen and no ear heard, and that there are pleasures that are great possessions and miseries that are perpetual torture."[94] Here, Avicenna's description of the afterlife as something that has not been seen or heard implies non-corporeal reward and punishment, which makes sense only if there is no bodily resurrection. On the other hand, he argues that parts of the body keep changing and replacing, so self-identity would not be based on the body.[95] Philosophers after Avicenna do not agree over attributing the rejection of bodily resurrection to Avicenna. For example, Ghazālī notoriously accuses both Fārābī and Avicenna of apostasy because of this issue, while Mullā Ṣadrā tries to exonerate Avicenna of such a charge by reinterpreting him.

In his *Incoherence*, Ghazālī summarizes philosophers' arguments for the impossibility of bodily resurrection and how they would hypothetically answer to objections. Ghazālī's report of Avicenna's position highlights the latter's view that given the disintegration of the body upon death, to believe in its return would lead to absurdities because when something becomes nonexistent, it cannot exist again as the same thing. In other words, when *x* perishes, any "return" of it would be nothing other than a copy. According to Avicenna, if the form of humanity in a person "ceases to exist in his matter and his matter returns to earth or to some other elements, then that human in himself ceases to exist. If then in that same matter a new human form is created, what comes into existence as a result is another human, not that [former] human."[96] A similar problem is addressed by the contemporary philosopher Derek Parfit in a famous thought experiment in which one's body is "destroyed and its blueprint is beamed to Mars" with all its makeup and memories. Parfit considers different scenarios and concludes that what looks like me, thinks like me, and feels like me is nothing but a "replica" of me, not myself. For example, what if something goes wrong in the teleportation process and I am still alive when my replica comes into existence and I can see her on the screen? Will I be just talking to myself? Parfit continues, "Dying when I know that I shall have a Replica is not quite as bad as simply dying. Even so, I shall soon lose consciousness forever."[97]

Ghazālī first attempts to expose the logical incoherencies in philosophers' reasoning, but more importantly for him, nothing is impossible for God, and no rational impediment whatsoever can stand in the face of God's power to bring us back in both body and soul, as promised in the Quran. He says,

93. Avicenna, *Ilāhiyyāt al-Najāt*, 2:152.
94. Avicenna, *Metaphysics of the Healing*, 366 (with a slight modification).
95. For a summary of Avicenna's argument in this regard and Ghazālī's critical report of it, see Marmura, "Ghazali and the Avicennan Proof," 195–205.
96. Cited in Jaffer, "Bodies, Souls and Resurrection," 169.
97. Parfit, *Reasons and Persons*, 200–201.

> The one who denies the resurrection does not give thought to [the question] of how he would know the confining of the causes of existence to what he has observed. For it is not improbable that in the resurrection of bodies there is a pattern other than what he observes. . . . What improbability is there for there being among the divine causes something . . . which we do not know, that results in the resurrection of bodies and their being rendered disposed to receive the resurrected souls?[98]

Bodily resurrection is not the only point of contention in Islamic philosophy. Fārābī argues that not every soul will enjoy an immortal life after the death of the body, and certain souls simply annihilate because the soul is not immortal by default, and it is the kind of life we live in this world that determines our fate after we die. His discussion of the afterlife takes place in association with his classification of societies into virtuous, wicked, and ignorant. Because of the acquisition and practice of morality in a rationally governed city, the souls of virtuous inhabitants get stronger in perfection to the extent that they can become independent of the body and enjoy the eternal life of the intellect. Fārābī believes that as generations of virtuous people die, their souls join with the previously deceased "in a way that one intelligible joins another intelligible—the more increases the self-enjoyment of each of them."[99] In contrast, the inhabitants of wicked cities will have an endless afterlife of misery. Fārābī argues that the souls of the wicked will survive the death of the body because they have knowledge of right and wrong, so their rational capacity would facilitate release from the body after death. However, their immoral actions, despite their knowledge, will result in their misery because after its detachment from their body, the rational soul will "become aware of the distress produced by these [unvirtuous] dispositions . . . and since the number of those who join each other is infinite, their distress too increases endlessly as time passes."[100] For Fārābī, one is to blame only if one has knowledge that the action is immoral. On the other hand, if for any reason one does not have knowledge of right and wrong—for example, in the case of the ignorant inhabitants of ignorant cities—then eternal punishment would not ensue. In such cases, the soul will annihilate after death because immortality is only acquired through the perfection of the rational soul.

The souls of those who lead a nonrational life never become independent from matter, so they "will proceed to nothingness, in the same way as cattle, beasts of prey, and vipers."[101] This position on the annihilation of some souls is a rarity among Islamic philosophers, as it is almost impossible to accord it with the Islamic scriptures, even if you approach the texts symbolically. One philosopher who expresses his strong feelings about Fārābī's view of the afterlife is the Andalusian Ibn Ṭufayl. According to his report, in some of his works, Fārābī has considered annihilation for the wicked souls too. Ibn Ṭufayl complains, "It puts the wicked on the same level with the good, for it makes nothingness the ultimate destiny for us all."[102] Still, Ibn Ṭufayl himself envisions the philosopher's paradise as a communion of rational souls. Like Avicenna, he believes in the individual

98. Ghazālī, *Incoherence*, 223.
99. Fārābī, *On the Perfect State*, 265.
100. Fārābī, *On the Perfect State*, 275.
101. Fārābī, *On the Perfect State*, 272–73.
102. Ibn Ṭufayl, *Ḥayy Ibn Yaqẓān*, trans. Goodman, 100.

afterlife experience, although his version of reward and punishment has a strong Sufi undertone, as he pictures Hell in terms of the pain of separation from God.

Ibn Ṭufayl's Andalusian successor, Averroes, argues that after the death of the body, the soul cannot be individuated because "the numerical plurality of individuals arise only through matter,"[103] and where there is no matter, there is no individuation. However, Averroes is aware of the conflict between his rejection of individual immortality and the numerous evidence in the Quran for its truth as an unquestionable article of Islamic faith. He assumes that what is "received from the prophets and lawgivers" leads average people to act virtuously, and the religious presentation of the afterlife in material terms is most useful in this regard. But in effect, what happens after death is in its reality not comparable to anything earthly, though it is a superior reality. On the other hand, he agrees with Avicenna that once the body perishes, it cannot return as numerically identical with the earthly body, and if it is supposed to return, the afterlife version would be only a kind of image of it, not the same body.[104] While not attesting to individual bodily resurrection, Averroes seems to leave the issue open to spiritual interpretation and allows himself the option of switching roles between someone seeking answers from their own reasoning and someone seeking answers from scripture.

Avicenna's arguments for the individual immortality of the soul were not questioned by his major followers in the Persian context. Both Suhrawardī and Mullā Ṣadrā agree with him despite their different metaphysical approaches. Both of them discuss the nature and quality of the afterlife experience based on their theories about the imaginative faculty of the soul. For Suhrawardī, the resurrection of the soul is unquestionable, since it is simply the freedom of the light of the soul from the darkness of the matter in this world and its return to the world of pure light. This ultimate bliss is for those souls who are striving toward the world of light in their thoughts and actions. Suhrawardī emphasizes the individual immortality of souls by arguing that mixture is possible only where there are bodies. His argument is very interesting, and it is based on the principle of self-knowledge. First, every light is manifest or present to itself, and the soul is light and incorporeal; therefore, it is present to itself. In other words, each soul has this unique and distinct awareness of its own existence. So,

> Do not imagine that the incorporeal lights become a single thing after separation from the body, for two things do not become one. . . . The incorporeals do not cease to be [individuals], for they are distinguished intelligibly through their cognizance of themselves, through their cognizance of their lights and illuminations of their lights.[105]

Suhrawardī also echoes a version of Fārābī's description of how the joy of the blissful afterlife is unending and increasing because infinite souls join in this experience.[106] This highest stage of salvation is beyond any bodily association, so Suhrawardī does not seem to be concerned about the problem of bodily resurrection at this high level.

103. Averroes, *Incoherence of the Incoherence*, 357.
104. Averroes, *Incoherence of the Incoherence*, 361–62.
105. Suhrawardī, *Philosophy of Illumination*, 148.
106. Suhrawardī, *Philosophy of Illumination*, 147.

As for the souls who have not reached the intellectual/spiritual perfection of sages, Suhrawardī falls back on his theory of the imaginal world to accommodate pleasure and pain similar to the way we experience them in this world. He imagines two groups of souls below the perfect ones, one group that has reached "an intermediate bliss and ascetics whose worship is pure," and the other group that includes evil souls. To explain the respective pleasure and pain for these two groups, Suhrawardī uses the notion of suspended forms, or images, which he previously introduced in relation to prophecy. These images reside in the imaginal world that is between the intellectual and the sensible worlds. After the death of their bodies, the previously mentioned two groups "will possess shadows of suspended forms in accordance with their moral qualities," so the good ones will find pleasure in bright and beautiful forms, while the evil ones will be with dark and ugly forms. As for the beautiful forms, though they are associated with sensory experiences, they are much better because of their perfection and their everlasting nature.[107]

Suhrawardī's description of the quality of the afterlife influenced Mullā Ṣadrā. However, Mullā Ṣadrā's position on bodily resurrection is also premised on his original thesis about the existential evolution of the soul. The sum of Mullā Ṣadrā's argument for bodily resurrection is that not only does the individual soul survive the death of the body; it also gathers enough existential force through substantial motion to create an imaginal body that mirrors its spiritual character. This body is neither material nor identical to the body before death, but it belongs to its soul because for Mullā Ṣadrā, the identity (*huwiyya*) of a body is fully dependent on the identity of its soul. Therefore, the resurrected person will be immediately recognized as the same person on earth. As he argues, despite all the transformations, "from the beginning of his life to the end, the individual is what it is bodily and spiritually due to the fact that the identity of his body is retained by his soul, which is its form in its totality."[108]

In addition to the substantial evolution thesis and the body's reliance on the soul for its identity, Mullā Ṣadrā's view of bodily resurrection also revolves around his theory of imagination, which was inspired by his predecessors, especially Ghazālī, Suhrawardī, and Ibn ʿArabī.[109] Mullā Ṣadrā argues for the existence of an imaginal domain that shares some characteristics with both the corporeal world below and the incorporeal world of the intellects above. The imaginal body that projects the spiritual reality of the individual human soul in the life after death belongs to this in-between domain of a higher degree of existence than material existence. The purely intellectual domain is only the destination of the perfect souls, but the imaginal body facilitates a purgatorial experience of pleasure and pain for the average souls, as well as the wicked ones. Let us summarize Mullā Ṣadrā's defense of bodily resurrection based on two major principles. First, existence is the principle of individuality and self-identity. As he says, "The specification of all things, whether incorporeal or corporeal, is in virtue of their specific existence."[110] In view of this, Mullā Ṣadrā refuses to accept death as annihilation because existence can never become

107. Suhrawardī, *Philosophy of Illumination*, 148–49.
108. Mullā Ṣadrā, *al-Shawāhid al-rubūbiyya*, 262.
109. See al-Kutubi, *Mullā Ṣadrā and Eschatology*, chapter 6; and Rustom, "Psychology, Eschatology, and Imagination," 9–22.
110. Mullā Ṣadrā, *al-Shawāhid al-rubūbiyya*, 262.

nonexistence. For him, death only "differentiates between what is [the real] you and not [the real] you and your unessential attributes."[111] Second, the faculty of imagination is capable of becoming independent from the body, and the existential evolution of the soul results in the intensification of the power of imagination to bring ideas into external existence. As long as we are attached to the earthly body, the products of our imagination have existence only in the mind, except for prophets and saints, who enjoy objective imagination even in this world. He argues, "The stronger and more substantial the power of this imaginal soul . . . the more manifestly will these [imaginal] forms appear in the soul and the stronger will be their being. . . . The complete [and objective] manifestations of these forms . . . occur only after death."[112] Based on these principles, Mullā Ṣadrā advocates a version of life after death that is most similar to what we can glean from Islamic scriptures. More than any other philosopher, he tries to reconcile his eschatology with the particularities of the experience of the afterlife.[113]

This was a brief account of the philosophers' attempts to accommodate the afterlife in their philosophical systems, or better say, their philosophical theologies. In a nutshell, apart from the importance of resurrection in the Islamic faith, they could also not have ignored divine justice regarding that part of His creation that is endowed with free will and moral responsibility. This brings us close to theories of morality and philosophical discourses on free will and its implications for the individual, social, and political spheres of existence. This is the topic of the next chapter.

111. Mullā Ṣadrā, *al-Shawāhid al-rubūbiyya*, 281.
112. Mullā Ṣadrā, *Wisdom of the Throne*, 138 (with slight modifications).
113. See al-Kutubi, *Mullā Ṣadrā and Eschatology*; Faruque, "Life After Life," 104–16; and Rustom, *Triumph of Mercy*, chapters 6–7.

4

Virtue and Governance

The discipline of philosophy has a great interest in ethical, social, and political questions. The relevance of such questions to our actual lives in an ever-changing world has resulted in the formation of interrelated fields of moral, social, and political philosophies with subfields such as gender studies, environmental studies, race studies, food studies, and so on. It is hardly possible to review centuries of Islamic philosophy on these issues, especially in a manner to show their immediate relevance in the contemporary world. Moreover, philosophical theories of morality, society, and politics have not been in a stable relationship with the mainstream interpretations of Islam regarding the relation of the Islamic law to ethical norms, social relations, and governance. This is because, on the one hand, religious scholars do not see eye to eye on the problems of human nature, free will, and justice. On the other hand, the actual history of Islam and real experiences of living under contending dynasties after the death of Prophet Muhammad, not to mention different forms of extremism in the name of Islam, do not exemplify the philosophers' ideals of morality and justice. Another caveat in this regard is the departure of some philosophers from basic egalitarian principles in the Quran due to their adoption of some Greek/Byzantine and Persian hierarchical and elitist conceptual frameworks. In this chapter, I try to cover some of the main philosophical ideas about morality, society, and politics offered by major Islamic philosophers.

MORAL TRUTH AND VIRTUE

Religions often place a great emphasis on moral codes, since morality lies at the heart of a religious system regarding its spiritual and practical implications. In the Islamic world, the sophisticated and expansive body of moral codes is, for the most part, based on certain narratives and principles in the Quran. Starting from its narrative of creation and the place of humanity in it, the Quran introduces human beings as moral agents whose freedom of choice determines their fates in the afterlife. This outlook explains the dominant orientation of moral philosophy in the Islamic world, which is in line with virtue ethics. Virtue ethics in general is characterized by explaining morality in terms of virtuous acts and their consequences rather than in terms of duty, as in deontological ethics. There are different forms of virtue ethics, and the Islamic kind fits into the eudemonic branch of virtue ethics, in which virtues are necessary for *eudemonia*, or "true happiness," which results from the flourishing of the soul.

Regardless of the meaning of virtue in one's normative ethics, philosophy of morality begins with the question of moral truth. Muslim theologians and philosophers both discuss the nature of moral truth. For theologians, the main question is whether the truth of a moral principle is determined by God or if it is true universally and objectively regardless of either human or divine subjects. There are a variety of answers to this question by different groups of Muslim theologians, but one group had a long-lasting influence on philosophers. This group consists of the Muʿtazilites, who are known for their unwavering adherence to rationality. From their point of view, a divine command such as "Do not take life which God has made sacred" (Q 6:151) is morally true because taking a life is wrong in itself, not because God has willed it to be so. It is believed that the Muʿtazilite theory of ethics primarily follows a philosophical method, since even the two Quranic concepts that they start from—that is, divine oneness and justice—can be "justified by independent rational reasoning."[1] Thus, it is no surprise that the Muʿtazilite position on the objectivity and universality of moral principles is attractive to Islamic philosophers, as they are committed to the use of reason.

In addition to the impact of the Muʿtazilite principle of moral rationalism on philosophers, the latter also followed in the path of Greeks and Persians, especially with respect to the meaning of virtue and the relation between ethics and politics. The Persian Zarathustra and the Greek Plato both depend on the notion of "the good" as a complex concept of metaphysical and moral quality. Zarathustra's teachings revolve around the good word, good thought, and good deed, and for Plato, the ultimate forms of justice and beauty are generated and sustained by the Supreme Good. On another Greek note, Aristotle subsumes ethics under practical philosophy, and his rationalization of virtue continues to have a special place in moral philosophy, especially virtue ethics. Islamic philosophers are significantly influenced by Greek ethics, both the Platonic and Aristotelian schools, in the typology, meaning, and criteria of virtue.

In the first section of *On First Philosophy*, al-Kindī points to the interrelation between metaphysical and moral truths by charging philosophers with the task of "acting truthfully," which is acting based on "the knowledge of things as they really are."[2] This suggests that moral truth is to be discovered by the intellect, hence its objectivity, independence, and universality. This is also confirmed by ʿĀmirī (d. 991) from Khorasan, who argues that by using intellectual methods, one can "distinguish completely between truth and falsehood in theoretical matters, and between good and bad in practical matters."[3] Thus, for al-Kindī and ʿĀmirī, the ultimate moral principles that should guide actions are true independently and universally because they derive from metaphysical truths about the nature of reality. However, their method of establishing ethical principles does not conform to how Aristotle formulates a rational ethics, in which balance is the key to success and the body is as important as the soul. Both al-Kindī and ʿĀmirī depart from Aristotle in adopting the Socratic way of making ethics all about the flourishing of the soul through denouncing the wishes of the body.

1. Hourani, *Reason and Tradition*, 19.
2. Adamson and Pormann, *Philosophical Works of Al-Kindī*, 10.
3. ʿĀmirī, *Knowledge*, 1:191.

Despite his Aristotelian metaphysics, al-Kindī's view of moral life is essentially Socratic with other Greek influences.[4] He emphasizes a spiritual life, denounces material pleasures, and considers as virtuous those actions that imitate God. This is also true about ʿĀmirī. He says, "We ought to grant that he who has recourse to pure intellect in all that he does has the bliss of finding—sufficiency in his Lord; but he who pursues the desires of the body, allows himself to be led by the biddings of nature, and goes along with the [physical] cravings of the soul, is far from his Lord and inferior in rank, since he does not hold fast to what the intellect enjoins."[5]

Al-Kindī even made a collection of Socrates's sayings in which Socrates's character is more similar to Diogenes of the Cynic school than Plato's Socrates, and he denounces physical pleasures and possessions. For example, in his *Sayings of Socrates*, he relates Socrates's disdain for physical pleasures by saying, "The things are not abominable to those who contend themselves with being like apes and with making their belly a graveyard of animals, and who prefer to have transient things rather than everlasting ones."[6] It is only in his treatise *On Definition* that al-Kindī refers to moral virtue based on Aristotle's principle of the mean between excess and deficiency, which is determined by practical reason.

In his *Nicomachean Ethics*, Aristotle provides examples of the mean. For instance, he considers the virtue of temperance as the rationally determined mean between self-indulgence and insensibility. His remarks in this regard imply that he does not denounce bodily pleasures, and earlier in the same text, he makes recommendations about physical health, which is well expected from his empirical practicality. Unlike Aristotle, al-Kindī prioritizes spiritual health, and his recommendations in this regard do not follow Aristotle's principle of a rational mean. The reason for this is that in Platonic versions of Islamic ethics, one can push spirituality beyond rational borderlines, and there is no such thing as "excess" when spiritual ventures are concerned. Nevertheless, no matter how ascetic their ethical philosophy may sound, the ultimate goal of philosophers is the purification of the soul for the sake of intellectual perfection, which facilitates an intellectual life in this world and the next; that is the summit of true happiness. This should be distinguished, at least in theory, from the Sufi journey toward unification with God, which I will discuss under their ethics.

The Socratic version of moral philosophy was expanded and modified by Abū Bakr Rāzī. In his *Spiritual Medicine*, after praising reason as our path to knowledge of everything and salvation in this life and after, he states, "We must not give Passion the mastery over it, for Passion is the blemish of reason, clouding it and diverting it from its proper path and right purpose, preventing the reasonable man from finding the true guidance and the ultimate salvation of all his affairs."[7] There are two points here that connect Rāzī to the philosophers discussed previously. First, from the fact that reason is capable of finding all truths, one can infer the rationality and objectivity of moral truth. Second, the goal of

4. For Socrates's presence in al-Kindī's ethics, see Adamson, *Al-Kindī*, 146–49; and Druart, "Al-Kindī's Ethics," 1:283–307.
5. ʿĀmirī, *On the Soul and Its Fate*, 1:214.
6. Adamson and Pormann, *Philosophical Works of Al-Kindī*, 269.
7. Rāzī, *Spiritual Physick of Rhazes*, 21.

ethics is the salvation of the soul, which is only possible if we suppress our passions. Later in the text, he argues, "Philosophers can put forward the very physique of man to prove pleasures and lusts, seeing how deficient he is in this respect compared with the irrational animals."[8] For Rāzī the physician, passion is not even beneficial in this life because it is the source of our anxieties and sadness. Bodily pleasures are transient, and we are never fulfilled, hence the unhappy state of the mind.[9]

However, a complete picture of Rāzī's ethical philosophy shows that his position is different from al-Kindī's in that he eventually adopts a more balanced approach to worldly affairs by renouncing only the uncontrolled pursuit of wealth and physical pleasures.[10] This makes sense given Rāzī's unfailing devotion to rationalism and natural sciences, which, at the practical level, requires an ethics that must avoid excess. For example, one would expect him to encourage people not to starve themselves but to avoid gluttony and have a moderate diet. Rāzī's moderate approach is based on his respect for "justice and knowledge," on the one hand, and disapproval of "pain," on the other hand.[11] One could think that he is more similar to Aristotle in this respect, but the truth is that for Rāzī, Socrates himself later turned to a more balanced life, as he says in *The Philosophical Way of Life*.[12]

Now we switch to those classical Islamic philosophers whose ethical philosophies are more influenced by Aristotle, though not completely disconnected from Plato. The moral philosophies of Fārābī and Avicenna are grounded in the foundations of their philosophical system, especially their cosmology and psychology, as well as relating to their views on society, religion, and politics. Yet it is only in Fārābī's case, not Avicenna's, that ethics and politics are inseparable. To begin with the question of moral judgments, for both Fārābī and Avicenna, objective truth is a necessary consequent of their view of human nature and its place in the cosmos. Like Aristotle and his followers, including the Neoplatonists, they believe that intellect is the core of humanity, its distinguishing feature and the medium of connecting to the divine. As such, they regard the intellect as the venue not only of theoretical wisdom but also of practical wisdom. On the religious side of ethics, too, core moral principles are received by perfect human intellects—namely, the prophets and their succeeding deputies, such as their companions and the Shiʿa Imams, who perform as moral guides.

The intellectual nature of humanity determines what Fārābī considers as a good life. For him, a good life is that which leads people to their eternal happiness in a purely intellectual afterlife. But for Fārābī, this cannot normally be achieved in a solitary way, since human beings are a social and political species, and our moral characteristics are best realized in relation to other beings. This view is as much influenced by the Quranic vision as by Aristotle. Fārābī's texts reveal the Quranic influence through his frequent usage of the term *umma*, which refers to the "Islamic community" in the Quran. As for the Aristotelian influence on Fārābī's social and political approach to ethics, Aristotle refers to

8. Rāzī, *Spiritual Physick of Rhazes*, 26.
9. For a summary of Rāzī's Platonic ethics, see Fakhry, *Ethical Theories in Islam*, 70–77.
10. See Butterworth, "Ethical and Political Philosophy," 272–75.
11. Adamson, *Al-Rāzī*, 179.
12. Rāzī, *Philosophical Way of Life*.

human beings as political by nature in the *Categories*, *Nicomachean Ethics*, and *Politics*, and he discusses a good life and happiness mostly within its communal context.

Famously, in the *Nicomachean Ethics*, Aristotle characterizes a "good life" as "the activity of the soul in accordance with virtue," and he believes that virtue is determined by reason as the mean between excess and deficiency. But to have knowledge of where the golden mean lies is not sufficient for acting virtuously. Like Aristotle, Fārābī emphasizes "choice" as a necessary factor for virtuous action, as well as moral training through "habit formation." He is very particular about the role of choice when he says that happiness can be achieved only if virtuous actions issue from a free agent who not only willfully chooses to act based on his "discernment" of what is good but also "discerns what he discerns at every moment of his life."[13] Thus, acquiring a virtuous character requires both a strong mind and a strong will.

For Fārābī, when we are born, we are not only potentially intellectual but also potentially moral, and these potentials equally require training to be actualized. The path to a moral life is through acquiring the "habit" of choosing virtue over vice. Fārābī argues that by repeating virtuous actions for a long time, one can acquire a disposition to always choose to act based on the knowledge of what is best; that is the golden mean between excess and deficiency.[14] This means that a good life is accomplished not by randomly choosing to act morally but through a constant practice that leads to the establishment of virtuous habits. This is comparable to having a healthy body, which is possible only if we are consistent in keeping a healthy diet. I end this brief account of Fārābī on virtue by adding that habit formation requires training through upbringing, education, and resisting urges and temptations. This means that virtuous life cannot happen outside of a virtuous society, and conversely, living in an unvirtuous society could annul, or at least diminish, the potential for virtuous disposition, not to mention acquiring the knowledge of right and wrong.[15]

Avicenna's best ideas about ethics are in his texts on the soul, especially where he talks about the conditions for its perfection. As we have seen earlier, for Avicenna, a human being is essentially identical with its soul, and the body is just a temporary instrument for living the earthly life. Moreover, the perfection of the human soul lies in its intellectual flourishment that can lead to an eternal intellectual afterlife. Given this principle, Avicenna's moral philosophy can be best understood in relation to his metaphysical psychology. As for his theory of virtues, in several places, he follows the Aristotelian rational principle of the golden mean and habituation and associates it with his theory about the human soul and the role of prophets in assisting it toward perfection. For example, he says in the last book of the *Metaphysics of the Healing*,

> It is necessary that the legislator should also prescribe laws regarding morals and customs that advocate justice, which is the mean. The mean in morals and customs is sought in two things. As for the one, involving the breaking of the dominance of the powers [of the passions], this is for the soul's purification and for

13. Fārābī, *Directing Attention*, 106.
14. Fārābī, *Directing Attention*, 108.
15. For Fārābī's theory of virtue, see Mittila, *Eudemonist Ethics*.

> enabling it to acquire the power of self-mastery so that it can liberate itself from the body untarnished. The other, involving the use of these powers, is for worldly interests.[16]

This is an important passage because it accommodates the Aristotelian ethics within a Platonic/ascetic theory. Avicenna's Platonic view of bodily attachments as obstacles in the path of a moral life also appears in his allegorical works.[17] For Avicenna, the noblest part of the human soul—namely, the intellect—is not only in charge of our theoretical life, as in science and philosophy, but also responsible for governing our practical life because of the soul's bodily attachments in this world. It is with regard to the latter aspect of human life that ethics becomes relevant to Avicenna's moral philosophy, which can be found in both his philosophical works and allegories. For Avicenna, a moral judgment such as "lying is bad" is universally true but not in the self-evident and logically necessary sense that "the whole is greater than the part" is true. This is because of the fact that in rare occasions, one might find it more reasonable not to follow the honesty principle—for example, as in the textbook case of lying to the Gestapo about hiding a Jewish family in your basement.

Nevertheless, as Janne Mattila argues, while Avicenna acknowledges the impact of particular social contexts on the application of moral judgments, which are not self-evident, moral reasoning is "ultimately founded on universal theoretical knowledge."[18] As Avicenna says, "All human actions are oftentimes assisted by the theoretical faculty, and the opinion is regarded universal by the theoretical faculty and particular by the practical faculty."[19] Thus, moral principles come to us from the intellectual realm even when we learn them from prophets because their knowledge, too, is at its base theoretical and comes to them through the conjunction of their perfect souls with the intellectual world above.

Ibn Miskawayh (d. 1030), a contemporary of Avicenna and, later, Fakhr al-Dīn Rāzī and Naṣīr al-Dīn al-Ṭūsī, devoted whole treatises to ethics. Born in a family who had converted from Zoroastrianism to Islam, Ibn Miskawayh was familiar with pre-Islamic Persian culture, and this is reflected in his ethical writings. Moreover, equipped with multicultural literacy, he tried to find connections among various ethical systems and produce a hybrid ethical discourse, which influenced later ethicists. His inclusive approach proves that he believed in the universality of moral principles rooted in human rationality. Of course, his sources are limited to the cultures he was familiar with—namely, "the Persians, the Indians, the Arabs, and the Byzantine,"[20] of which the latter refers to Greek philosophers. In his passages on the treatment of moral diseases such as anger and the fear of death, he mentions the example of religious figures and quotes from some, especially Prophet Muhammad. As for Islamic philosophers, his citations of al-Kindī are quite significant.

Like the previously discussed thinkers, Ibn Miskawayh follows the Platonic model of eudemonic virtue ethics, which is based on the immortality of the soul and happiness as

16. Avicenna, *Metaphysics of the Healing*, 377. Brackets in the original.
17. For an excellent study of Avicenna's ethical allegories, see Zargar, *Polished Mirror*, chapter 2.
18. Mittila, *Eudemonist Ethics*, 188.
19. Avicenna, *al-Mabda ʾ wa'l-ma ʿād*, 96.
20. Ibn Miskawayh, *Jāwīdān-khirad*, 1:326.

the ultimate end of a virtuous life. In his most important ethical work, *The Refinement of Character*, Ibn Miskawayh builds his ethical system on what he believes to be the nature and function of the soul and what makes it reach its perfection. Like Avicenna, he believes in soul-body dualism and the superiority of the rational soul, with the ultimate human happiness being the perfection of the intellect. Moreover, he considers moral perfection as a stage in the journey toward intellectual perfection.[21] Again, like Avicenna, his interpretation of intellectual perfection has strong Neoplatonic undertones, which makes it fit for Sufi ethics as well. For example, he is believed to have influenced the Sufi ethics of Muḥammad Ghazālī and Muḥsin Fayḍ Kāshānī (d. 1680).[22] Ibn Miskawayh notes that as long as the soul is attached to the body, they are in a mutual relationship. What he offers is a holistic ethics that considers virtues of both the body and the soul:

> Now, as the soul is a divine, incorporeal faculty, and as it is, at the same time, used for a particular constitution and tied to it physically and divinely in such a way that neither of them can be separated from the other except by the will of the Creator (mighty and exalted is He!), you must realize that each one of them [i.e., the soul and the constitution] is dependent upon the other, changing when it changes, becoming healthy when it is healthy, and ill when it is ill.[23]

This soul-body relation guides Ibn Miskawayh's definition of virtue and its typology, in which he synthesizes Plato, Aristotle, and Neoplatonism with some Persian and Islamic ethical norms. In the manner of Aristotle's *Nicomachean Ethics*, he considers virtue to be a mean between excess and deficiency, so all virtuous acts are facilitated by moderation. The special attention he pays to the virtue of justice must have been as much a Shiʿa legacy as Greek,[24] though the Shiʿa influence became explicit only in the political philosophy of his successor in ethical theory, Naṣīr al-Dīn Ṭūsī. It is particularly in his discussion of justice that Ibn Miskawayh resonates with Fārābī in emphasizing the social aspect of human beings and connecting the cultivation of individual virtues to society. He makes this connection in discussing not only the virtue of justice but also the virtue of friendship. Moreover, there is a central place for God and the divine law in Ibn Miskawayh's ethics, at both individual and social levels.

In between the times of Ibn Miskawayh and Ṭūsī, the philosophical theologian Fakhr al-Dīn Rāzī, who is known for his critical approach to Avicenna, constructs a sophisticated ethical theory. As Ayman Shihadeh shows, Rāzī's earlier consistency with Ashʿarism, the theological school to which he belonged, gives way to a more synthetic approach under the influence of philosophers and Sufis. In his later works of ethics, he developed a "character-oriented [moral] perfectionism" in which "something is said to be 'good' if it serves human perfection."[25]

For Rāzī, the ultimate human perfection, or ultimate happiness, is attainable through knowledge and shunning physical attachments. The latter aspect that concerns character

21. See Fakhry, *Ethical Theories in Islam*, 119.
22. Nasr, "Abū ʿAlī Aḥmad ibn Muḥammad Miskawayh," 1:324.
23. Ibn Miskawayh, *Refinement of Character*, 1:356.
24. For the Greek influence, see Fakhry, *Ethical Theories in Islam*, 113–15.
25. Shihadeh, *Teleological Ethics*, 113.

building is only an instrument for facilitating an intellectual life but on its own cannot lead to happiness:

> Virtuous character traits do not produce happiness; for their objective is that the soul does not become firmly attached to the body. Their effect is only that the soul does not become tormented; as for [the attainment of] happiness, [they do not have any effect].[26]

One of the philosophers who had a strong influence on Fakhr al-Dīn Rāzī was Abū al-Barakāt al-Baghdādī (d. before 1165), a philosopher-physician of Jewish descent from Baghdad.[27] For lack of space, I have not mentioned his ideas before in this volume, but I will come back to him a second time in the next section on free will. Rāzī adopts al-Baghdādī's notion of the human soul, which is different from Avicenna's account. According to al-Baghdādī's model, there are essentially different species of human souls, like there are different animal species. There are souls who belong to the opposite poles of good and evil and souls that occupy a spectrum between the extremes. Perfection is impossible for souls that are essentially evil, but those in between may make progress toward perfection.[28]

In contrast to Fakhr al-Dīn Rāzī, Naṣīr al-Dīn Ṭūsī, for the most part, follows the Aristotelian-Avicennian tradition of ethics. In his famous *Nasirean Ethics*, he follows Ibn Miskawayh's *Refinement of Character* in analyzing the nature and faculties of the soul. Although the content of his analysis is more in line with Avicenna's psychology, his description of the soul in its hierarchies resembles Isma'īlī narratives, especially when he draws on the Isma'īlī notion of "instruction" and the more general Shi'a notion of the imamate. Furthermore, his reference to the noblest instantiation of the soul's perfection resonates with Sufi narratives.[29] Ṭūsī's eudemonic virtue ethics is presented through a synthesis of Greek and Islamic notions. For example, the Aristotelian definition of virtue as a golden mean is juxtaposed with the Quranic view of human nature, according to which moral choices can raise one to the level higher than angels or drag them down to a beastly status.

Ṭūsī's key notion in his virtue ethics is "equilibrium," which, on the one hand, connects ethics to metaphysics because for him, the whole universe relies on equilibrium for its existence. On the other hand, as equilibrium is best exemplified in the supreme virtue of justice, it relates ethics to politics. Following the Aristotelian tradition, Ṭūsī emphasizes habituation as a method of becoming virtuous, and like Ibn Miskawayh, he compares virtue to healthiness and vice to disease, which can be cured if one acquires knowledge of its cause and seeks help from moral guides. As a Shi'a, for Ṭūsī, the best examples of moral guides who can heal the diseases of the soul are the Shi'a Imams.[30]

On the Andalusian side of Islamic philosophy, despite all differences, the three major figures—Ibn Bājja, Ibn Ṭufayl, and Averroes—all regard moral truth as objective. Even Ibn

26. Shihadeh, *Teleological Ethics*, 125. Brackets in the original.
27. For Abū al-Barakāt al-Baghdādī's life, work, and influence, see Griffel, *Post-Classical Philosophy*, 203–25.
28. Shihadeh, *Teleological Ethics*, 118–20.
29. Ṭūsī, *Nasirean Ethics*, 47–52. See also Meisami, *Naṣīr al-Dīn Ṭūsī*, 82–83.
30. Ṭūsī, *Nasirean Ethics*, 126–49. For Ṭūsī on the method of becoming virtuous, see Meisami, *Naṣīr al-Dīn Ṭūsī*, 89–91.

Ṭufayl, who is the least Aristotelian of the three, believes in the independence and universality of ethical principles. As Cyrus Zargar points out, the path to understanding Ibn Ṭufayl's virtue ethics is through his conception of universals in metaphysics.[31] His ethics unfolds in terms of the human threefold likeness to animals, heavenly bodies, and God. He considers the human being as the most balanced animal whose likenesses to heavenly beings and to God make him "dedicated to a great task which no animal could undertake."[32] This cannot be merely the task of leading a moral life through following religious laws for the sake of attaining happiness—namely, the ethics of the masses. Rather, for Ibn Ṭufayl, ultimate goodness is possible only through imitating God. The main character of his philosophical fiction, Ḥayy, while considering the superficial ethics of the masses necessary for them, finally leaves it behind and takes refuge in a form of life that he considers most similar to the divine. While Ibn Ṭufayl considers all the truths to reside in prophecy too, he sounds approving of Ḥayy's disdain for the religiosity of the masses: "If people understood things as they really are, Ḥayy said, they would forget these inanities and seek the Truth. They would not need all these laws."[33] At this point, Ibn Ṭufayl's moral philosophy resembles that of some Sufis for whom religious laws are merely associated with the outer layer of faith, not the hidden truth of it.

Sufis are masters of ethics because their spiritual journey must follow an intricate pattern of practices and conduct both inner and outer. Islamic history has seen a multitude of such masters, both male and female, across its diverse lands from Asia to Africa, so the number of Sufi narratives and texts on ethics cannot even be enumerated in this study. As for theoretical Sufism, a brief sketch of Ghazālī's and Ibn ʿArabī's moral philosophies can give us an idea about the general approach to moral truth and the nature of a good life. Although for Sufis, everything including human actions have a predetermined place in the divine scheme of creation, this does not contradict moral responsibility and the voluntary pursuit of happiness. I will outline the Sufi attempts to resolve the paradoxicality of this position in the next section.

To begin, in Ghazālī's Sufi ethics, the guiding principle of his moral philosophy is the necessity of knowledge and genuine intention behind moral actions. The necessary relation between conduct and religious knowledge in the pursuit of happiness in this life and the next is frequently repeated and delineated in Ghazālī's most important ethical treatise, *The Balance of Conduct* (*Mīzān al-ʿamal*). In this treatise, he regards knowledge as presiding over conduct, with the latter being the "servant" that "bears and elevates knowledge."[34] In the same text, Ghazālī also follows the philosophical principle that moral conduct can result from subordinating passions to the rule of the rational faculty.[35] However, it is important to note that Sufis' scale weights for both knowledge and conduct are heftier than those of other ethicists. For Ghazālī, any form of knowledge that would not eventually lead to God is not worthwhile, not to say that it is a mere distraction; true knowledge must be beneficial in the afterlife. Furthermore, true moral conduct is ideally ascetic. In

31. Zargar, *Polished Mirror*, 122.
32. Ibn Ṭufayl, *Ḥayy Ibn Yaqẓān*, trans. Goodman, 141–42.
33. Ibn Ṭufayl, *Ḥayy Ibn Yaqẓān*, trans. Goodman, 162.
34. Ghazālī, *Mīzān al-ʿamal*, 194.
35. Ghazālī, *Mīzān al-ʿamal*, 190–92.

Ghazālī's case, our inner and outer conduct can lead us either toward God or away from God. There are virtues and vices of different kinds and stages of virtuosity and viciousness, with the former raising us to the level of angels and the latter to that of beasts.[36] To reach the goal of moral elevation, people need the moral guidance of prophets and saints, sincere intention, and constant practice. Thus, we are back to the Quranic picture of humankind's dual nature and their need for divine guidance through prophets and saints, with their religious laws and rituals. Moreover, following their guidance is to be accompanied by knowledge and realization; otherwise, it would be mere conformism (*taqlīd*), with no moral and spiritual value. There is one thing that all Sufis have in common, and that is their contempt for superficiality in belief and practice. Ghazālī quotes Prophet Muhammad in an aphoristic style: "All people are dead but the knowers; all who know are dead but those who act [on their knowledge]; all who act are dead but those who are sincere; and the sincere ones are in great peril."[37] By saying that the last and the best group are in danger, Ghazālī refers to the Sufi idea that one cannot succeed without "God's giving success," a position that is also based on Ashʿarite theology, according to which all acts are created by Allah.

In a manner similar to Ghazālī, Ibn ʿArabī's moral philosophy is built on the Quran, although his interpretation of the scriptures is offered in a far more enigmatic style. Moreover, his doctrine of the unity of being makes his moral philosophy more complicated because it is hard to reconcile moral responsibility with the fact that everything that exists is a manifestation of God. Inspired by biblical knowledge and several sayings attributed to Prophet Muhammad, Ibn ʿArabī frames human existence as the most "comprehensive" existence in creation and hence capable of rebellion. In describing human creation, he says, "God unites the polarity of qualities only in Adam. . . . His outer form He composed of the cosmic realities and forms, while his inner form He composed to match His own Form."[38] One can infer from this polarity the dual disposition of humans, which makes them capable of both perfection and imperfection. In Ibn ʿArabī's worldview, morality fits into the grander scheme of the God-world relationship, and moral truth can be understood in terms of both the reality of things and the rightful dues of things.

Averroes, a contemporary of Ibn ʿArabī, seems as remote from him in ethics as in any other aspects of his philosophy. Averroes's moral philosophy can be extracted from his scattered words across his commentaries on Plato and Aristotle, but that is enough for proving his objectivism in ethics. Given his dedication to Aristotelian rationalism and his battle against the Ashʿarite worldview, for Averroes, moral truth is objective and independent of both divine and human minds. For example, he argues that God is just because justice is good in itself.[39] As for his ideal of a good life, like his philosophical predecessors, both Greek and Islamic, he explains it in terms of the perfection of the rational soul through a philosophical life of contemplation. However, for him, religion can also play an important part in facilitating a moral life and the attainment of happiness, especially

36. For Ghazālī's ethical approach and typology of virtues, see Fakhry, *Ethical Theories in Islam*, 193–206.
37. Ghazālī, *Mīzān al-ʿamal*, 269.
38. Ibn ʿArabī, *Bezels of Wisdom*, 56.
39. See Hourani, *Reason and Tradition*, 252.

because of the essential relation between individual and social aspects of a moral life. This relation is believed to be in agreement with both Aristotelian and Islamic views of happiness for human beings at large.[40]

Mullā Ṣadrā does not have a treatise that is devoted to ethics per se, but his moral philosophy can be culled from his philosophical works and commentaries on the scripture. Overall, his philosophy of morality is grounded in his metaphysical principles—namely, the primacy and gradation of existence as the only reality and the existential movement of the soul from its bodily origination toward spiritual perfection. Like Avicenna, Mullā Ṣadrā subsumes ethics under the practical sciences and defines it in terms of individual happiness. He also mentions several steps for the purification of the practical intellect and characterizes ethics as the purification of the inner self (as distinct from Islamic law, which is concerned with purifying the outer self). Ethical purification is necessary for achieving the final stage of human flourishing and happiness, which is "annihilation of the self from itself."[41]

Mullā Ṣadrā's position on the objectivity of moral truth can be easily inferred from his statements regarding the reality of virtue and vice. He argues that virtue and vice are "existential attributes." This also means that just like existence, they are not only real but also graded. There are degrees of virtuosity and degrees of viciousness, with the intellectual virtues being the noblest and intellectual vices being the most despicable. He proceeds to identify the noblest form of intellectual virtue as "the perception of universals and intelligibles which are unchanging in their existence." Intellectual virtue does not follow the principle of the Aristotelian golden mean, as "it is better to go to excess in it," while all moral virtues are the mean between deficiency and excess. Like his predecessors, Mullā Ṣadrā glorifies the virtue of "justice" and calls it the sum total of all moral virtues.[42]

Mullā Ṣadrā discusses natural temperaments and bodily habits as factors in the development of a morally good life. The importance of the soul-body interaction in Mullā Ṣadrā's ethical theory is further bolstered by his view on the origination of the soul and its evolution according to his metaphysics of substantial motion. As we have seen, he characterizes the human soul as bodily in origin, though capable of substantially moving beyond the body and becoming fully realized as the soul that can survive the death of the body. The original unity of the soul with the body amounts to the fact that our original natural temperaments and the bodily habits we gradually acquire can impact the soul in its moral development. For Mullā Ṣadrā, the more balanced the mixture of our temperaments, the better chances we have for adopting a way of life that fits our noble status as human beings.[43] This means that our manner of living can either increase or decrease our capacity for living an ethical life. On the other hand, leading an ethical life facilitates the existential growth of the soul toward perfection by making it more capable of an intellectual life that is its ultimate happiness. Conversely, a lifestyle that is immersed in satisfying the needs of the body can divest the soul of its humanity and bring it down to the level of beasts. Once again, we are back to the Quranic narrative of the two extreme destinies

40. See Leaman, *Averroes and His Philosophy*, 157.
41. Faruque, *Sculpting the Self*, 215–16.
42. Mullā Ṣadrā, *Asfār*, 4:115–16.
43. Mullā Ṣadrā, *Asfār*, 8:76–77.

of human beings. Islamic philosophers, as well as certain groups of theologians, understand this narrative in association with people's moral accountability, which is entailed by the fact that their path toward either extreme is freely chosen.

MORAL ACCOUNTABILITY AND FREEDOM

It is common sense that we cannot be held accountable for actions that are forced. In other words, having the freedom to choose what we do is the prerequisite for moral accountability. But the complexity of human experiences due to the role of natural and environmental forces, not to mention the supernatural forces, for those who believe in them, gives rise to a variety of problems regarding the nature and scope of human free will. I discuss this topic under ethics because in the Islamic context, free will is addressed mostly in relation to moral responsibility. But more broadly speaking, free will is often discussed in metaphysics because it involves questions about human nature and the mind/soul-body relation. Roughly speaking, those contemporary metaphysicians who support the existence of free will in the face of determinism conceptualize it in terms of choice, intention, character formation, and absence of external and/or internal compulsion. Since contemporary metaphysics relies heavily on findings in modern sciences, a neat application of its conceptual framework to understand free will in the Islamic context is not feasible.

Moreover, understanding free will in Islamic philosophy is always associated with questions about God's relation to the world, a theistic assumption that is absent from contemporary Western metaphysics for the most part. However, for mere pedagogical convenience, I would like to apply the modern term "compatibilism" to theories of free will in Islamic philosophy. In my usage of the term in the present context, "compatibilism" refers to the theological/philosophical view that human free will is a reality, though it is not absolute. Most Islamic philosophers are advocates of human free will, and their arguments in this respect are influenced by Islamic theology.

The middle-ground or compatibilist position that is supported mostly by Shiʿa philosophers is a legacy of Shiʿa theology and an attempt to avoid the two extremes of considering human action as either completely autonomous or created by God. For the Muʿtazilite theologians, human beings are the independent creators of their own actions. According to one of the proofs they offer, the experience of "willing" is as immediately evident to us as "believing and thinking." Moreover, we can even "will" to do something when we know that it is not beneficial to us, which means that our choice is not determined even by any internal factors such as knowledge. They see their position in agreement with the belief in divine justice because if we were not the real agents of our actions, God would not be just in holding us accountable and either rewarding or punishing us.

The opposite of the Muʿtazilite position would be vulgar determinism in the sense of all our actions being determined by God in eternity. But the Muʿtazilites' rivals, the Ashʿarites, tried to explain their rejection of libertarianism while avoiding vulgar determinism. The Ashʿarites' belief in God's unique and all-encompassing causal power is accompanied by their famous doctrine of "acquisition" (*kasb*) regarding human actions. While denying human beings the real causal power to create their own acts, the doctrine is supposed to avoid vulgar determinism, which leaves no space for moral accountability. The Ashʿarite doctrine "refers to the acquisition from God of a created power of efficient causality by the human agent. . . . But, God is not involved in the acts of which He is the ultimate cause and agent."[44] The Ashʿarites believe that their doctrine does not violate moral accountability because whereas God creates all actions, humans actually choose certain actions over others.[45] They have a number of sophisticated arguments for their position, but it seems that for them, some human actions are voluntary because, although they are ultimately created by God and we could not have done otherwise, they are not compulsory. One can understand this in terms of the difference between the voluntary motion of pulling the trigger intentionally and being forced to shoot because the motion of fingers is being controlled by an external force.

The Ashʿarite doctrine of "acquisition" is addressed extensively by Muḥammad Ghazālī in both his theological and Sufi texts. Although he does not follow each and every one of the Ashʿarite doctrines, and in his Sufi phase he goes beyond theology as such, Ghazālī always remains faithful to the doctrine of acquisition, which he regards as a "middle course" between Muʿtazilite libertarianism and vulgar determinism. For the Ashʿarite Ghazālī, human voluntary actions are differentiated from involuntary ones due to the interaction among desire, knowledge, and motivations, all created by God and resulting in a final resolution to act. Ghazālī is aware of the paradoxicality of this position, but he seems to have decided that his Sufi approach can offer a resolution. As Marmura argues, Ghazālī's use of Ashʿarite theology in his Sufi works is not "an end in itself" but "an aid to the *sālik*, the Sufi wayfarer" in his spiritual journey.[46]

Classical Islamic philosophers affirm the efficacy of causal powers in the created world. Nevertheless, in their position on free will, they avoid the naive libertarianism of the Muʿtazilites. This is because they endorse the Aristotelian/Neoplatonic view of the universe as dominated by necessary causation. In some cases, they may even sound like determinists, but in effect, they simply tend to acknowledge the causal power of human choices against the background of a universe where necessary causation rules all through. For example, in contrast to the Ashʿarites, al-Kindī endorses the efficacy of causes in the universe and considers the heavens as causes of events and actions in this world. In this context, his emphasis on the necessary causal link among events may deceptively present him as a determinist regarding human choices. For example, in one of his cosmological texts, *On Rays*, al-Kindī regards the belief in free will as a result of "man's deficiency in understanding things." For him, this misunderstanding is resolved when we follow philosophers who "realize that the things of this world proceed by necessity in relation to the latter [sc. Heavenly harmony] . . . [and] use human reason to infer that the same is true in all other cases."[47] Nevertheless, for al-Kindī, even the causal impact of the heavens on human actions "does not rule out the efficacy and reality of our voluntary choices."[48] Whether or not he manages to clarify his position sufficiently regarding free will and determinism, one can

44. Frank, "Structure of Created Causality," 27.
45. See Belo, "Freedom and Determinism," 326–27.
46. Marmura, "Ghazālī and Ashʿarism Revisited," 1:258–78.
47. Adamson and Pormann, *Philosophical Works of Al-Kindī*, 228–29.
48. Adamson, *Al-Kindī*, 203–4.

still see that the Sunni principle of predestination has a strong hold on al-Kindī, and he freely uses theological terms in this context. Perhaps, as is usually the case in his works, he is simply trying his best to reconcile reason and revelation.

As explained in the previous section, "choice" has a central place in Fārābī's ethical philosophy, and he regards it as a necessary condition for happiness.[49] In agreement with this principle, Fārābī strongly defends free will. He distinguishes between the kind of will as a natural inclination that motivates animals and the act of choice (*ikhtiyār*), which is "the outcome of deliberation or rational thought" and is only possessed by the human beings.[50] Fārābī's affirmation of free will is backed by his position on the contingency of future events.[51] Famously, in his commentary on Aristotle's *On Interpretation*, he tries to solve a problem that Aristotle puts forward regarding future events, which, according to Fārābī, is mistakenly interpreted as upholding determinism.[52] Fārābī's discussion on this topic engages linguistic and logical matters, which are beyond the limits of this study.[53] For the sake of the present discussion, it suffices to say that for Fārābī, contingency is a reality, and one of the motivations behind his defense of the reality of contingency regarding future events is his seriousness about the existence of free will. He does not see free will in conflict with God's knowledge of the future and tries to solve some of the problems in this regard. He argues that if we reduce the contingency of future events to our mental states, then free will disappears, and "all religions will be committed to the conclusion that man does not choose to do whatever he does. . . . [and] It would follow that God Most High, who rewards and punishes, acts unjustly."[54]

Fārābī's acknowledgment of future contingency and free will does not mean that he was opposed to his predecessors and successors about the necessary relation between cause and effect. His cosmos is strictly ordered with the First Cause on top of the descending chain of intermediary causes. However, the human being who is also part of this picture has a soul with a rational faculty "that distinguishes good and evil."[55] The ability to discern good from evil is necessary for being held accountable for our actions, but it is not sufficient without free will.

Free will did not receive a focused study by Avicenna. His position on free will can be extracted from his texts on divine predetermination, especially in relation to the problem of evil. It is not certain whether he regards free will as a reality because for him, nothing comes into existence unless it is necessitated. If we add this principle to his acknowledgment of God's measuring out of particular events, Avicenna may appear as a nuanced determinist, and many Avicenna scholars do not hesitate to call him a determinist. However, a minority of scholars believe that he was not a determinist with regard to human actions and embraced free will.[56] Avicenna's accommodation of free will in his deterministic cos-

49. Fārābī, *Directing Attention*, 106.
50. Fārābī, *On the Perfect State*, 205.
51. Belo, "Freedom and Determinism," 330.
52. Zimmermann, *Al-Fārābī's Commentary*, 78.
53. For a critical analysis of Fārābī's discussion, see Adamson, "Arabic Sea Battle," 168–88.
54. Zimmermann, *Al-Fārābī's Commentary*, 93.
55. Fārābī, *On the Perfect State*, 165.
56. For a review of these contending positions, see Belo, *Chance and Determinism*, 14–16.

mos is also described as a form of compatibilism.[57] The most recent scholarship on this topic defends Avicenna's adherence to free will in the light of God's predetermination of particular events and the controversial role that matter plays in this respect.[58] Whatever the nature of free will and its place in the cosmos, one thing we can say for sure is that Avicenna does not deny human beings moral responsibility.

Almost a century after Avicenna, Abū al-Barakāt al-Baghdādī tries to expose some logical and theological problems in the endeavors to reconcile divine foreknowledge with human free will. He argues against the possibility of God's knowledge of events in the natural world, including voluntary actions. This is because he is adamant that either God has foreknowledge (namely, knowledge of future events) or humans are free in their actions. Humans are morally responsible according to the Quran, hence free; therefore, God does not have foreknowledge. To have knowledge of future events is the same as predetermining them, which would contradict any contingency. To save himself from the accusation of attributing limitation and imperfection to God, he says, "The argument that God, exalted be He, would not fully know does not necessarily implicate deficiency or incapacity in His knowledge, because the impediment is rather from the side of the known object than from the side of the one who knows." Future events as such cannot be known, not even by God.[59] However, it is argued that for al-Baghdādī, it is only God's foreknowledge that is not compatible with human freedom. Other causal chains, whether inside or outside of humans, which can also conflict with one another, hold true alongside free will. Even God Himself and His angels can be among these causes, but as long as God does not have foreknowledge of them, human free will is intact.[60] Al-Baghdādī's coupling of foreknowledge with predetermination is not compelling because voluntary actions are temporal and spatial events, while God's foreknowledge is outside of time and space. Even in the case of human clairvoyance, to know that something will happen is not the same as making it happen.

Neither of the two famous commentators of Avicenna, Fakhr al-Dīn Rāzī and Ṭūsī, follows al-Baghdādī's position on God's foreknowledge and free will. Rāzī's Ashʿarite background obligates him to treat the question of free will and determinism with caution. In some places, he calls it a mystery or a matter that leads to contradictory results.[61] But in his later works, he seems to be quite distanced from the Ashʿarite theological determinism, especially regarding the denial of natural causality. Influenced by Avicenna, he endorses the secondary power of natural causes, including human agency, but he clarifies that all these powers are brought into existence by God.[62] As for Ṭūsī, he claims that his position follows a statement from the sixth Shiʿa Imam, Jaʿfar al-Ṣādiq (d. 765), which is a middle path between libertarianism, or the absolute delegation of power to human beings, and vulgar determinism. In effect, he uses Avicenna's metaphysics to support the Shiʿa position between libertarianism and determinism. In an essay on this topic, Ṭūsī defines "will" as "that which when joined with power implies preference of an action, which means that

57. McGinnis, *Avicenna*, 225.
58. See De Cillis, *Freewill and Predestination*.
59. Shehata, "Abul-Barakāt al-Baghdādī," 124.
60. Shehata, "Abul-Barakāt al-Baghdādī," 128.
61. See Shihadeh, *Teleological Ethics*, 38–39.
62. Shihadeh, *Teleological Ethics*, 42–43.

when power and will exist, the realization of an action is necessary, and the lack of action is an impossibility."[63] Like Avicenna, he argues that all secondary causes, including the internal causes of our voluntary actions, come from God, since He is the one who created our psychology this way. In simple terms, we are destined by God to make free choices and attempt toward our chosen course of action based on a certain desire that rises in us due to figuring out the possible benefits of it with the help of our imagination and intellect.[64] Thus, we are morally responsible because our choices are conscious and knowledge based.

The question of free will and determinism also seriously engages Averroes. While his departure from Avicenna on the manner of divine causality gives him more room for free will in his metaphysics, in his theological works, he seems to "deny full autonomy to human actions."[65] The apparent contradiction may resolve if we consider his method of accommodating truths from both reason and revelation. However, even in his philosophical works, Averroes does not ascribe full autonomy to human action in the manner of Muʿtazilite libertarianism. Like Avicenna, Averroes believes in an ordered universe that is ruled by causal order. But more like Aristotle, he understands the existence of things and events in terms of final causality, with God being the ultimate final cause rather than the efficient cause as the Giver of existence. In Averroes's universe, all things "exist because of one thing, and that their actions tend toward this one which is the first cause because of which the world exists."[66] This emphasis on final causality, when considered with respect to agents of voluntary action, can save them a degree of autonomy because, as Catarina Belo argues, "the stress is here placed on the internal constitution, and nature of the agent, rather than on external causes."[67] Thus, regardless of their different cosmologies, Fārābī, Avicenna, and Averroes may fit into compatibilism broadly construed. In general, compatibilism tends to reconcile determinism with free will in the sense that while living in a deterministic universe, we are responsible for some of our actions because we have the ability to deliberate and intend.

In contrast to philosophers, most Sufi thinkers do not shy away from acknowledging determinism, but their determinism is rooted in their unique position on the God-world relationship. In the Sufi phase of his intellectual journey, Ghazālī goes beyond Ashʿarism as such and develops a Sufi reading of the Ashʿarite position. With regard to free will, the Sufi Ghazālī shifts from "denying power to creatures to denying existence itself to them."[68] In his *Niche of Lights*, after identifying God as the Real Light and Existence and all the universe as manifestations of Him, he says,

> Existence can be classified into the existence that a thing possesses in itself and that which it possesses from another. When a thing has existence from another, its existence is borrowed and has no support in itself. When the thing is viewed

63. Morewedge, *Metaphysics of Ṭūsī*, 25.
64. Morewedge, *Metaphysics of Ṭūsī*, 31–34.
65. Belo, "Freedom and Determinism," 334.
66. Averroes, "Commentary on Aristotle's Metaphysics, Book Lām," 200.
67. Belo, *Chance and Determinism*, 152.
68. Mayer, "Theology and Sufism," 274.

> in itself and with respect to itself, it is pure nonexistence. It only exists inasmuch as it is ascribed to another [i.e., God].[69]

According to an avid reader of Ghazālī, ʿAyn al-Quḍāt, whether we choose or do not choose a course of action, in both cases, we *are* compelled to make a choice. But as Mohammed Rustom shows, ʿAyn al-Quḍāt can "see the hand of divine destiny in the very freedom of human action itself, thereby positing human will alongside divine will."[70] In other words, for him, God has created human beings as compelled to make choices, so although this is in accordance with God's will, they are still responsible for their actions. As we shall see later, there are traces of this thought in Mullā Ṣadrā's treatment of free will.

One implication of denying real existence to things other than God is that in the human domain of actions and choices, the real agent will be God rather than human beings. So what seems to be our will from the human perspective is actually a manifestation of divine will. Ibn ʿArabī has a more intricate argument in this regard, which William Chittick explains based on the doctrine of God's "self-disclosure" in His creation and the method of switching perspectives from human to God and vice versa. He says, "Since God's attributes are within him (i.e., human being), he manifests God's desire and power. Inasmuch as he is the form of God and not Himself, his decisions and acts belong to himself."[71] For Ibn ʿArabī, the evidence for our accountability is to be found in the Quran, where we are "commanded" to embrace good and avoid evil by following God's commands: "For the servant is commanded, and a command is only given to someone who possesses power."[72] Ibn ʿArabī's reconciliation of God's power with human power is captured by his report of what a major early Sufi figure said in this regard, which filled him with joy:

> Which proof of the attribution and ascription of the act to the servant and of self-disclosure within him is stronger than the fact that his attribute is that God has created him upon His own form? Were the act to be disengaged from him, it would no longer be correct for him to be upon His own form. . . . But it is established for you and for the People of the Path without any disagreement that man is created upon the form.[73]

As previously mentioned in this volume, Ibn ʿArabī's thought, and theoretical Sufism in general, was a great influence on later Islamic philosophy. The Sufi vision of free will that we find in Ghazālī and Ibn ʿArabī shaped Mullā Ṣadrā's metaphysics of free will. Yet in his discussion of free will, surprisingly, he does not cite Ibn ʿArabī. Mullā Ṣadrā's argument for his position is systematically premised on his principle of the gradational unity of existence. For Mullā Ṣadrā, all realities are there only in relation to the One Reality, or God, so all the attributes of relational existences (including causal powers and actions) are relative to the One Absolute Existence.[74] In sum, he maintains that we have free will because we are like God, but unlike ours, God's free will is absolute and perfect.[75]

69. Ghazālī, *Niche of Lights*, 16.
70. Rustom, *Inrushes of the Heart*, 84.
71. Chittick, *Sufi Path of Knowledge*, 208.
72. Chittick, *Sufi Path of Knowledge*, 207.
73. Chittick, *Sufi Path of Knowledge*, 209.
74. Mullā Ṣadrā, *Asfār*, 6:373–74.
75. On this topic, see Meisami, "Ghazālī's Influence."

Regardless of the metaphysical nature of free will, Islamic philosophy and Sufism each find their own way of holding people responsible for their actions, which is crucial for maintaining a belief in a just God. Now whatever form and degree of agency we possess, both reason and revelation tell us that we have an active role in the type of individual and social lives we lead. In the following section, I will therefore turn to some of the key discussions in Islamic philosophy centered on one's leading a good life not only as a social and political being but also as an inhabitant of the universe at large.

AUTHORITY AND GOVERNANCE

The questions of what is the best method of governance and who is qualified to govern Muslim affairs became crucial and controversial in Islamic history after the death of Prophet Muhammad in 632 CE. Muhammad's establishment of an Islamic polity, his uncontested leadership of the early Muslim community, and his death without appointing a successor, according to majority opinion, paved the ground for a tumultuous political history. The complex history of Islamic politics and its challenges to date, especially in the face of colonial and postcolonial encroachments, as well as reformist attempts from within, has made politics the most visible, not to mention contested, aspect of Islam. Likewise, the history of ideas around Islamic politics is multidimensional, as it engages with diverse cultural, ethnic, theological/legal, and philosophical discourses, including Greek, Arabic, and Persian. The question of governance in Islamic philosophy is often accompanied by questions about divine justice, human nature, salvation, and most importantly, degrees of rationality among people. In this section, I will draw a sketch of the key aspects of political philosophy by focusing on authority and governance in the works of a selected number of philosophers.

It is common knowledge among scholars that Fārābī discusses politics in a very systematic manner in relation to his cosmology and philosophy of human nature. Like Aristotle, who regards the human being "by nature a political animal," Fārābī is adamant that human beings cannot flourish as humans outside of a political community that is governed according to principles of reason. For both philosophers, the criterion of human flourishing is intellectual growth, which is attainable in a rational society. Moreover, influenced by the Greek and Persian forms of intellectual elitism and social hierarchy, Fārābī offers a political philosophy that can be characterized as salvific authoritarianism. All his texts on politics show the influence of both Plato and Aristotle, but his ideal city, which he calls "the virtuous city" (*al-madīna al-fāḍila*), is mostly modeled on Plato's *Republic*. Fārābī's discourse on authority also reflects a complex of Islamic ideas, such as the role of prophets, caliphs, emirs, and Imams in governance.

In both his *Political Regime* and *On the Perfect State*, Fārābī discusses society and politics in relation to both moral and intellectual virtues. Not only do we need a society/polity that facilitates virtuous life, but also acquiring the habit of virtuosity by individuals is necessary for the sustenance of social and political order. A society that lives according to intellectual principles devised by a perfect ruler—namely, a person who possesses all moral and intellectual virtues—is a society that finds eternal happiness through immortality. Thus, as Charles Butterworth says, Fārābī's political philosophy "fuses statecraft with soulcraft."[76] Clearly, in his political philosophy, authority lies only with those who have perfect knowledge of what is best for their people, to whom Fārābī sometimes refers, inter alia, as "the chief" or "the king." But regardless of what the perfect rulers are called, what they all have in common is that they receive infallible knowledge from the Active Intellect, or in other words, they are true philosophers. As explained earlier, Fārābī bases the prophets' authority on their intellectual powers, though assisted by their powerful imagination in conveying philosophical truths to the masses. The following passage captures the gist of Fārābī's theory of absolute authority:

> The supreme ruler without qualification is he who does not need anyone to rule him in anything whatsoever, but has actually acquired sciences and every kind of knowledge, and has no need of a man to guide him in anything. . . . He is able to guide well all others to everything in which he instructs them, to employ all those who do any of the acts for which they are equipped, and to determine, define, and direct these acts toward happiness. This is found only in the one who possesses great and superior natural dispositions, when his soul is in union with the Active Intellect. . . . This man is the true prince according to the ancients; He is the one of whom it ought to be said that he receives revelation.[77]

Similar to Plato, Fārābī classifies cities and ranks the inhabitants of them based on their intellectual states and the functions they serve. While there can be several virtuous cities, they all belong to one type because, despite their diverse cultural and religious codes, they are all directed according to rules of reason by philosophers, who receive their knowledge from the same source—namely, the Active Intellect. In contrast, what Fārābī regards as "the opposite of the virtuous city" has subdivisions. The three main divisions are the ignorant city, the immoral city, and the erring city. Broadly speaking, what makes these cities the opposite of virtuous is either the citizens' ignorance of the right path or their neglecting of it, whether deliberately or due to the misguidance of deceitful rulers.[78] While following Plato in broad strokes, Fārābī's characterization of the divisions and subdivisions of societies can be read against his own cultural context. After all, it would be simplistic to consider any philosophical text immune from the powerful impact of cultural, political, and religious discourses of the time.

The Platonic elitism of Fārābī's political philosophy seems to be inconsistent with the egalitarian message of the Quran and the early period of Islamic history after Prophet Muhammad, when leaders were selected through the consensus of the community. However, by Fārābī's time, Islamic politics had adopted some pre-Islamic political paradigms and practices from the Persian and Byzantine Empires. The hierarchical structure of Fārābī's virtuous city and its intellectual hierarchy does not resemble Muhammad's community, where the best people are those who have a greater awareness of God and live their lives in conformity with His will. Over the course of a few centuries, the rather small God-fearing and egalitarian Islamic community transformed into expansive caliphates and competing princedoms of either Arab or Persian heritage.

76. Butterworth, "Ethical and Political Philosophy," 280.
77. Fārābī, *Political Regime*, 36.
78. Fārābī, *Political Regime*, 41–53; Fārābī, *On the Perfect State*, 253–59.

Of course, Fārābī does not theorize hereditary monarchy, and he could defend himself by arguing that his perfect state is just an ideal one, with the only real example of the Prophet's community. In any case, his theory of absolute power supported by perfect knowledge can be easily interpreted in favor of a political system where only the elect know what is best for all, which is a perfect recipe for autocracy. In effect, Islamic history until today has witnessed many examples of such autocratic claims and systems around the Muslim world, albeit without the rational aspects that Fārābī idealized.

Avicenna, on the other hand, argues that only a prophet who is sent by God can possess perfect knowledge because he receives it from the emanation of the Angel of Revelation. And in his capacity as a messenger to humanity, he guides his people "in whatever mode of expression is deemed best for achieving through his opinions the good of the sensory world by political governance and of the intellectual world by [theoretical] knowledge."[79] Thus, Avicenna regards a prophet as both a political leader who governs his community's worldly affairs and a philosopher who guides them toward intellectual/spiritual perfection. In the *Metaphysics of the Healing*, Avicenna explains that after Prophet Muhammad, political authority and governance are to fall in the hands of the most qualified leader—namely, a caliph who best exemplifies the virtues of intelligence, courage, temperance, and knowledge of the religious law (*al-sharīʿa*). Once such a person is either designated by his predecessor or elected through scholarly and communal consensus, his rule is uncontestable.[80]

The fact that Ghazālī's criticism of Avicenna does not target his position on governance is indirect evidence of Avicenna's political orthodoxy. This is noteworthy in view of Ghazālī's concentrated efforts to support the authority of the caliph in its relation to the sultanate, on the one hand, and in defense against the Ismaʿīlī Shiʿa threats of the time, on the other hand. Concerning the first challenge, Ghazālī's approach was a conciliatory one. As for the second challenge, he summoned all his intellectual power to refute the Ismaʿīlī arguments for the Shiʿa Imam's divine right to governance. In this regard, I agree with the statement that "Al-Ghazālī may have done more to enhance the long-term prospects for a stable Sunni order than could have been achieved by religio-political strategy alone."[81] Ghazālī lived under the Abbasid Caliphate and the Seljuq Sultanate (r. 1055–1300), so he discussed the relation between the caliph and sultan in several of his works, and there seems to be an overall consistency across his different texts, even his Sufi writings. An analysis of his texts on authority shows that for Ghazālī, the caliph is the ultimate source of authority according to the Islamic law, and any other political power, such as the sultanate, is legal as long as they obey the caliph.[82] Ghazālī's life as a faithful subject of the caliph and sultan serves as an example of his theory of authority.

As a Sufi, Ghazālī praises the position of governance as "the vice-regency of the Transcendent God" only if it is "by way of justice." In the *Alchemy of Happiness*, he advises the governor to seek both knowledge and practice. As for the knowledge requirement, the governor must have awareness of the transience of this life and know that his position

79. Avicenna, *On the Proof of Prophecies*, 115.
80. Avicenna, *Metaphysics of the Healing*, 374–75.
81. Black, *Islamic Political Thought*, 110.
82. See Hillenbrand, "Islamic Orthodoxy or Realpolitik?," 81–94.

matters only if he considers it as a religious duty, since "according to the Messenger of Allah, one day of justice that issues from a just sultan is better than sixty years of constant worship."[83] Ghazālī's advice on good practice consists of ten principles that he explains using many traditions and anecdotes. To summarize, a just governor must (1) act toward people the way he would want them to act toward him if they were in power; (2) prioritize his service to people over anything personal, even his religious rituals; (3) avoid an extravagant lifestyle; (4) treat his people with tolerance rather than violence; (5) be kind and generous; (6) prioritize the religious law over anyone's personal preferences; (7) always be on guard against unethical actions and injustices by constant self-examination and consulting the Quran; (8) seek council from virtuous scholars of Islam and avoid those scholars who are greedy for earthly goods and flatter him for the purpose of gaining those goods; (9) make those close to him, like his ministers and servants, accountable according to the same rules as he does for all people; and (10) keep his wrath under control by practicing patience toward people.[84]

Ghazālī's influence on the Islamic Iberian world, or Andalusia, was far and wide both as a theologian and as a Sufi. However, some of the followers of his Sufi teachings therein were not as optimistic about those in power as he was. Andalusia has an interesting political history that impacts the relation among philosophy, Sufism, and politics. Among different Islamic rules in Andalusia, the Almohad dynasty (r. 1121–1269) is believed to have been the most reliant on mingling theology with politics and legal affairs, with Ghazālī's style of Ashʿarism as their favorite theological approach. Even their political campaign against the previous regime, the Almoravids, centered on theological claims. For example, they accused the Almoravids of an anthropomorphic understanding of God and tried to build a more rational image of themselves in contrast to them.[85] Most of the Almohad rulers avoided antagonism with philosophers, and some philosophers were affiliated with the Almohad court, often in the capacity of court physicians. This is true about two major Islamic philosophers of Andalusia: Ibn Ṭufayl and Averroes.

I assume that it is not despite their experience with the contemporary politics of their time but *because* of it that Ibn Ṭufayl and his predecessor, Ibn Bājja, looked down upon political life and were disappointed with the society of men altogether. In their writings, they depart from Fārābī's ideal of contribution to a perfect society and do not embrace the Platonic/Aristotelian view that bases happiness and individual flourishment on social and political membership. Instead, they consider solitary life as conducive to intellectual and spiritual salvation. In his *Governance of the Solitary One*, Ibn Bājja affirms the possibility of perfection and happiness outside of a polity. As Erwin Rosenthal argues, although fully aware of the importance of a social and political life to his Greek and Muslim predecessors, Ibn Bājja's political philosophy is actually a road map for withdrawal from politics and taking refuge to a solitary life as the best life for a philosopher.[86]

In Ibn Ṭufayl's *Ḥayy Ibn Yaqẓān*, the protagonist, Ḥayy, who manages to understand the secrets of the universe and finds the One God all by himself, decides to join the society of

83. Ghazālī, *Kīmīyā*, 1:525–27.
84. Ghazālī, *Kīmīyā*, 1:527–42.
85. Stroumsa, *Andalus and Sefarad*, 129.
86. See Rosenthal, *Political Thought*, 171–74.

men as a guide to happiness but becomes disillusioned by the "ignorance" of "the masses." He returns to his only intellectual and spiritual companion and stays with him in their "island" to lead a mystic life away from the "defective" society against which his friend had already warned him.[87] The ultimate choice of Ibn Ṭufayl's Ḥayy was actually appealing to the Almohad policy of respecting Sufis as long as they remain outside of the realpolitik. The previous caliphate, Almoravid, which was challenged by Sufis, reacted by burning Sufi books like those of Ghazālī's and banning Sufi practices. In contrast, the Almohad integrated Sufi culture, which helped keep Sufi political influence in check. It is reasonable to believe that Ḥayy's ultimate seclusion from involvement in politics is what the Almohads expected and encouraged in their relation with Sufis. A secluded Sufi is not much of a political threat.[88]

Averroes was introduced into the Almohad court by Ibn Ṭufayl and succeeded in his position as the court physician. He was not only a physician and a philosopher but also engaged with society and politics as a judge and jurist. Averroes's political philosophy may sound more conservative than Ibn Bājja's and Ibn Ṭufayl's. For one thing, he does not agree with them that a virtuous life is possible outside of society and uses Aristotle's characterization of the human being as a political animal to support his arguments. While his approach to politics is a mixed adaptation of Plato and Aristotle, for Averroes, a society and polity that is qualified for the flourishing of people is one that is governed by the prophetic law. Averroes often clarifies that there is no authority above that of the Islamic law, and the best government is the one that guarantees its implementation. In his commentary on Plato's *Republic*, Averroes clarifies that the Islamic state is the best form of the ideal state, where all people can attain happiness by following the religious law. Of course, religious laws in their particular implementations are not always understood literally. He follows Plato on likening rulers to physicians who help their patients case by case. At their core, principal religious laws must be in agreement with human nature in general, a fact that philosophers must be able to understand. Averroes agrees with Plato that under certain circumstances, a perfect state can deteriorate, and his example is the first Umayyad ruler, Muʿāwiya, who damaged the virtuous state of early and pre-Umayyad Islamic rule:

> You may understand what Plato states concerning the transformation of the ideal constitution into the timocratic, and that of the excellent [man] into the timocratic man, from the case of the government of the Arabs in the earliest period. For they used to imitate the ideal constitution, and then were transformed in the days of Muʿāwiya into timocratic men. It seems to be the case with the constitution that exists now in these islands.[89]

What preserves a state from deteriorating is adherence to the Islamic law, which for Averroes is the perfect religion. This means that Averroes is not a pluralist like Fārābī, who gives equal status to different religions and practices as long as they are rational. One could differentiate their approaches to interpreting Plato's *Republic* in view of the

87. Ibn Ṭufayl, *Ḥayy Ibn Yaqẓān*, trans. Goodman, 162–65.
88. On the relation between Sufism and politics in Andalusia, see Akhtar, *Philosophers, Sufis, and Caliphs*, part 2.
89. Cited in Rosenthal, *Political Thought*, 194.

sociopolitical conditions of their times. While Fārābī grew up as a person and scholar in the vast Abbasid Empire, which was inclusive of numerous cultures, as well as some Shiʿa communities and princedoms, the Almohad was the centralized state of a peninsula attached to the Mālīkī school, a strict school of Sunni law and extremely protective against other legal schools, particularly against political Shiʿism.

Speaking of political Shiʿism, it was not just the Andalusian rulers who did not want to have anything to do with it. The Seljuqs, as previously mentioned, not only fought the Shiʿas on a theoretical battleground—for example, through Ghazālī's writings—but also literally struggled against their missionaries and warriors. The fear of Shiʿism as a political force was to the extent that even vague textual suggestions of the Shiʿa view of governance would get philosophers in trouble. The case of Shihāb al-Dīn Suhrawardī may serve as a good example of the situation. The execution of this philosopher upon the order of the Ayyubid sultan, Saladin, in 1191 CE is often explained from an ideological perspective. According to official accounts of the events prior to the execution order, Suhrawardī's Illuminationist philosophy, along with accusations of sorcery, was considered heretical and corrupting. According to this account, some religious scholars reported him to Saladin as an immediate danger to the faith of Suhrawardī's patron, the prince of Aleppo in Syria, who happened to be Saladin's son, Malik al-Ẓāhir. However, the real story may be more complicated than this. Suhrawardī's writings suggest a theory of absolute authority based on divine wisdom. In the *Philosophy of Illumination*, Suhrawardī directly addresses the question of political authority, and the terminology he uses in this context has Shiʿa undertones. For example, he says that at times, the manifest divine Imam is "with authority" and "government," and sometimes a "hidden" Imam possesses that authority. The concept of "hidden Imam" is familiar to both Ismaʿīlīs and Twelver Shiʿas, and in the same passage, he refers to the hidden Imam as the "Pole" (*quṭb*), which is also a Sufi term. The referent of the "Pole" in Sufi literature is sometimes regarded as identical with that of the "Shiʿa Imam."[90] Indeed, it is not far-fetched to assume that a fervent Sunni leader like Saladin was alarmed by the Shiʿa undertones of Suhrawardī's position on governance and thus had him executed on that account.[91]

The fact that in Twelver Shiʿism the imamate ends with the Twelfth Imam, who is believed to have been in occultation for centuries, makes the problem of political leadership more complicated. One major Twelver philosopher who theorizes authority and governance is Mullā Ṣadrā. His texts on the imamate are a synthesis of philosophy, Sufism, and spiritual interpretations of Islamic scriptures, especially the Shiʿa tradition. At the center of his theory of leadership is the Sufi notion of the "perfect human." For Mullā Ṣadrā, while the Prophet and the twelve Imams are the original perfect humans who have absolute authority over their followers, in the absence of the Twelfth Imam, there should be guides who can teach people the true meaning of the Quran and uphold the Islamic law accordingly. In the absence of the Imam, only those religious scholars who acquire knowledge from the divine source are qualified for guiding people. It is true that Mullā Ṣadrā sets the bar too high for this position for it to be accredited to just any religious scholar or jurist. However, he claims, "It is necessary that at all times there should be a

90. Nasr, "Shiʿism and Sufism," 235.
91. For Suhrawardī's political philosophy, see Ziai, "Source and Nature," 304–44.

Friend of God/Guardian who is in charge of preserving the Quran and knows the secrets and mysteries of it so as he can teach the believers."[92]

There is no evidence that Mullā Ṣadrā ever pointed out anyone in particular who is qualified as such a perfect guide and leader, and it was not until the twentieth century that his theory of a perfect leader was taken advantage of in actual politics. I would indeed contend that the theory of the absolute "guardianship of the jurist" (*wilāyat-i faqīh*), which became the religio-political core of the Islamic Republic of Iran, was a discursive stretch of the synthesis of Sufism and Shiʿism in Mullā Ṣadrā's treatment of authority. While Mullā Ṣadrā's theory of guardianship can be interpreted as spiritual guardianship by a perfect soul, it is also possible to use it for legitimizing a person's absolute religio-political authority. For example, Ayatollah Khomeini (d. 1989) credited the jurist with "guardianship" (*wilāya*) and commanded Muslims to obey these "proofs of the Imām to the people."[93] It is true that Mullā Ṣadrā himself was not affiliated with the political power of his time and criticized the jurists who did that.[94] Nevertheless, one cannot ignore how discourses work in relation to power, especially given Khomeini's background in teaching Mullā Ṣadrā. By synthesizing, in the *wilāyat-i faqīh* thesis, the religious authority of the jurist and the spiritual authority of a superior soul, Khomeini and some of his students promoted a narrative of absolute authority that is above the consensus of the community and immune to criticism. To be sure, Khomeini himself never stopped his followers from calling him "the representative" of the Twelve Imams.

Apart from the rise of Shiʿa authoritarianism and theocracy in Iran, over the past two centuries, we have witnessed the emergence of politically active forms of fundamentalism around the Muslim world. One can think of the establishment of Wahhabism in the birthplace of Islam, today's Saudi Arabia; the Muslim Brotherhood in Egypt; the spread of Salafism; and the formation of violent extremist groups such as al-Qaida, the Taliban, and ISIS across the Middle East. To find an explanation for such retrogressive developments, one needs to look to the modern history of the Middle East following the dissolution of the Ottoman Empire alongside the devastating legacies of colonialism in the Muslim world, the partition of India, the Cold War, and various economic paradigm shifts across the globe.

92. Mullā Ṣadrā, *Sharḥ Uṣūl al-kāfī*, 2:611.
93. Cited in Meisami, *Knowledge and Power*, 195.
94. See Toussi, *Political Philosophy*.

Conclusion

Care for Others, Care for the World

As we bring *Exploring Islamic Philosophy* to a close, some comments are in order concerning the scope of Islamic philosophy vis-à-vis two important issues in contemporary times—namely, that of social justice and the ecological crisis. All social justice discourses center on the notion of equality with respect to factors such as gender, race, ethnicity, class, and their intersections. Islamic discourses since the advent of the religion have gained their social strength from their emphasis on the inherent equality of people in the eyes of God. For the sake of avoiding anti-contextual evaluations of the premodern views of the Islamic philosophers based on our contemporary notions of equity and inclusivity, I only wish to problematize here the question of equality from a metaphysical point of view in philosophy and Sufism. I also try to show that Sufi narratives of humanity have the strongest potential for upholding gender equity.

It is true that philosophers' glorification of rationality as the distinguishing essence of humanity may sound like a recipe for elitism and inequality in society. But if we look at this issue from a purely metaphysical point of view, there is nothing inborn in human nature that could necessarily prevent it from actualizing its rational potential. When Fārābī speaks of the perfect ruler who possesses sovereignty mainly based on acquired rational qualifications, he uses the term "human being" (*insān*), which is gender neutral. Even when he speaks of "natural dispositions," all he means is leadership potential, and nowhere does he restrict rational perfection to male citizens. I find it interesting, not to say ironic, that the gender-inclusive rhetoric of Fārābī's *On the Perfect State* is lost through its English translation, where *insān* is rendered into "man" throughout the passages on the perfect ruler.[1] I do not mean to regard Fārābī as gender conscious, but how classical texts are translated definitely contributes to our collective vision of equality with the passage of time. For Fārābī, to occupy the "perfect rank of humanity," one has to unite with the Active Intellect, and average citizens of a perfect city can equally reach ultimate human happiness through immortality. The rationalist view of human perfection and leadership makes hereditary status rather irrelevant to Fārābī, as an irrational king can lead a city to its destruction as any commoner would in the absence of wisdom. As for women's right to leadership, it is possible only based on the absence of any statements against it in Fārābī's writings.

It is more difficult to consider the possibility of women's social and political significance in Avicenna's philosophy. Beginning with his natural philosophy, first he follows Galen in attributing an active reproductive role to the female body, but he eventually

1. See Fārābī, *On the Perfect State*, 239–53.

returns to Aristotle's position that the female partner has a mere passive function in reproduction.[2] At the metaphysical level, Avicenna does not differentiate between male and female souls in terms of their psychic faculties and potential for perfection. And although the historical examples of prophets and philosophers are all men, he does not restrict conjunction with the Active Intellect to them alone. That being said, when it comes to practical matters such as divorce, Avicenna does argue that a woman cannot decide on separation from a marriage because "she is of a feeble intellect and is quick to follow passion and anger." But he goes on to add that asking for divorce must still be a possibility for women in certain circumstances, and in such cases, the matter must be "relegated to the judges,"[3] who happen to be only men in Islamic societies.

On a brighter note, Avicenna is of the position that women have a greater share in sexual pleasure than men in that they are capable of enjoying sex more than them (a view, incidentally, that stands in stark contrast to that of most medieval Western thinkers). Moreover, concerning the parent-child relationship, Avicenna recognizes both parents' rights to educate their children and expect obedience and respect from them.[4] More importantly, for him, the main purpose of forming a family is "love," which is acquired through forming the habit of "friendship." Since friendship and love equally involve both parties, at least Avicenna does not consider married women as mere objects of lust and instruments of reproduction. However, love, respect, and education are limited to the private sphere of one's home. Avicenna argues against women participating in the public sphere—for example, having a job—because "she is much inclined to draw attention to herself and . . . is easily deceived and is less inclined to obey reason."[5] It seems that in these passages, Avicenna is simply following the mainstream reading of Islamic law that determined the legal practice of the day.

Despite the fact that the Quran and the practice of Prophet Muhammad do not suggest the inferiority of women, later legal texts do not necessarily follow suit. Furthermore, the sexist aspects of Aristotle's natural and social philosophy had a deep impact on classical Islamic philosophers. For example, in his books on ethics, Naṣīr al-Dīn Ṭūsī offers a patriarchal ethical theory in which women are less intelligent than men and inclined to jealousy, sloth, and idleness.[6] This "ethical" approach to women within the context of family and polity has recently been denounced by one scholar as "gendered morality."[7]

A surprising deviation from Aristotelian sexism among classical Islamic philosophers is Averroes. This is surprising because Averroes was a practicing jurist, and as a philosopher, he was a dedicated follower of Aristotle. In this regard, his different position on women appears mainly in his commentary on Plato's *Republic*, and scholars have interpreted him differently on this topic. What cannot be denied is Averroes's affirming of the possibility of intellectual, social, political, and artistic activities for women. Averroes

2. Hall, "Intellect, Soul and Body," 83–84.
3. Avicenna, *Metaphysics of the Healing*, 372–73.
4. Avicenna, *Metaphysics of the Healing*, 372–74.
5. Avicenna, *Metaphysics of the Healing*, 373.
6. See Meisami, *Naṣīr al-Dīn Ṭūsī*, 91–92.
7. For a thorough analysis and critique of this approach exemplified in the Persian genre of *akhlāq*, see Ayubi, *Gendered Morality*.

slams Andalusian society for confining women to the private sphere and wasting their social and political capacities:

> In these states, however, the ability of women is not known, because they are only taken for procreation there. They are therefore placed at the service of their husbands and (relegated) to the business of procreation, for rearing and breast-feeding. But, this undoes their (other) activities. Because women in these states are not being fitted for any of the human virtues, it often happens that they resemble plants. That they are a burden on the men in these states is one of the reasons for the poverty of these states. They are found there in twice the number of men, while at the same time they do not, through training, support any of the necessary activities; except for a few which they undertake mostly at a time when they are obliged to make up their want of funds, like spinning and weaving. All this is self-evident.[8]

Belo tries to show that when Averroes refers to women as weaker than men, what he means is only physical weakness. Also, she highlights a degree of consistency between Averroes's commentary on Plato and his work in Islamic jurisprudence.[9] For example, contrary to many jurists of his time, Averroes gives women the right to divorce and contract their marriage and does not even reject the possibility of women acting as judges and leaders of prayers. Thus, whether we consider Averroes's position on women as a sign of his "political realism"[10] or his "stark rationalism,"[11] he is a great case for tracing an early gender equality discourse in classical Islamic philosophy.

But this is the furthest we can get in classical Islamic philosophy regarding the possibilities for gender equality, which is confined to a limited number of women's rights. To go beyond this, one needs to look into Sufism from the following interrelated perspectives: first, the intellectual and social presence of women in Sufi history; second, the metaphysical doctrine of the unity of being; and third, the rich philosophical poetry, which is replete with narratives of male and female beauty and inclusive love that is based on Sufi metaphysics.

From the early days of Islam, women have been recognized as sources of religious knowledge and spirituality. For example, Muhammad's wife ʿĀisha is frequently referred to as an authentic source in the chain of transmission of prophetic traditions, and there are plenty of reports of men being trained under female scholars of prophetic traditions.[12] And this is to say nothing of the emergence of female Sufi exemplars such as Rābīʿa al-ʿAdawiyya (d. 801)[13] and Āʾisha al-Bāʿūniyya (d. 1517).[14] There are several stories about Rābīʿa's spiritual status, her choice of asceticism, and her celibate life, which was not the social norm for women of her time. To this, we can add her criticism of male superiority complexes and, most importantly, furthering a feminine narrative of the love for God,

8. Rosenthal, *Political Thought*, 191.
9. Belo, "Some Considerations," 13–17.
10. Rosenthal, *Political Thought*, 191.
11. Belo, "Some Considerations," 20.
12. The role of women in knowledge transmission in premodern Islam is thoroughly documented in Sayeed, *Transmission of Religious Knowledge*.
13. For Rābīʿa al-ʿAdawiyya, see Cornell, *Rabiʿa*.
14. See Bāʿūniyya, *Principles of Sufism*.

which is in fact evidenced in many poems by female Sufi figures.[15] In reports about her, Rābiʿa is frequently described as intoxicated with God's love and shunning the whole world for this profound spiritual passion. For example, she was once seen "staggering like one inebriated," and the observer asks about the cause. She replies, "Last night I was intoxicated with love for my Lord and woke up inebriated from it."[16] Rābiʿa constantly warns other Sufis against loving anything or anybody other than God and criticizes them when they seem to do otherwise.[17]

What happens in the Sufi context regarding female roles is unique, and it is founded on Sufi metaphysics of unity. From the Sufi metaphysical perspective, all beings are manifestations of God, so there is no theoretical excuse for giving men a higher rank in humanity. As for the spiritual dynamics, anyone, regardless of gender, can be a Sufi master and channel divine knowledge and grace to the disciple. In this regard, Ibn ʿArabī is an interesting example. Not only did he study under two major female Sufis from Andalusia, but his metaphysics and Sufi theology have strong implications for an inclusive approach to humanity in its diversities.[18] He also mentions his female disciples in some of his poems,[19] and the historical record of sessions wherein his works were read publicly demonstrates that many of the attendees and participants in these reading sessions were women and that he also dedicated sessions to exclusive female audiences.[20]

In Ibn ʿArabī's cosmos, "no property becomes manifest within existence without a root in the Divine Side by which it is supported."[21] In the last book of *The Bezels of Wisdom*, which is on the "Word of Muḥammad," Ibn ʿArabī gives a metaphysical explanation for why women were beloved to the Prophet of Islam:

> When man contemplates the Reality [God] in woman, he beholds Him in a passive aspect, while when he contemplates Him in himself, a being that from which the woman is manifest, he beholds Him in an active aspect. When, however, he contemplates Him in himself, without any regard to what has come from him, he beholds Him as passive to himself directly. However, *his contemplation of the Reality in woman is the most complete and perfect* because in this way he contemplates the Reality in both active and passive modes, while by contemplating the Reality only in himself, he beholds Him in a passive mode particularly. . . . Because of this the Apostle loved women by reason of the possibility of perfect contemplation of the Reality in them.[22]

This text's potential for feminist readings is great. Ibn ʿArabī has transformed the image of women as a mere venue for procreation to a necessity for reaching true knowledge of God. One may object that even in this role accorded to women by Ibn ʿArabī, they are still instruments for male perfection. Yet Ibn ʿArabī uses polar concepts in his theory

15. See Dakake, "'Guest of the Inmost Heart,'" 72–97.
16. Sulamī, *Early Sufi Women*, 78.
17. For an excellent pedagogical and linguistic study of Rābiʿa's poetry, see Albertini, "Meanings, Words, and Names," 219–43.
18. For a detailed exposition of gender relationships in Islamic cosmology, see the excellent study by Murata, *Tao of Islam*.
19. Shaikh, *Sufi Narratives of Intimacy*, 229.
20. See the paper trail in Hirtenstein, "In the Master's Hand," 101n60.
21. Chittick, *Sufi Path of Knowledge*, 39.
22. Ibn ʿArabī, *Bezels of Wisdom*, 275 (emphasis mine).

of creation without intending them to refer to separate gendered realities. He uses the notion of differentiation to explain creation out of the purely simple reality of God. For him, Adam symbolizes all of humanity in its reflection of the divine spirit in the universe. Before humanity, the universe was "an undifferentiated thing without anything of the spirit in it."[23] So when he speaks of man's activity and woman's passivity, these are interdependent aspects of creation and are ontologically rooted in divine qualities—namely, God's attributes of majesty (male) and beauty (female).[24] From the metaphysical Sufi principle of the unity of being in the sense of all diversities being manifestations of the same divine reality, one can deduce the equal status of all.

We can also turn to the teachings of the celebrated Persian poet Jalāl al-Dīn Rūmī (d. 1273), whose poetry is a perfect example in this discussion because of its complex use of both male and female body imagery. And on many occasions, our poet uses sexual intimacy as a metaphor for spiritual unification. But there are too many carnal images in Rūmī's poetry to deny the importance of the body in his philosophy of love. While the beautiful body often appears in female form, male beauty also has a place in Rūmī's poetry, which, as William Chittick notes, is usually associated with the beauty of Joseph from the story of Joseph in the Quran.[25] Indeed, for Rūmī, each beauty is a manifestation of divine beauty, and every act of loving is part of the infinite love of God.

Similar to gender, reading premodern texts on the topic of the environment is prone to anti-contextualization. The environmental crisis today is the result of a global greed for profit at the expense of destroying nature. One classical text that is interesting in its treatment of nature is Ibn Ṭufayl's philosophical fiction *Ḥayy Ibn Yaqẓān*. In his gradual progress toward actualizing his rational and spiritual potentials on his deserted island, Ḥayy considers the quality and quantity of his diet. He figures out that wasting away the earth's resources is equal to the evil of opposing God because the earth, plants, and animals are God's creation. He decides that he must limit himself to meaty fruit and feed on seeds—that is, nuts—only if the former is not available. Only in case these foods are not available can he eat animal produce and meat, and only those that are abundant. As for the amount of consumption, "It should be enough to stave off hunger, but no more."[26] While nature is valued as God's creation by Ibn Ṭufayl, Ibn ʿArabī praises it as manifesting God's name the Living (*al-Ḥayy*). He says in the *Meccan Revelations*, "The name Alive is an essential name of the Real. Therefore, nothing can emerge from Him but living things. Hence, all the cosmos is alive."[27] Not only is the earth alive, but it is regarded as blessed, hence Ibn ʿArabī's high respect for it as "the locus of every good."[28]

Moreover, the Sufis consider human beings as the representatives of God on earth; hence they are stewards rather than owners and unlimited consumers. The trust of the earth given to humanity comes with responsibilities toward nature, and the primary responsibility is to preserve the harmony between humans and their environments. In this regard, Seyyed Hossein Nasr states,

23. Ibn ʿArabī, *Bezels of Wisdom*, 50.
24. See Murata, *Tao of Islam*, chapter 6.
25. Chittick, *Sufi Path of Love*, 289.
26. Ibn Ṭufayl, *Ḥayy Ibn Yaqẓān*, trans. Goodman, 144–45.
27. Chittick, *Lost Heart*, 262.
28. Murata, *Tao of Islam*, 140.

> On the basis of principles drawn from the Quran and *Ḥadīth*, Islamic architecture grew with full awareness of the necessity of preserving harmony and balance with the natural environment. The use of space, building materials, water, heat and cold, sunlight and shade, the wind, the creation of gardens and many other elements in Islamic architecture and city planning were based on the balance and harmony between man and nature, in contrast to today's cities, which are out of balance with nature and their very existence depends on the intrusion into and destruction of the natural world.[29]

The Sufi approach is the exact opposite of the Cartesian mechanistic worldview, which reduces animals and plants to soulless objects. The same worldview marks the modern age picture of human beings as owners of the universe with full rights to use its resources without limits. In contrast, Islamic texts are replete with narratives about the human responsibility to take care of nature. The earth is regarded as a trust given to humanity; all that is in nature is a sign of God, and according to the Quran, all living things are constantly engaged in praising Him.[30] Moreover, there are numerous traditions that invite Muslims to be grateful for God's gift of natural resources and to avoid wasting and overconsumption.

Strongly influenced by Sufism, the metaphysical framework of later Islamic philosophy opens a new vista on the relation between humans and their natural environment.[31] As I discussed before, Mullā Ṣadrā's universe consists of one existence in gradations. Using the light analogy, he pictures different existences unified as one reality and diversified as various degrees of the same reality. From this metaphysical perspective, all that exists—including organic and inorganic objects, humans, animals, plants, and pebbles—are different only by their degree of existence. On the other hand, existence (*wujūd*) and consciousness (*wijdān*) are two sides of the same coin, which means that everything in the universe, however great or small, is implicated in the Great Chain of Consciousness.[32]

Yet a strong sense of environmental ethics in the Muslim world is still lacking. The will to dominate nature for increases in profit is often seen as a marker of progress, and many Muslims, like countless others, have fallen prey to the seductiveness of this wasteful ideology. In my home country, Iran, for example, wildlife, rivers, and various kinds of natural greenery are vanishing before our very eyes, all in the name of "development."

With hopes for a brighter future, I would like to bring this book to a close with some pertinent lines courtesy of the beloved Iranian poet Sohrab Sepehri (d. 1980), who was greatly inspired by nature and celebrated its beauty in his verse:

When knowledge
Still nestled by springs,
Humankind
Indulged himself in his azure philosophy

29. Nasr, "Environmental Crisis," 160–61.
30. For explorations of this theme, see Murad, "Inner and Outer Nature," 117–37; and Rustom, "Density of Man," 56–76.
31. See Nasr, *Man and Nature*; Nasr, *Order of Nature.*
32. On this subject, see Rustom, "Great Chain of Consciousness," 49–60.

In the delicate indolence of a meadow.
His thoughts flew with the bird.
He breathed with trees.
He was submissive to the poppy's conditions.
Intrepid meanings of the waters
Roared in the depths of his speech.
Humankind
Slept
In the text of the elements
And woke up
In dawning fear.

But sometimes
The strange music of growth
Echoed
In the frail joints of his joys
And dust settled
On his struggling knees.
Then
His creative fingers,
Idled and got lost
In precise geometrical grief.[33]

33. Sepehri, "Sohrab Sepehri" (with one slight change).

Bibliography

Adamson, P. "Abū Bakr Al-Rāzī (d. 925), *The Spiritual Medicine*." In El-Rouayheb and Schmidtke, *Oxford Handbook*.

Adamson, P. *Al-Kindī*. Oxford: Oxford University Press, 2006.

Adamson, P. *Al-Rāzī*. Oxford: Oxford University Press, 2021.

Adamson, P. *The Arabic Plotinus: A Philosophical Study of the "Theology of Aristotle."* London: Duckworth, 2002.

Adamson, P. "The Arabic Sea Battle: al-Farabi on the Problem of Future Contingents." *Archiv für geschichte der philosophie* 88.2 (2006): 168–88.

Adamson, P. "Averroes on Divine Causation." In *Interpreting Averroes: Critical Essays*, edited by P. Adamson. Cambridge: Cambridge University Press, 2018.

Adamson, P. "From the Necessary Existent to God." In Adamson, *Interpreting Avicenna*.

Adamson, P., ed. *Interpreting Avicenna: Critical Essays*. Cambridge: Cambridge University Press, 2013.

Adamson, P. *Philosophy in the Islamic World*. Vol. 3, *A History of Philosophy Without Any Gaps*. Oxford: Oxford University Press, 2016.

Adamson, P., and A. Lammer. "Fakhr al-Dīn al-Rāzī's Platonist Account of the Essence of Time." In *Philosophical Theology in Islam: Later Ashʿarism East and West*, edited by A. Shihadeh and J. Thiele. Leiden: Brill, 2020.

Adamson, P., and P. E. Pormann, trans. *The Philosophical Works of Al-Kindī*. Karachi: Oxford University Press, 2012.

Adamson, P., and R. C. Taylor, eds. *The Cambridge Companion to Arabic Philosophy*. Cambridge: Cambridge University Press, 2005.

Akhtar, A. H. *Philosophers, Sufis, and Caliphs*. Cambridge: Cambridge University Press, 2017.

Albertini, T. "Meanings, Words, and Names: Rābīʿa's Mystical Dance of the Letters." In *Ineffability: An Exercise in Comparative Philosophy of Religion*, edited by T. D. Knepper and L. E. Kalmanson. Dordrecht: Springer, 2017.

Aminrazavi, M. "Mīr Dāmād on Time and Temporality." In *Timing and Temporality in Islamic Philosophy and Phenomenology of Life*, edited by A. T. Tymieniecka. Dordrecht: Springer, 2007.

ʿĀmirī, Abū al-Ḥasan. *Knowledge and the Religious Sciences*. Translated by S. H. Nasr. In Nasr and Aminrazavi, *Anthology of Philosophy in Persia*, vol. 1.

ʿĀmirī, Abū al-Ḥasan. *On the Soul and Its Fate*. Translated by E. K. Rowson. In Nasr and Aminrazavi, *Anthology of Philosophy in Persia*, vol. 1.

Aristotle. *On the Soul*. In McKeon, *Basic Works of Aristotle*.

Aristotle. *Metaphysics*. In McKeon, *Basic Works of Aristotle*.

Audi, R. *Epistemology: A Contemporary Introduction to the Theory of Knowledge*. 2nd ed. New York: Routledge, 2003.

Averroes. "Commentary on Aristotle's Metaphysics, Book Lām." In Genequand, *Averroes's Metaphysics.*

Averroes. *The Incoherence of the Incoherence.* Translated by S. van den Bergh. Reprint. Middlesex: Gibb Memorial Trust, 2012.

Averroes. *Long Commentary on the De Anima of Aristotle.* Edited by R. C. Taylor and T. A. Druart. Translated by R. C. Taylor. New Haven: Yale University Press, 2009.

Avicenna. *al-Ishārāt wa'l-tanbīhāt.* Edited by S. Dunya. 3 vols. Cairo: Dār al-Iḥyā' al-Kutub al-ʿArabiyya, 1983–94.

Avicenna. *al-Mabda' wa'l-ma'ād.* Edited by A. Nūrānī. Tehran: McGill Institute of Islamic Studies, 1984.

Avicenna. *al-Ta'līqāt.* Edited by A. Badawī. Cairo: al-Hay'a al-Miṣriyya al-ʿĀmma li'l-Kitāb, 1973.

Avicenna. *Book of Demonstration.* In McGinnis and Reisman, *Classical Arabic Philosophy.*

Avicenna. *Ilāhiyyāt al-Najāt.* Edited by A. ʿAmayra. Vol. 2. Beirut: Dār al-Jīl, 1992.

Avicenna. *Metaphysics of the Salvation.* In McGinnis and Reisman, *Classical Arabic Philosophy.*

Avicenna. *The Metaphysics of the Healing.* Translated by M. E. Marmura. Provo: Brigham Young University Press, 2005.

Avicenna. *On the Proof of Prophecies and the Interpretation of the Prophets' Symbols and Metaphors.* Translated by M. E. Marmura. In Lerner and Mahdi, *Medieval Political Philosophy.*

Avicenna. *On the Soul.* In McGinnis and Reisman, *Classical Arabic Philosophy.*

Avicenna. *The Physics of the Healing.* Translated by J. McGinnis. Provo: Brigham Young University Press, 2009.

Avicenna. *Remarks and Admonitions, Part One: Logic.* Translated by S. Inati. Toronto: Pontifical Institute of Mediaeval Studies, 1984.

Axworthy, M. *A History of Iran.* New York: Basic Books, 2008.

ʿAyn al-Quḍāt. *The Essence of Reality: A Defense of Philosophical Sufism.* Translated by M. Rustom. New York: New York University Press, 2023.

Ayubi, Z. *Gendered Morality: Classical Islamic Ethics of the Self, Family, and Society.* New York: Columbia University Press, 2019.

Azadpur, M. *Analytic Philosophy and Avicenna: Knowing the Unknown.* New York: Routledge, 2020.

Bāʿūniyya, Ā'isha al-. *The Principles of Sufism.* Translated by Th. Homerin. New York: New York University Press, 2016.

Belo, C. *Chance and Determinism in Avicenna and Averroes.* Leiden: Brill, 2007.

Belo, C. "Essence and Existence in Avicenna and Averroes." *Al-Qantara* 30.2 (2009): 403–26.

Belo, C. "Freedom and Determinism." In Taylor and López-Farjeat, *Routledge Companion.*

Belo, C. "Some Considerations on Averroes' Views Regarding Women and Their Role in Society." *Journal of Islamic Studies* 20.1 (2009): 1–20.

Benevich, F. "The Essence-Existence Distinction." *Oriens* 45.3–4 (2017): 203–58.

Benevich, F. "The Reality of the Non-Existent Object of Thought: The Possible, the Impossible, and Mental Existence in Islamic Philosophy (Eleventh–Thirteenth Centuries)." *Oxford Studies in Medieval Philosophy* 6 (2018): 31–61.

Black, A. *The History of Islamic Political Thought.* Edinburgh: Edinburgh University Press, 2011.

Black, D. L. "Avicenna on Self-Awareness and Knowing That One Knows." In Rahman, Street, and Tahiri, *Unity of Science*.

Black, D. L. "Certitude, Justification, and Principles of Knowledge in Avicenna's Epistemology." In Adamson, *Interpreting Avicenna: Critical Essays*.

Black, D. L. "Estimation (*wahm*) in Avicenna: The Logical and Psychological Dimensions." *Dialogue: Canadian Philosophical Review* 32.2 (1993): 219–58.

Black, D. L. "Imagination and Estimation: Arabic Paradigms and Western Transformations." *Topoi* 19.1 (2000): 59–75.

Black, D. L. "Knowledge (*ʿilm*) and Certitude (*yaqīn*) in al-Fārābī's Epistemology." *Arabic Sciences and Philosophy* 16 (2006): 11–45.

Black, D. L. "Psychology: Soul and Intellect." In Adamson and Taylor, *Cambridge Companion*.

Brown, K. "An Analytical Summary of the Second and Third *Qabas in Mīr Dāmād's Kitābu ãl-Qabasāt*." *International Journal of Shīʿī Studies* 3.2 (2005): 11–74.

Butterworth, C. E. "Ethical and Political Philosophy." In Adamson and Taylor, *Cambridge Companion*.

Campanini, M. *An Introduction to Islamic Philosophy*. Translated by C. Higgitt. Edinburgh: Edinburgh University Press, 2008.

Chatti, S. "Avicenna on Possibility and Necessity." *History and Philosophy* 35.4 (2014): 332–53.

Chittick, W. C. "Ibn ʿArabī." In Nasr and Leaman, *History of Islamic Philosophy*, vol. 1.

Chittick, W. C. *In Search of the Lost Heart: Explorations in Islamic Thought*. Edited by M. Rustom, A. Khalil, and K. Murata. Albany: SUNY Press, 2012.

Chittick, W. C. *The Sufi Path of Knowledge: Ibn al-ʿArabī's Metaphysics of Imagination*. Albany: SUNY Press, 1989.

Chittick, W. C. *The Sufi Path of Love: The Spiritual Teachings of Rumi*. Albany: SUNY Press, 1983.

Corbin, H. *History of Islamic Philosophy*. Translated by L. Sherrard. London: Keagan Paul, 1993.

Cornell, R. *Rabiʿa from Narrative to Myth*. London: Oneworld, 2019.

Dakake, M. "'Guest of the Inmost Heart': Conceptions of the Divine Beloved Among Early Sufi Women." *Comparative Islamic Studies* 3.1 (2007): 72–97.

D'Ancona, C. "Greek into Arabic: Neoplatonism in Translation." In Adamson and Taylor, *Cambridge Companion*.

Daryaee, T. "Zoroastrianism Under Islamic Rule." In *The Wiley Blackwell Companion to Zoroastrianism*, edited by M. Stausberg, Y. Vevaina, and A. Tessman. West Sussex: Wiley-Blackwell, 2015.

Davidson, H. A. *Alfarabi, Avicenna, and Averroes on Intellect*. Oxford: Oxford University Press, 1992.

De Cillis, M. *Freewill and Predestination in Islamic Thought*. New York: Routledge, 2014.

Druart, T. A. "Al-Kindī's Ethics." In Netton, *Islamic Philosophy and Theology*.

Druart, T. A. "Al-Rāzī's Conception of the Soul: Psychological Background to His Ethics." *Medieval Philosophy and Theology* 5 (1996): 245–63.

Druart, T. A. "Averroes: The Commentator and Commentators." In *Aristotle in Late Antiquity*, edited by L. P. Schrenk. Washington, DC: Catholic University of America Press, 1994.

Elders, L. *Thomas Aquinas and His Predecessors: The Philosophers and the Church Fathers in His Work*. Washington, DC: Catholic University of America Press, 2018.

El-Rouayheb, K., and S. Schmidtke, eds. *The Oxford Handbook of Islamic Philosophy*. Oxford: Oxford University Press, 2017.

Fakhry, M. *Al-Fārābī: Founder of Islamic Neoplatonism: His Life, Works and Influence*. Oxford: Oneworld, 2002.

Fakhry, M. *Ethical Theories in Islam*. Leiden: Brill, 1991.

Fārābī, A-N. *Book of Demonstration*. In McGinnis and Reisman, *Classical Arabic Philosophy*.

Fārābī, Abū Naṣr. *Book of Letters*. Translated by Ch. Butterworth. Berkeley: Zaytuna College Press, 2024.

Fārābī, Abū Naṣr. *Directing Attention to the Way to Happiness*. In McGinnis and Reisman, *Classical Arabic Philosophy*.

Fārābī, Abū Naṣr. *On the Intellect*. In McGinnis and Reisman, *Classical Arabic Philosophy*.

Fārābī, Abū Naṣr. *On the Perfect State*. Translated by R. Walzer. Reprint. Oxford: Oxford University Press, 1998.

Fārābī, Abū Naṣr. *The Political Regime*. Translated by F. M. Najjar. In Lerner and Mahdi, *Medieval Political Philosophy*.

Fārābī, Abū Naṣr. *The Principles of Existing Things*. In McGinnis and Reisman, *Classical Arabic Philosophy*.

Faruque, M. U. "Life After Life: Mullā Ṣadrā on Death and Immortality." *Religious Studies* 60.1 (2024): 104–16.

Faruque, M. U. *Sculpting the Self: Islam, Selfhood, and Human Flourishing*. Ann Arbor: University of Michigan Press, 2021.

Frank, R. M. "The Structure of Created Causality According to Al-Aš'arî: An Analysis of the *Kitâb al-Lum'a*." *Studia Islamica* 25 (1966): 13–75.

Gannage, E. "The Rise of *Falsafa*." In El-Rouayheb and Schmidtke, *Oxford Handbook*.

Genequand, C., trans. *Averroes's Metaphysics: A Translation with Introduction of Averroes's Commentary on Aristotle's Metaphysics, Book Lām*. Leiden: Brill, 1986.

Ghazālī, M. *Freedom and Fulfilment*. Translated by R. J. McCarthy. New York: Twayne Publishers, 1980.

Ghazālī, Muhammad. *The Incoherence of the Philosophers*. Translated by M. E. Marmura. Provo: Brigham Young University Press, 2000.

Ghazālī, Muhammad. *Kīmīyā-yi sa ʿādat*. Edited by H. Khadīv-Jam. Vol. 1. Tehran: Intishārāt-i ʿIlmī Farhangī, 1996.

Ghazālī, Muhammad. *Mīzān al- ʿamal*. Edited by S. Dunya. Cairo: Dār al-maʿārif, 1964.

Ghazālī, Muhammad. *The Niche of Lights*. Translated by D. Buchman. Provo: Brigham Young University Press, 1998.

Ghazālī, Muhammad. *Revival of Religious Sciences*. Translated by M. M. Al-Sharīf. Vol. 4. Beirut: Dār al-kutub al-ʿilmmiyya, 2011.

Gohlman, W. E. *The Life of Ibn Sina*. Albany: SUNY Press, 1974.

Griffel, F. "Al-Ghazālī's (d. 1111) *Incoherence of the Philosophers*." In El-Rouayheb and Schmidtke, *Oxford Handbook*.

Griffel, F. "Fakhr al-Dīn al-Rāzī." In *Encyclopedia of Medieval Philosophy: Philosophy Between 500 and 1500*, edited by H. Lagerlund. Dordrecht: Springer, 2011.

Griffel, F. *Post-Classical Philosophy in Islam*. Oxford: Oxford University Press, 2021.

Gutas, D. *Avicenna and the Aristotelian Tradition: Introduction to Reading Avicenna's Philosophical Works*. Leiden: Brill, 1988.

Ha'irī Yazdi, M. *The Principles of Epistemology in Islamic Philosophy: Knowledge by Presence*. Albany: SUNY Press, 1992.

Hall, R. E., "Intellect, Soul and Body in Avicenna: Systematic Synthesis and Development of the Aristotelian, Neoplatonic and Galenic Theories." In *Interpreting Avicenna: Science and Philosophy in Medieval Islam*, edited by J. McGinnis and D. C. Reisman. Leiden: Brill, 2004.

Hillenbrand, C. "Islamic Orthodoxy or Realpolitik? Al-Ghazālī's Views on Government." *Iran* 26 (1988): 81–94.

Hirtenstein, S. "In the Master's Hand: A Preliminary Study of Ibn 'Arabī's Holographs and Autographs." *JMIAS* 60 (2016): 65–106.

Hodges, W., and T. A. Druart. "Al-Farabi's Philosophy of Logic and Language." In *Stanford Encyclopedia of Philosophy*, edited by E. Zalta and U. Nodelman. Stanford: Metaphysics Research Lab, Center for the Study of Language and Information, Stanford University, 2020. https://plato.stanford.edu/archives/fall2020/entries/al-farabi-logic/.

Hourani, G. F. "Averroes on Good and Evil." *Brill Studia Islamica* 16 (1962): 13–40.

Hourani, G. F. *Reason and Tradition in Islamic Ethics*. Cambridge: Cambridge University Press, 1985.

Ibn 'Arabī. *The Bezels of Wisdom*. Translated by R. W. J. Austin. New York: Paulist Press, 1981.

Ibn 'Arabī. *The Meccan Revelations*. Edited by M. Chodkiewicz. 2 vols. New York: Pir Press, 2002–4.

Ibn Miskawayh. *Jāwīdān-khirad*. Translated by A. Giese. In Nasr and Aminrazavi, *Anthology of Philosophy in Persia*, vol. 1.

Ibn Miskawayh. *The Refinement of Character*. Translated by C. K. Zurayk. In Nasr and Aminrazavi, *Anthology of Philosophy in Persia*, vol. 1.

Ibn Ṭufayl. *Ḥayy Ibn Yaqẓān*. In McGinnis and Reisman, *Classical Arabic Philosophy*.

Ibn Ṭufayl. *Ḥayy Ibn Yaqẓān: A Philosophical Tale*. Translated by L. E. Goodman. New York: Twayne Publishers, 1972.

Ivy, A. L. *Al-Kindī's Metaphysics*. Albany: SUNY Press, 1974.

Jaffer, T. "Bodies, Souls and Resurrection in Avicenna's *Ar-risala al-Aḍḥawiya fī amr al-ma'ād*." In *Before and After Avicenna: Proceedings of the First Conference of the Avicenna Study Group*, edited by D. Reisman and A. al-Rahim. Leiden: Brill, 2003.

Kalin, I. *Knowledge in Later Islamic Philosophy: Mullā Ṣadrā on Existence, Intellect and Intuition*. New York: Oxford University Press, 2010.

Kargar, D. "Irānšahri." In *Encyclopaedia Iranica*, vol. 13, fasc. 5. https://www.iranicaonline.org/articles/iransahri-abul-abbas-mohammad-b-mohammad/.

Kaukua, J. *Self-Awareness in Islamic Philosophy: Avicenna and Beyond*. Cambridge: Cambridge University Press, 2015.

Kaukua, J. *Suhrawardī's Illuminationism: A Philosophical Study*. Leiden: Brill, 2021.

Kirmānī, Ḥamīd al-Dīn. *al-Maṣābīḥ fī ithbāt al-imāma*. Edited and translated by P. Walker. New York: I. B. Tauris, 2007.

Kirmānī, Ḥamīd al-Dīn. *Rāḥat al-'aql*. Edited by K. Husain and M. Ḥilmī. Cairo: Dār al-Fikr al-'Arabī, 1953.

Kutubi, E. al-. *Mullā Ṣadrā and Eschatology: Evolution of Being*. New York: Routledge, 2015.

Leaman, O. *Averroes and His Philosophy*. Oxford: Clarendon Press, 1988.

Leaman, O. *An Introduction to Classical Islamic Philosophy*. 2nd ed. Cambridge: Cambridge University Press, 2002.

Lerner, R., and M. Mahdi, eds. *Medieval Political Philosophy: A Sourcebook*. Ithaca: Cornell University Press, 1963.

Lizzini, O. "Representation and Reality: On the Definition of Imaginative Prophecy in Avicenna." In *The Parva naturalia in Greek, Arabic and Latin Aristotelianism*, edited by B. Bydén and F. Radovic. Dordrecht: Springer, 2018.

López-Farjeat, L. X. *Classical Islamic Philosophy: A Thematic Introduction*. New York: Routledge, 2022.

Loux, M. J. *Metaphysics: A Contemporary Introduction*. 2nd ed. New York: Routledge, 2002.

Marmura, M. E. "Avicenna's Chapter on Universals in the *Isagoge* of His *Shifā*." In *Islam, Past Influence and Present Challenge*, edited by P. Cachia, W. M. Watt, and A. T. Welch. Albany: SUNY Press, 1979.

Marmura, M. E. "Ghazālī and Ashʿarism Revisited." In Netton, *Islamic Philosophy and Theology*.

Marmura, M. E. "Ghazali and the Avicennan Proof from Personal Identity for an Immaterial Self." In *A Straight Path: Studies in Medieval Philosophy and Culture; Essays in Honor of Arthur Hyman*, edited by R. Hyman. Washington, DC: Catholic University of America Press, 1988.

Mayer, T. "Theology and Sufism." In *Classical Islamic Theology*, edited by T. Winter. Cambridge: Cambridge University Press, 2008.

McGinnis, J. *Avicenna*. Oxford University Press, 2010.

McGinnis, J. "Avicenna's Naturalized Epistemology and Scientific Method." In Rahman, Street, and Tahiri, *Unity of Science*.

McGinnis, J. "Making Abstraction Less Abstract: The Logical, Psychological, and Metaphysical Dimensions of Avicenna's Theory of Abstraction." *Proceedings of the American Catholic Philosophical Association* 80 (2007): 169–83.

McGinnis, J., and D. Reisman, eds. *Classical Arabic Philosophy: An Anthology of Sources*. Indianapolis: Hackett, 2007.

McKeon, R., ed. *The Basic Works of Aristotle*. New York: Modern Library, 2001.

Meisami, S. "Ghazālī's Influence on Mullā Ṣadrā's View of Causal Necessity and Freewill." *Journal of World Philosophies* 9 (Winter 2024): 39–52.

Meisami, S. *Knowledge and Power in the Philosophies of Ḥamīd al-Dīn Kirmānī and Mullā Ṣadrā Shīrāzī*. London: Palgrave-Macmillan, 2018.

Meisami, S. "Light/Darkness Dualism and Islamic Metaphysics in Persianate Context." In *Islamic Thought and the Art of Translation: Texts and Studies in Honor of William C. Chittick and Sachiko Murata*, edited by M. Rustom. Leiden: Brill, 2023.

Meisami, S. *Mulla Sadra*. Oxford: Oneworld, 2013.

Meisami, S. "Mullā Ṣadrā on the Efficacy of Prayer." *Journal of Sufi Studies* 4.1–2 (2015): 59–83.

Meisami, S. "Mullā Ṣadrā Shīrāzī and the Meta-Theory of Logic." In *Women's Contemporary Readings of Medieval (and Modern) Arabic Philosophy*, edited by S. Chatti. Dordrecht: Springer, 2022.

Meisami, S. *Naṣīr al-Dīn Ṭūsī: A Philosopher for All Seasons*. Cambridge: Islamic Texts Society, 2019.

Meisami, S. "The Point of Reality and the Circle of Appearance: The Sufi Philosophy of Maḥmūd Shabistarī's *Gulshan-i rāz* Through the Lens of Shams al-Dīn Lāhījī's *Mafātīḥ al-iʿjāz*." *Journal of Sufi Studies* 9.1 (2020): 30–51.

Mīr Dāmād, M. B. *The Book of Blazing Brands*. Translated by K. Brown. New York: Global Scholarly Publications, 2009.

Mittila, J. *The Eudemonist Ethics of al-Fārābī and Avicenna*. Boston: Brill, 2022.

Morewedge, P., ed. and trans. *The Metaphysics of Ṭūsī*. New York: Society for the Study of Islamic Philosophy and Science, 1992.

Mullā Ṣadrā. *al-Ḥikma al-mutaʿāliya fī asfār al-ʿaqliyya al-arbaʿa*. Edited by M. R. Muẓaffar. Beirut: Dār al-Iḥyāʾ al-turāth al-ʿArabī, 1981.

Mullā Ṣadrā. *al-Mabdaʾ waʾl-maʿād*. Edited by S. J. Āshtīyānī. Qum: Markaz-i Inthishārāt-i Tablīgh-i islāmī, 2001.

Mullā Ṣadrā. *al-Shawāhid al-rubūbiyya*. Edited by S. J. Āshtiyānī. Mashhad: Markaz-i Nashr-i Dānishgāhī, 1981.

Mullā Ṣadrā. *al-Taʿlīqāt ʿalā ilāhiyyāt al-Shifāʾ li al-shaykh al-raʾīs Abū ʿAlī Ḥusayn Avicenna*. Edited by N. Ḥabībī. Vol. 2. Tehran: Bunyād-i ḥikmat-i Ṣadra, 2006.

Mullā Ṣadrā. *al-Taʿlīqāt ʿalā Sharḥ Ḥikmat al-ishrāq*. Edited by H. Ziai. Costa Mesa: Mazda Publishers, 2010.

Mullā Ṣadrā. *al-Tanqīḥ fiʾl-manṭiq*. In *Majmūʿa-yi rasāʾil-i falsafī-i Ṣadr al-mutaʾallihīn*, edited by H. Nājī-Isfahānī. Tehran: Intishārāt-i Ḥikmat, 2006.

Mullā Ṣadrā. *The Book of Metaphysical Penetrations*. Translated by S. H. Nasr. Annotated by I. Kalin. Provo: Brigham Young University Press, 2014.

Mullā Ṣadrā. *Risala fʾl-qaḍāʾ waʾl-qadar*. In "Mullā Ṣadrā and the Problem of Freedom and Determinism: A Critical Study of the *Risālah fiʾl-qaḍāʾ waʾl-qadar*," by D. Ede. PhD diss., Institute of Islamic Studies, McGill University, 1978.

Mullā Ṣadrā. *Sharḥ Uṣūl al-kāfī: Kitāb faḍl al-ʿilm wa Kitāb al-ḥujja*. Edited by M. Khājawī and A. Nūrī. Vol. 2. Tehran: Pizhūhishgāh-i ʿulūm-i insānī wa muṭālaʿāt-i farhangī, 2004.

Mullā Ṣadrā. *The Treatise on Conception and Belief*. Translated by J. Lameer. Tehran: Iranian Institute of Philosophy, 2006.

Mullā Ṣadrā. *The Wisdom of the Throne*. Translated by J. Morris. Princeton: Princeton University Press, 1981.

Murad, M. "Inner and Outer Nature: An Islamic Perspective on the Environmental Crisis." *Islam & Science* 10.2 (2012): 117–37.

Murata, S. *The Tao of Islam: A Sourcebook on Gender Relations in Islamic Thought*. Albany: SUNY Press, 1992.

Najjar, F. M. "Fārābī's Political Philosophy and Shiʿism." *Brill Studia Islamica* 14 (1961): 57–72.

Nasr, S. H. "Abū ʿAlī Aḥmad ibn Muḥammad Miskawayh." In Nasr and Aminrazavi, *Anthology of Philosophy in Persia*, vol. 1.

Nasr, S. H. "The Environmental Crisis in the Islamic World: Pertinence of the Teachings of Traditional Islam." In *Handbook of Islamic Ethics, Economics, and Finance*, edited by A. Mirakhur, Z. Iqbal, and S. K. Sadr. Berlin: De Gruyter, 2020.

Nasr, S. H. *Man and Nature: The Spiritual Crisis in Modern Man*. Chicago: ABC International, 1997.

Nasr, S. H. "The Qur'ān and Ḥadīth as Source and Inspiration of Islamic Philosophy." In Nasr and Leaman, *History of Islamic Philosophy*, vol. 1.

Nasr, S. H. *Religion and the Order of Nature*. New York: Oxford University Press, 1996.

Nasr, S. H. "Shiʿism and Sufism: Their Relation in Essence and History." *Religious Studies* 6.3 (1970): 229–42.

Nasr, S. H., and M. Aminrazavi, eds. *An Anthology of Philosophy in Persia*. 5 vols. London: I. B. Tauris in association with the Institute of Ismaili Studies, 2008–15.

Nasr, S. H., and O. Leaman, eds. *History of Islamic Philosophy*. New York: Routledge, 2001.

Netton, I. R., ed. *Islamic Philosophy and Theology*. Vol. 1. New York: Routledge, 2007.

Parfit, D. *Reasons and Persons*. Oxford: Clarendon Press, 1984.

Pourjavady, R. "Introduction." In *Philosophy in Safavid Iran: The Late Period (1652–1736)*, edited by R. Pourjavady. Leiden: Brill, forthcoming 2026.

Rahman, F. *Avicenna's Psychology*. Oxford: Oxford University Press, 1952.

Rahman, S., T. Street, and H. Tahiri, eds. *The Unity of Science in the Arabic Tradition: Science, Logic, Epistemology and Their Interactions*. Dordrecht: Springer, 2008.

Rāzī, Abū Bakr. *The Philosophical Way of Life*. Translated by P. Adamson. In Rustom, *Sourcebook in Global Philosophy*.

Rāzī, Abū Bakr. *The Spiritual Physick*. Translated by A. J. Arberry. In Nasr and Aminrazavi, *Anthology of Philosophy in Persia*, vol. 1.

Rāzī, Abū Bakr. *The Spiritual Physick of Rhazes*. Translated by A. J. Arberry. London: Murray, 1950.

Richardson, K. "Avicenna's Conception of the Efficient Cause." *British Journal for the History of Philosophy* 21.2 (2013): 220–39.

Rizvi, S. "Mīr Dāmād's (d. 1631) *al-Qabasāt*: The Problem of the Eternity of the Cosmos." In El-Rouayheb and Schmidtke, *Oxford Handbook*.

Rizvi, S. *Mullā Ṣadrā and Metaphysics: Modulation of Being*. New York: Routledge, 2009.

Rosenthal, E. I. J. *Political Thought in Medieval Islam: An Introductory Outline*. Cambridge: Cambridge University Press, 1962.

Rosenthal, F. *Knowledge Triumphant: The Concept of Knowledge in Medieval Islam*. Leiden: Brill, 2007.

Rowson, E. K. *A Muslim Philosopher on the Soul and Its Fate: al-ʿĀmirī's Kitāb al-amad ʿala'l-abad*. New Haven: Yale University Press, 1988.

Rustom, M., ed. "The Great Chain of Consciousness: Do All Things Possess Awareness?" *Renovatio* 1.1 (2017): 49–60.

Rustom, M. *Inrushes of the Heart: The Sufi Philosophy of ʿAyn al-Quḍāt*. Albany: SUNY Press, 2023.

Rustom, M. "Islam and the Density of Man." *Sacred Web* 46 (2020): 56–76.

Rustom, M. "Psychology, Eschatology, and Imagination in Mullā Ṣadrā Shīrāzī's Commentary on the *Ḥadīth* of Awakening." *Islam & Science* 5.1 (2007): 9–22.

Rustom, M. *A Sourcebook in Global Philosophy*. Sheffield: Equinox Publishing Ltd., 2025.

Rustom, M. "Storytelling as Philosophical Pedagogy: The Case of Suhrawardī." In *Knowledge and Education in Classical Islam: Religious Learning Between Continuity and Change*, edited by Sebastian Günther, vol. 1. Leiden: Brill, 2020.

Rustom, M. *The Triumph of Mercy: Philosophy and Scripture in Mullā Ṣadrā*. Albany: SUNY Press, 2012.

Sayeed, A. *Women and the Transmission of Religious Knowledge in Islam*. New York: Cambridge University Press, 2013.

Sepehri, S. "Sohrab Sepehri: Selected Poems [English]." A. Salami. 2023. https://alisalami.com/2023/01/sohrab-sepehri-selected-poems-english/.

Shaikh, S. *Sufi Narratives of Intimacy: Ibn ʿArabī Gender, and Sexuality*. Chapel Hill: University of North Carolina Press, 2012.

Shehata, M. M. "Abul-Barakāt al-Baghdādī on Divine Foreknowledge and Human Free Will." *Nazariyat* 6.2 (2020): 99–131.

Shihadeh, A. "Avicenna's Corporeal Form and Proof of Prime Matter in Twelfth-Century Critical Philosophy: Abū l-Barakāt, al-Masʿūdī and al-Rāzī." *Oriens* 42.3–4 (2014): 364–96.

Shihadeh, A. *The Teleological Ethics of Fakhr al-Dīn al-Rāzī*. Leiden: Brill, 2006.

Sijistānī, Abū Yaʿqūb. *The Book of Wellsprings*. In Nasr and Aminrazavi, *Anthology of Philosophy in Persia*, vol. 2.

Sijistānī, Abū Yaʿqūb. *Le dévoilment des choses chachées*. Translated by H. Corbin. Paris: Éditions Verdier, 1988.

Stroumsa, S. *Andalus and Sefarad: On Philosophy and Its History in Islamic Spain*. Princeton: Princeton University Press, 2019.

Stroumsa, S. *Freethinkers of Medieval Islam: Ibn Rāwandī, Abū Bakr al-Rāzī, and Their Impact on Islamic Thought*. Leiden: Brill, 1999.

Suhrawardī, Shihāb al-Dīn. *The Philosophy of Illumination*. Translated by J. Walbridge and H. Ziai. Provo: Brigham Young University Press, 1999.

Suhrawardī, Shihāb al-Dīn. *Risāla-yi Hayākil al-nūr*. Edited by M. K. Zanjānī-Aṣl. Tehran: Nashr-i Nuqṭa, 2000.

Suhrawardī, Shihāb al-Dīn. *The Shape of Light*. Translated by T. Bayrak. Louisville: Fons Vitae, 1998.

Sulamī, ʾAbd al-Raḥmān. *Early Sufi Women*. Translated by R. Cornell. Louisville: Fons Vitae, 1999.

Taylor, R. C. "Averroes." In *A Companion to Philosophy in the Middle Ages*, edited by J. J. E. Garicia and T. B. Noone. Oxford: Wiley-Blackwell, 2005.

Taylor, R. C. "Averroes and the Philosophical Account of Prophecy." *Studia graeco-arabica* 8 (2018): 287–304.

Taylor, R. C. "The Epistemology of Abstraction." In Taylor and López-Farjeat, *Routledge Companion*.

Taylor, R. C., and L. X. López-Farjeat, eds. *The Routledge Companion to Islamic Philosophy*. New York: Routledge, 2016.

Toussi, S. K. *The Political Philosophy of Mullā Ṣadrā*. New York: Routledge, 2020.

Ṭūsī, Naṣīr al-Dīn. *Nasirean Ethics*. Translated by G. M. Wickens. New York: Routledge, 1964.

Ṭūsī, Naṣīr al-Dīn. *The Paradise of Submission*. Edited and translated by S. J. Badakhchani. New York: I. B. Tauris, 2005.

Ṭūsī, Naṣīr al-Dīn. *Sharḥ al-Ishārāt wa'l-tanbīhāt*. Edited by S. Dunya. 3 vols. Cairo: Dār al-maʿārif, 1983–94.

Walbridge, J. "Suhrawardī's (D. 1191) *Intimations of the Tablet and the Throne*: The Relationship of Illuminationism and the Peripatetic Philosophy." In El-Rouayheb and Schmidtke, *Oxford Handbook*.

Wisnovsky, R. "Final and Efficient Causality in Avicenna's Cosmology and Theology." *Quaestio* 2.1 (2002): 97–124.

Wisnovsky, R. "Notes on Avicenna's Concept of Thingness (*šhay ̓iyya*)." *Arabic Sciences and Philosophy* 10 (2000): 181–221.

Wisnovsky, R. "Towards a Genealogy of Avicennism." *Oriens* 42.3–4 (2014): 323–63.

Zaehner, R. C. *Zurvan: A Zoroastrian Dilemma*. Oxford: Clarendon Press, 1972.

Zargar, C. A. *The Polished Mirror: Storytelling and the Pursuit of Virtue in Islamic Philosophy and Sufism*. London: Oneworld, 2017.

Ziai, H. "The Source and Nature of Authority: A Study of Suhrawardī's Illuminationist Political Doctrine." In *The Political Aspects of Islamic Philosophy*, edited by M. Mahdi and C. E. Butterworth. Cambridge, MA: Harvard University Press, 1992.

Zimmermann, F. W. *Al-Fārābī's Commentary and Short Treatise on Aristotle's De Interpretatione*. Oxford: Oxford University Press, 1981.

Further Reading

Adamson, P. *Philosophy in the Islamic World*. 3 vols. Oxford: Oxford University Press, 2015–18.

Adamson, P., and F. Benevich, ed. *The Heirs of Avicenna: Philosophy in the Islamic East, 12th–13th Centuries*. Vol. 1, *Metaphysics and Theology*. Leiden: Brill, 2024.

Campanini, M. *An Introduction to Islamic Philosophy*. Translated by C. Higgitt. Edinburgh: Edinburgh University Press, 2008.

Chittick, W. C. *Science of the Cosmos, Science of the Soul*. Oxford: Oneworld, 2007.

Haʾirī Yazdi, M. *Universal Science: An Introduction to Islamic Metaphysics*. Translated by J. Cooper. Edited by S. N. Ahmad. Leiden: Brill, 2017.

Izutsu, T. *Creation and the Timeless Order of Things*. Ashland: White Cloud Press, 1994.

Leaman, O. *An Introduction to Classical Islamic Philosophy*. 2nd ed. Cambridge: Cambridge University Press, 2002.

López-Farjeat, L. X. *Classical Islamic Philosophy: A Thematic Introduction*. New York: Routledge, 2022.

Nasr, S. H. *What Is Metaphysics?* Sheffield: Equinox Publishing Ltd., 2025.

Nusseibeh, S. *The Story of Reason in Islam: Cultural Memory in the Present*. Stanford: Stanford University Press, 2017.

Index

Abbasid Caliphate, 2, 104
accidents, 9–13
acquired intellect, 46
acquisition (*kasb*), 96–97
Active Intellect: authority, 103, 109, 110; cosmology, 23–28; immortality of the soul, 35; prophecy, 73–75; source of knowledge, 41–45
ʿAdawiyya, Rābīʿa al-, 111–12
ʿĀisha, 111
Alexander of Aphrodisias, 5
Almohads, 105–7
Almoravids, 105–6
ʿĀmirī, Abū al-Ḥasan, 6, 86, 87
Āmulī, Sayyid Ḥaydar, 77
Angel of Revelation, 44, 74–76, 104
annihilation, 81, 83, 95
Aquinas, St. Thomas, 13
assent, 41, 53, 55, 56
Averroes: afterlife, 79, 82; Almohad court, 105–6; essence and existence, 13–15; eternity, 25; evil, 71; free will, 100; God as final cause, 25; immortality, 35; morality, 92, 94–95; natural world, 28–29; prophecy, 74; theory of knowledge, 40, 42, 47–48; women, 110–11
Avesta, 6
Avicenna, 2; Active Intellect, 26, 27; afterlife, 79–80; authority, 104–5; essence and existence, 12–19; evil, 71; free will, 98–99; God's causality, 68; God's existence, 59–61; God's knowledge, 63–64; individual immortality, 34–35; intellects, 25; modalities, 19–20; morality, 88–90; Necessary Being and eternity, 23; prayer, 77–78; predetermination and providence, 70; prime matter, 28; prophecy, 73–74; soul, 33; theory of knowledge, 38–55; time, 29; universals, 11–12; women, 110
ʿAyn al-Quḍāt, 44, 101
awareness, 33–34, 49, 55, 82, 103, 104, 114
Ayyubid dynasty, 107

Baghdādī, Abū al-Barakāt al-, 92, 99
Bāʿūniyya, Āʾisha al-, 111
Bīrūnī, Abū Rayḥān, 7
bodily form, 28, 50
Breath of the Merciful, 68
Byzantine, 85, 90, 103

certitude, 55–56
common sense, 18, 39, 41, 96
compatibilism, 96, 99–100
compositive imagination, 39, 41
conception, 36, 41, 53, 55–56, 77, 78, 93
conformism (*taqlīd*), 94
consciousness, 52, 80, 114
contingent existent, 21, 61, 66
creation out of nothing, 4

determinism, 96–100
dispositional intellect, 46
divine predetermination, 70, 98

emanationism, 25, 60
essence. *See* quiddity
estimation (*wahm*), 38–41
eudemonia, 85
evil (*sharr*), 70–72, 77, 78, 83, 92, 98, 101
external senses, 39, 41

Fārābī, Abū Naṣr: Active Intellect, 42–44, 103; afterlife, 79, 81; divine attributes, 65; emanationism, 60; First Cause, 23; free will, 98; gender, 109–10; God's transcendence, 58; matter and form, 27;

Fārābī, Abū Naṣr (*continued*): morality, 88–89; politics, 102–4; prophecy, 73; sources of knowledge, 41; structure of knowledge, 53; truth and justification, 54; universals, 10
Firdawsī, Abū al-Qāsim, 6
fixed entities (*al-aʿyān al-thābita*), 68
formative imagination, 39
foundationalism, 52, 55–56
free will, 6, 67, 84, 85, 92, 93, 98–102
Friends of God (*awliyāʾ Allāh*), 43, 74–76

Galen, 29, 110
Gathas, 6
gender, 85, 109–13
generation and corruption, 17, 22, 26, 31, 60
Ghazālī, Abū Ḥāmid: acquisition (*kasb*), 97; bodily resurrection, 34, 80; divine causality, 60; divine knowledge, 66; divine oneness, 68; eternity, 24; free will, 100–101; hierarchy of lights, 61; knowledge and intellect, 43; morality, 93–94; politics, 104–5
Ghaznavids, 7

Holy Spirit, 26, 73
hypostasis, 42

Ibn ʿArabī: divine attributes or names, 62–68; free will, 101; morality, 94; perfect human, 76–77; unity of being, 61; women, 112–13
Ibn Bājja, 5, 66, 92, 105
Ibn Isḥāq, Ḥunayn, 14
Ibn Miskawayh, 90–92
Ibn Rāwandī, 3
Ibn Rushd, 5. *See also* Averroes
Ibn Sīnā, Abū ʿAlī, 2. *See also* Avicenna
Ibn Ṭufayl: afterlife, 81; environment, 113; eternity, 24; morality, 92–93; politics, 105–6; prophecy, 93; ultimate happiness, 44
Illuminationism, 8, 14, 16
imagination, 38–43, 73–76, 83–84
imamate (*imāma*), 72, 76–77, 92, 107
immortality, 32, 34–35, 73, 79, 81–82, 90, 102, 109
incomparability (*tanzīh*), 66–67
intermediary causes, 68, 79, 98
internalism, 52, 56
internal senses, 39
intuition (*ḥads*), 48–49
Islamic law (*al-sharīʿa*), 71, 76, 85, 95, 104, 106–7, 110
Ismaʿīlīs, 7, 57, 58, 107

justice, 73, 79, 84, 85–86, 88, 89, 91, 92, 94, 95, 96, 104, 105, 109, 111
justification, 38, 51–56
Justinian, 5

Khomeini, Ayatollah, 108
Kindī, Abū Yūsuf Yaʿqūb al-: First Cause, 22–23; free will, 97; human soul and immortality, 33, 79; knowledge, 42; morality, 86–87; predestination, 98; translation movement, 4; universals, 10
Kirmānī, Ḥamīd al-Dīn, 4, 26, 35, 58, 76, 77
knowledge by presence, 49

libertarianism, 96–97, 99, 100
Light of Lights (*al-nūr al-anwār*), 16, 21, 60, 69, 71
logical secondary intelligibles, 42

Maimonides, 66
Mālīkī, 107
material intellect, 45–48, 60
matter and form, 27–28, 50, 63
methodic experience (*tajriba*), 54–55
Mīr Dāmād, Muḥammad Bāqir, 5, 14, 16–17, 19, 26, 27, 30–31, 79
Mongols, 2, 7
motion, 6, 18, 32–36, 38–39, 41, 57, 59–60, 62, 71, 97
Muʿāwiya, 106
Muḥtasham, Nāṣir al-Dīn, 2
Muʿtaṣim, al-, 2
Muʿtazilites, 14, 86, 96, 97

names of Beauty (*jamāl*), 65
names of Majesty (*jalāl*), 65
natural universals, 11–12, 16
Necessary Existent (*al-wājib al-wujūd*), 20, 59–66, 70

necessity, 20–24, 59, 60, 62, 67, 69
Neoplatonism, 3, 5, 42, 58, 91
nominalism, 9
Nūḥ ibn Manṣūr, 6

particulars, 8, 9, 11, 40, 45, 58, 64, 66
passive intellect, 43, 48, 75
perception, 10, 11, 34, 38–40, 43–46, 49–50, 55, 64, 69
perfect human (*al-insān al-kāmil*), 74, 75–77, 88, 107
Peripatetic philosophy, 8, 10, 14, 15, 51, 64
philosophical secondary intelligibles, 42
Platonism, 16, 32
Plotinus, 4, 19, 42, 47, 57–58
Porphyry, 4, 10–11
predestination, 98
primary intelligibles (*al-maʿqūlāt al-ūlā*), 41–42, 45–46
prime matter, 27–28, 45, 72
property, 10–11, 112
providence, 12, 13, 70–73, 77–79
Pythagoras, 32

Qajar dynasty, 2
quiddity, 12–17, 51, 59, 62–63, 65
Qūnawī, Ṣadr al-Dīn, 77

Rāzī, Abū Bakr, 2, 6, 27, 29, 32, 87–88
Rāzī, Fakhr al-Dīn, 3, 14, 15–16, 29, 90, 91–92, 99
resurrection, 35, 79–84
Rūdakī, 6
Rūmī, Jalāl al-Dīn, 113

Sabziwārī, Hādī, 49
Ṣādiq, Jaʿfar al-, 99
Safavid dynasty, 2, 16, 17, 66, 67
Saladin, 107
Samanid dynasty, 5–7
Sasanian Empire, 5
secondary intelligibles (*al-maʿqūlāt al-thāniya*), 41–42, 45, 46
self-awareness, 33–34
Seljuq Sultanate, 7, 104, 107
sensation, 40, 44, 48, 55
sensible forms, 39, 41, 43
Shabistarī, Maḥmūd, 58
Shīrāzī, Mullā Ṣadrā: Active Intellect, 51, 55; divine agency, 69–70; divine knowledge, 64–65; environment, 114; essence and existence, 17–18; evil, 71–72; free will, 101; God's attributes, 67; God's existence, 61–62; graded unity of being, 50, 67–69, 77, 114; imaginal world, 83; imamate, 77; intellects, 26; justification, 55; knowledge and unification, 50–51; knowledge as existence, 56; modalities, 21–22; morality, 95; perfect humans, 107; Platonic Ideas, 5, 18–19; politics, 107–8; prayer, 78–79; prophecy, 75; resurrection, 83–84; secondary intelligibles, 42; substantial motion, 31, 35, 83–85, 95; time and eternity, 31
Shīrāzī, Quṭb al-Dīn, 72
Sijistānī, Abū Yaʿqūb, 58
similarity (*tashbīh*), 66–67
Socrates, 32, 87–88
substance, 12–13, 18, 27–29, 31
substantial motion, 31, 35, 83–85
Sufism, 65, 70, 76–77, 93, 101, 102, 105, 107, 108, 109, 111, 114
Suhrawardī, Shihāb al-Dīn: afterlife, 82; divine knowledge, 64, 69; essence and existence, 14–16; evil, 71; God, 60–61; hierarchy of lights, 21, 26, 60; imaginal world, 74–75, 83; knowledge, 49; mode of necessity, 21; Platonism, 19; politics, 97; prayer, 78; prophecy, 75
supplication (*duʿāʾ*), 72, 77–78
suspended images (*al-ṣuwar al-muʿallaqa*), 75

Transcendentalism, 8
translation movement, 2, 4
Ṭūsī, Naṣīr al-Dīn, 2, 16, 29, 41, 49, 64, 77, 90, 91–92, 99, 110

Umayyad Caliphate, 106
universals, 8–12, 49, 58, 64, 66, 93, 95

virtue, 85–87, 89–96

Ẓāhir, Malik al-, 107
Zoroastrianism, 5–7, 90

www.ingramcontent.com/pod-product-compliance
Lightning Source LLC
Chambersburg PA
CBHW051434270326
41935CB00018B/1820
* 9 7 8 1 8 0 0 5 0 6 8 2 4 *